A Chef's Tale (with Richard Flaste and Bryan Miller)

Pierre Franey's Cooking in America (with Richard Flaste)

Cuisine Rapide (with Bryan Miller)

The Seafood Cookbook (with Bryan Miller)

Pierre Franey's Low-Calorie Gourmet (with Richard Flaste)

Cooking with Craig Claiborne and Pierre Franey (with Craig Claiborne)

Pierre Franey's Kitchen (with Richard Flaste)

The New York Times 60-Minute Gourmet

Craig Claiborne's Gourmet Diet (with Craig Claiborne)

The New York Times More 60-Minute Gourmet

Classic French Cooking (with Craig Claiborne)

Veal Cookery (with Craig Claiborne)

Craig Claiborne's The New York Times Cookbook (with Craig Claiborne)

Pierre Franey's Cooking in France

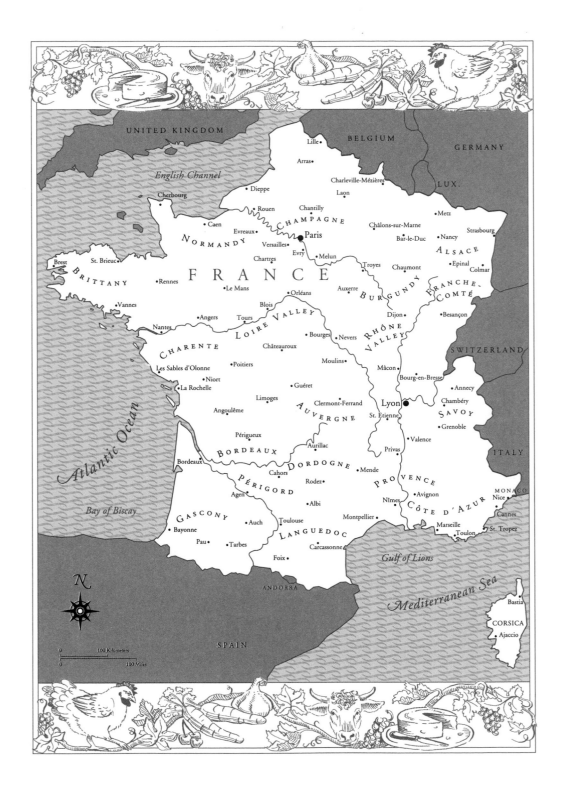

Pierre Franey's Cooking in France

BY PIERRE FRANEY

AND RICHARD FLASTE

ALFRED A. KNOPF   NEW YORK   1996

THIS IS A BORZOI BOOK
PUBLISHED BY ALFRED A. KNOPF, INC.

Copyright © 1994 by Pierre Franey and Richard Flaste
Maps copyright © 1994 by Claudia Carlson
All rights reserved under International and Pan-American
Copyright Conventions. Published in the United States by
Alfred A. Knopf, Inc., New York, and simultaneously in
Canada by Random House of Canada Limited, Toronto.
Distributed by Random House, Inc., New York.

Library of Congress Cataloging-in-Publication Data
Franey, Pierre.
Pierre Franey's cooking in France / by Pierre Franey
and Richard Flaste. — 1st ed.
p.   cm.
Includes index.
ISBN 0-679-43157-8
1. Cookery, French.   1. Flaste, Richard.   11. Title.
111. Title: Cooking in France.
TX719.F784 1994
641.5944—dc20   94-292
CIP

Manufactured in the United States of America
Published August 30, 1994
Second Printing, July 1996

For Luc

CONTENTS

ACKNOWLEDGMENTS

This book owes its greatest debt, its reason for being, to the public television series of the same name. The idea for the TV series came from Michel Roux, whose Carillon importers along with the Grand Marnier Foundation were its primary benefactors. The series was directed and produced by Charles Pinsky. The executive producer was John T. Potthast of Maryland Public Television.

Georgette Farkas, a Lausanne-trained hotel and restaurant authority, was central to the entire endeavor, functioning as both logistical wizard for the series and a food reporter for the book.

The French government tourist office in New York worked hard and long to provide assistance in facilitating travel throughout France and pointing us toward some of the most interesting of our experiences. Michel Bouquier, George L. Hern, Jr., and Marian Fourestier were our closest tourist-office contacts. I am also grateful to the people of the hotel and restaurant association Relais et Châteaux, and to the representatives of all of the local tourist offices throughout France who saw to it that we moved smoothly from one destination to another. Organizational assistance was also provided by Patricia Barroll of Carillon.

Two highly professional editorial assistants, Ana Deboo and, on several occasions, Melissa Clark, made it possible to produce this book as rapidly as its tight deadline required.

A great many others were gracious and helpful along the way, most of whom are mentioned in the course of this book and in the listing of establishments at the end.

As always, I want to express deep gratitude for the wise and expert guidance of my longtime friend, Jonathan B. Segal, vice president and senior editor of Knopf, whose affection for France matches my own.

Pierre Franey's Cooking in France

Introduction SO MUCH TO TRY

I was visiting Lyon, home of some of France's finest restaurants, when I ran into a friend of many years, Paul Bocuse. He was driving his Mercedes, dressed in a white chef's jacket, and had three passengers in the car, all chefs in uniform. He spotted me as I was shopping at a vegetable stand, on a break from filming *Cooking in France* for public television, a program—like this book—intended to share with Americans as much of today's culinary France as possible.

"Pierre, why aren't you coming to see me?" Paul called out. "You're going every place else." So Paul already knew about the show, probably knew exactly where I had been in the country and where I was headed. Sometimes I think top French chefs are born with antennae; they always know what's going on. I stepped away from the green beans and the zucchini and explained to him that he was already too famous back in the States (the man even runs a restaurant at Disney World!); I told him I was on a mission to see the whole of France in a way that I had never experienced it before, to visit places old and new that might hold surprises for viewers, readers of this book, and even for a veteran traveler in France like me. I know (I think, anyway) that Paul understood; he laughed and drove off.

The France I was in the midst of visiting was one flourishing with cooks of every category, from the practitioners of traditional peasant cuisine to the most innovative chefs. And there was so much I wanted to do. Certainly, I wanted to try out Pierre Gagnaire's place in St. Etienne, the restaurant that had recently received the coveted Michelin third star, but just as important was to discover places I had never heard about and never would have visited except for the opportunity afforded by the wide range of this trip—and I ultimately succeeded. I found my way, for instance, to the establishment of Chef Jean-Marie Miquel in Najac, a cook who is decidedly underappreciated by any guidebook I have ever seen. I wanted to spend time with people cooking in the humbler restaurants and also to drop in on the farmers and processors responsible for the cheese, wine, meat, fish, herbs, vegetables—everything that makes eating in France the great joy it is today. For the American reader and cook, a greater appreciation of this French ardor for produce underlines the principle—too often paid only lip service—that at the heart of great food is the use of the best possible ingredients, fresh as can be and with a minimum of processing.

Not so long ago, I felt sorely disappointed in the way French cuisine was evolving. This was the time of *nouvelle cuisine,* which took over in the 1970s and left its mark, even in its declining years, into the 1980s. It was a kind of dark age, if you will, that had this country in its grip, a time when many chefs in France—small-time and big-time alike—thought they had to produce dishes that existed almost entirely for their looks, their showmanship. A little of this would be neatly arranged with a little of that, on a huge plate that was meant to be a canvas for the chef's painting, without any evident effort to cause flavors and ingredients to work in concert. (It might be a steamed bit of fish composed with some warmed cherry tomatoes, snow peas in ginger butter, maybe a few deep-fried strips of leek, all of it arranged so carefully by hand and pretty, but no expert cooking here, a concoction of garnishes.)

It looked to me as if regional cooking, the engine of the French culinary masterwork, had been forced into a period of neglect. Even Bocuse, a pioneer of *nouvelle,* came to think that he was inadvertently participating in the demise of the great French cuisine, and he started to distance himself from it. On top of being pretentious and often foolish, *nouvelle* was driving cooks away from the reasonably priced cuts of meat, from the reliance on fine old soups and stews and ample portions of vegetables and breads. So it was expensive, too—for the chef as well as for the customer.

Ironically, you might say the recession that began in the late 1980s wasn't all bad for cooks: throughout France, it forced many of them to go back to some of the time-honored food, just to save money. But, in hindsight, I think the reaction against *nouvelle*—because it was simply bad cooking—was inevitable. Exactly when it would take place and how thoroughly was an open question.

Clearly, as I could see for myself again and again on this recent trip, it is behind us now. There is a renewed reverence for true cooking that should inspire home cooks. Go to Alsace and notice how proud the people are of their *choucroute garnie* (the time-honored sauerkraut and sausage dish) or go to Carcassonne for a *cassoulet,* as wonderful a *cassoulet* as ever. Try the herbed dishes of Provence and the *foie gras* of the Périgord. It is clear that regional cooking, which had been holding its head low, is laughing its head off now.

But there are other trends that this trip around all of France allowed me to discern, too: young people are coming into the business with an energy and optimism I can't recall seeing in decades. France not long ago set up a vocational high-school system in which the youngsters attend two years of cooking school that includes regular "stages" at various restaurants so that they can practice what they learn in an internship. When they graduate they seek out salaried beginners' jobs in restaurants and work their way up. Alain Ducasse, one of the most spectacular of the new breed of French cooks—maybe the best there is today—has set up, in effect, his own graduate program for these young people in his restaurant at the Hôtel de Paris in Monte Carlo, taking them for a year at a time after they leave vocational school, imbuing them with his reverence for ingredients and true cooking, then sending them on their way. You see his graduates all over the country: Richard Coutanceau, in La Rochelle, is one spectacularly successful example. I don't want to say that this approach—vocational school and internships—is better than the old apprenticeship period that I served (three years of brutally hard work starting at the age of fourteen), but it comes close and it seems successful.

With all this attention to professionalism and the big new crop of restaurant workers, the forgotten art of skilled table service is happily returning—a roast carved or a sauce flambéed at tableside. I had thought that this kind of service was gone forever. In the aftermath of World War II, it seemed so hard to get trained dining-room personnel that it was necessary to finish every dish on the plate before it was brought to the dining room; that situation did not improve until recently.

It takes years of training to learn the more elaborate serving techniques, of course, but home cooks should seize the chance to learn from masters. They possess, to the utmost, a respect for careful presentation that is essential to keep in mind, no matter what one's level of skill. (Don't hurl rice on the plate, mold each serving in a cup first; don't just place the sliced beef any which way, place it in a symmetrical pattern, and so on.)

Despite the renewed focus on tradition in cooking and presentation, I don't want to convey the impression that innovation is dead—it certainly is not, as you will see in the ensuing pages—nor has France turned a deaf ear to modern nutritional thinking. Many French chefs are lightening their cooking, using less fat and relying more vigorously on the less-embellished wonderful ingredients themselves.

Another heartening development is that as the young people cascade into the business, invigorating it in such a dynamic way, they are doing so as couples, with astounding frequency. It used to be that the restaurant business just about killed romance; it was terribly hard for young men and women to find time together, given those demanding hours. The business also used to be almost entirely male. Now, because both men and women are entering restaurant work, you will see them combining work and social life by opening restaurants. I'm thinking of delightful people like Regis and Fabienne Ongaro at La Belle Étoile in the Dordogne Valley, who work as hard as any two people possibly could, he in the kitchen and she in the dining room. I find all this very amusing because it is reflective, a mirror image of the modern trend at home—both in France and America—where it was men who rarely entered the kitchen before. Now young men and women work together at the range all the time, a happy couples' pursuit.

And one more salutary development: the bistros are going stronger than ever. In Paris, you will find that great chefs like Joël Robuchon and Michel Rostang have opened bistros to coexist with their loftier establishments. In St. Etienne, Pierre Gagnaire runs one in addition to his Michelin three-star restaurant, and in Lyon, there is an absolute explosion of bistros, thanks in some good measure to the work of Jean-Paul Lacombe, who has almost single-handedly ignited the renewal. I can't help but believe that this revival will make its way right into the American home, too, as bistro food—the hearty stews, *pâtés,* and roasts—take on a new and deserved cachet.

If you asked me for just two words to describe what this whirlwind tour of France taught me about the nation's cooking, they would be: alive again! French cooking is truly a dynamic process, as many of the recipes and discussions in this book will serve to illustrate, and I expect the cuisine's dynamism will make sure it remains alive as the example to follow elsewhere in the world, especially in the United States.

Paris

Onion soup, especially in Les Halles area

Steak frites, steak, usually a strip steak, served with thin, crunchy french fries

Pot-au-feu, boiled beef and vegetables

Fruits de mer platter, a colorful presentation of raw oysters and clams on the half shell, steamed mussels, and boiled *langoustines* and shrimp; available widely

Couscous served with stewed vegetables and Merguez sausages, now a Parisian staple

Creative dishes and great wines at countless temples of *haute cuisine*

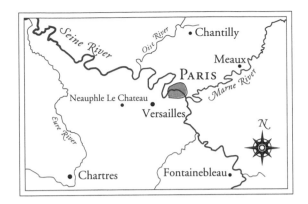

ALL THE VOICES
OF FRANCE

Some books on French cooking or guidebooks on France barely—if at all—mention the general cooking of Paris. They may name the world-renowned restaurants, but they don't speak about Parisian cooking itself. It's as if Paris, unlike Provence or Burgundy, were just too big and chaotic to contemplate. Or perhaps it is that Paris isn't so much French as it is part of the same country that includes New York, Rome, and Tokyo, so cosmopolitan now, with so many influences, that it must be taken on its own. The Paris I see today, it is true, is a cacophony of cooking voices each shouting to be heard. And yet, maybe because I visit so often and maybe because my daughter Claudia and her husband Rick live there, the city does seem more harmonious and welcoming, more comprehensible to me now. It is as much my home as St. Vinnemer in Burgundy, or East Hampton in New York. And when I go back, I like what I see, very much.

Although Paris, like the rest of France, has gone through periods when there seemed to be very little diversity in its culinary offerings, the truth is, in the long view, one sees that it has always been willing to move on. This observation holds especially among the temples of *haute cuisine.* Not so very long ago every chef had to abide by the dictates of Escoffier. If, for instance, he was preparing something called a *poularde Lucullus*—braised chicken stuffed with nine ounces of forcemeat and five ounces of grated truffle—that was precisely what the dish had to contain. Four ounces of truffle would be unacceptable. Although the culinary mastery in France was unmatched, thanks to Escoffier, there was no tolerance for innovation. Today, the mastery is still there but influences from all over France (many of which will be alluded to elsewhere in this book) have taught the practitioners of *haute cuisine* that militaristic devotion to rules can be abandoned to good effect, that,

after they ground themselves well in the basics and *At home, again, in Paris*
virtues of the past, they can start to trust themselves.

The result is that, from one great Paris restaurant to
the next, you will find offerings that are lighter than
they were in Escoffier's day, dishes that emphasize eye appeal more than they ever
did, and that are often smaller in serving size, in recognition of the changing desires
of today's diners. You won't see the classical *faisan souvaroff,* for instance (a pheasant
with truffles and *foie gras,* baked with a brown sauce and Cognac and sealed in
dough). It's all too rich, too ostentatious.

What you will see is an idiosyncratic delight in creativity, one taboo after another
broken. If Escoffier used more than one sauce on each half of a plate, he made sure
they would harmonize, like a cream sauce and a lobster sauce for grilled salmon.
Now you will find combinations that in the past could only have been described as
bizarre: for instance, *filet mignon* served with paprika sauce on one side and a truffle
sauce on the other. The effect is to offer contrast, counterpoint—and yet it works in
a traditional sense, by which I mean the dish is a single statement and not a lot of
individual bits of this and that failing to join in the larger effort.

In a way the *haute cuisine* of Paris is a powerful illustration to the home cook of a

A cook in the expansive kitchen of Les Ambassadeurs at the Hôtel de Crillon, one of the grand Parisian hotels noted for haute cuisine

lesson I always try to impart: start out by following a recipe to the letter, so you understand what its creator meant it to be. Then, armed with that bit of education, try your own variations, have fun, assert yourself.

As much as the cuisine of Paris is evolving and displaying its willingness to innovate, it has not been at the expense of plainer cooking. The great bistro dishes that deserve to last forever, like a fine onion soup or a rabbit stew, are going strong. The bistros in Montparnasse and the whole Left Bank are vibrant again, after what seemed to me to be a moribund period. The regional cooking I have enjoyed recently all over France—with each area so proud and so determined in presenting its own cooking—is strongly represented in Paris as a kind of buffet of regions: Alsatian cooking, Southwestern cooking, a bit of Provence or, perhaps, Normandy. Take your pick. And, if a break from France is needed, there's a Thai place, or a whole pack of Vietnamese establishments (there is far more Vietnamese food than Chinese in Paris, because of the historic link with Southeast Asia). Italian restaurants abound now, although few would be regarded as upscale the way they frequently are in New York. And who in the past would have predicted that the couscous of North Africa would become one of the Parisian staples of the day? All of this is incredible to me, and thrilling; you must understand that when I was a boy apprenticing in Paris in the 1930s I had never even heard of spaghetti, much less lemongrass.

This explosion of influences is in some good measure due to Rungis, the wholesale market that replaced the hallowed Les Halles. When I was young, I often went to Les Halles in central Paris, and then one might have been able to buy some products from the various regions of France. Perhaps there was some produce from Spain or Brussels. But mostly the foodstuffs came from nearby environs.

Most of Les Halles (that is, the marketplace) is gone now, although the old neighborhood is still vibrant with restaurants that evoke the area's recent past. The bistros are still there, and Les Halles is often the first place a Parisian in the mood for bistro food would choose, because it feels so right. A restaurant owner named Jacques Paul runs A La Tour de Montelhéry much as he always has since 1966, although his clientele has changed, it's true. The patrons once stopped in all night long, coming directly from backbreaking work at the market, but now the customers are more likely to be of the white-collar variety, businessmen and -women. The bawdiness that was once routine here is mostly a gleeful memory now, recalled over and over again in stories by the staff and owners. But the menu hasn't changed, still leaning toward the meat dishes that so satisfied the butchers of Les Halles streaming in from the market. It's the perfect place to go for a serious skirt steak, called *onglet,* or a terrific *côte de boeuf* (rib steak).

The contrast between the old Les Halles, the earthy market it once contained, its stalls and vendors selling their wares in a personal way, and the industrial, super-efficient market that has replaced it is as sharp as can be. Rungis's size and the volume of its business take your breath away. About a half hour's drive south from the center of Paris, Rungis is the largest single commercial food market in Europe. Three thousand trailer trucks pass through each day, and 15,000 individual buyers. In 1992, 2.2 million tons of food were sold.

It can be an intimidating place, with huge chilly hangars, each dedicated to one product or another—fish, meat, dairy, fruit, vegetables, flowers. And when I stepped into the fish hangar, which opens at 4:00 a.m. and has already dispatched much of its seafood to shops, restaurants, and elsewhere in Paris and

Europe by 6 a.m., I found the cold air so briny that it actually smelled like the sea.

I was surprised to see that the provincialism of old Paris has receded to the extent that at Rungis there is smoked fish from Denmark, citrus fruit from Florida, lamb from Poland, and, believe it or not, chanterelles (called *girolles* in France) from the Pacific Northwest of the United States.

So comfortable is this new Paris with its eclecticism that you even find the princes of *haute cuisine* mingling with the skilled practitioners of the *cuisine bourgeoise,* and doing so with unbridled admiration rather than the condescension I saw not so many years ago. One of the most enjoyable times we had in Paris on a recent excursion was at a restaurant called La Régalade, a robust representative of southwestern France's country cooking. There we ate the tripe sausages called *andouillettes* and country *pâté* and the cured ham of Bayonne—homey stuff. But we were joined for a joyous meal by the likes of Christian Constant, chef of the august Hôtel de Crillon; Guy Legay of the Hôtel Ritz; Gabriel Biscay of the Lapérouse; and Manuel Martinez of La Tour d'Argent. And I must tell you that there, among the simple *pâtés* and the simpler decor (bentwood chairs, red vinyl banquettes), these famed chefs devoured the meal with gusto.

For anyone new to this complex Paris, or in search of rewarding eating experiences that can cross the ocean to our kitchens, it helps to have a bit of insiders' knowledge. To be reasonably certain that a bistro is worth your time and money, it is sensible here, as in other important restaurant areas of the world, to note whether a place is crowded with locals, as most of the good ones will be. Some restaurants, like La Coupole on the Left Bank, may be more noted for their casual, bistro ambience than the food, but the cuisine isn't bad either, particularly the festive seafood platter called *fruits de mer.*

For good, inexpensive lunches, if you happen to be in a business neighborhood, the *boulangeries* (bakeries/gourmet shops) will serve delicious light meals at a counter or, often, at small tables in a tiny room at the back or upstairs. Frequently, they will have daily specials, like beef stew, steak and potatoes, roast chicken, or a *brandade* (salt cod and mashed potatoes); almost always it will be something simple, without fanfare, meant for eating-on-the-go. At the other end of the spectrum, the legendary restaurants, it makes the most sense to order the specials, or from the prix fixe menu (often a restaurant will allow substitutions, so don't be timid about asking). The idea is to request the sort of dish that won't be found elsewhere, something unique to a great restaurant—the price will be high enough.

❧ In the bistro spirit, I used the facilities of the Crillon kitchen to prepare a saddle of rabbit; rabbit deserves greater popularity in the United States because it is so lean and flavorful. It's marvelous with sautéed wild mushrooms added to the sauce, as I have done here, or on the side.

Rable de Lapin à la Moutarde

(SADDLE OF RABBIT WITH MUSTARD)

2 saddles of rabbit, about 1½ pounds total

Salt and freshly ground pepper to taste

2 teaspoons olive oil

1 tablespoon shallots, finely chopped

½ cup pearl onions, peeled

1 cup carrots, trimmed, peeled, cut into 2-inch pieces, and then quartered lengthwise

1 cup dry white wine

Bouquet garni tied with string and consisting of:

2 sprigs thyme

4 sprigs parsley

1 small sprig rosemary

1 bay leaf

½ cup heavy cream

1 tablespoon Dijon mustard

Sautéed mushrooms (recipe follows)

4 sprigs chervil, for garnish

1. Split the saddles in half by cutting across the backbone. Season on all sides with salt and pepper to taste.

2. In a skillet large enough to hold the rabbit pieces in one layer, heat the olive oil over medium-high heat. Add the rabbit, backbone side down, and cook until lightly browned. Turn and cook on second side. (Total browning time about 3 minutes.) Add the shallots, pearl onions, carrots, white wine, and *bouquet garni*. Cook, stirring, for a minute or two. Reduce to a simmer, cover, and cook for about 15 minutes. Do not allow it to return to a boil. Remove the rabbit pieces from the cooking juices and keep warm.

3. Bring the cooking juices to a boil and reduce by half. Add the cream and mustard and blend well. Incorporate the sautéed mushrooms (recipe follows). Check the sauce for seasoning. Return the rabbit and any juices that have accumulated around it to the sauce and cook until heated through, coating with the sauce. Remove and discard the *bouquet garni*.

4. Place 1 piece of rabbit on each of 4 warmed serving plates. Spoon the sauce and vegetables around and garnish with sprigs of chervil.

YIELD: 4 SERVINGS

Sauté de Champignons

(SAUTÉED WILD MUSHROOMS)

1 tablespoon butter
1 cup chanterelles (or other wild
   mushrooms), trimmed and
   cleaned
1 cup shiitake (or other wild mush-

rooms), trimmed and cleaned
1 tablespoon shallots, finely chopped
Salt and freshly ground pepper to
   taste

1. In a heavy-gauge skillet, melt the butter over high heat and add all the mushrooms, stirring well, until lightly browned and all the moisture has evaporated.

2. Add the shallots and salt and pepper to taste and continue to cook, stirring, until wilted (about 3 or 4 minutes). Check for seasoning.

YIELD: 4 SERVINGS

❧ Among the more elegant restaurants we visited in Paris was the Bistro Chez Pauline, with its chef André Génin; it has been run by members of the Génin family since 1952. Unlike the sorts of places that choose a single culinary niche and stick to it, André likes to mix things up a bit, with bistro and more refined classics mingled. Take, for instance, his classic oysters and spinach.

Note: Although I offer guidance on shucking oysters in the recipe, a simpler option is to ask the fishmonger to do it for you shortly before you prepare the dish (be sure to save the oyster liquor).

Huîtres Panées aux Epinards

(BREADED OYSTERS WITH SPINACH)

12 oysters
1 egg
1 cup toasted fresh French bread
   crumbs, pressed through a fine
   sieve

Juice of ½ lemon
6 tablespoons butter

2 cups spinach leaves (about ½
    pound), washed, drained, and
    trimmed

Salt and pepper to taste
Pinch of paprika, for decoration

1.   Cover the palm of your hand with a folded kitchen towel and place an oyster in it. Using an oyster knife, scrape any dirt from the oyster. Thrust the point of the knife into the hinge of the shell and run the knife around the oyster, forcing it open. Once the shell has been opened, scrape the oyster and its juices from the bottom shell into a small saucepan. Repeat until all oysters are removed from their shells.

2.   Place the saucepan containing the oysters over medium heat and poach them in their juices for about 1 minute. Turn once during the cooking time. Be sure not to overcook. Remove the saucepan from the heat and transfer the oysters to a plate. Reserve the cooking juices.

3.   In a small mixing bowl, beat the egg.

4.   Dip each oyster first in the beaten egg and then in the bread crumbs, tapping to remove any excess.

5.   Strain the reserved cooking juices through a fine sieve into a small saucepan and cook over medium heat until reduced to ¼ cup. Using a wire whisk, beat in the lemon juice and 3 tablespoons of butter, adding it one small piece at a time.

6.   In a large nonstick skillet, over medium-high heat, melt 1 tablespoon butter and add the spinach. Cook, stirring, just until wilted. Remove and keep warm.

7.   In another nonstick skillet large enough to hold the oysters in a single layer, melt the remaining 2 tablespoons butter over high heat. When the butter begins to bubble, add the oysters and cook on the first side until lightly browned. Turn and cook on second side. You should not cook the oysters for more than 1 to 2 minutes on each side.

8.   Divide the spinach onto 2 warmed serving plates. Spoon the sauce around it. Arrange 6 oysters on each plate around the spinach. Sprinkle a pinch of paprika on the plate borders for decoration.

YIELD: 2 SERVINGS

❧ *At La Régalade, Yves Candeborde prepared the most typical and enduring of bistro desserts, a* clafouti *(custard tart) with pears, although it is well known with other fruits, especially cherries. You might want to try figs, or apples. Yves replaces the traditional flour with cornstarch to make it lighter.*

Important note: In this version of a clafouti, *the batter is partially cooked on the range top so that it will set a bit and the fruit will not fall directly to the bottom. Then it is moved into the oven. So it is imperative that you use an ovenproof skillet for the entire procedure.*

Clafouti aux Poires

(CUSTARD TART WITH PEARS)

2 ripe pears, about 2½ cups	1 egg yolk
6 tablespoons sugar	1 cup *crème fraîche* or heavy cream
2 tablespoons cornstarch	2 tablespoons butter
10 tablespoons ground almonds	1 tablespoon Poire William liqueur
3 eggs	Raspberry *coulis* (see recipe page 65)

1.   Heat the oven to 400°.

2.   Peel the pears and cut them into quarters. Using a paring knife, cut away the cores and seeds. Cut the fruit into ¼-inch cubes.

3.   In a mixing bowl, using a flexible wire whisk, combine the sugar, cornstarch, and ground almonds and blend well. Add the whole eggs, and continue to beat with a wire whisk until the mixture is completely smooth. Add the egg yolk and blend well. Incorporate the *crème fraîche* or cream and blend well, once again. Be careful not to beat too much once the cream has been added or it will turn to butter.

4.   In a nonstick skillet, cook 1 tablespoon of butter over medium-high heat until it begins to take on a hazelnut color. Add the pears and toss them in the butter, cooking briefly. Add the Poire William and again cook briefly without flaming.

5.   In a 9-inch nonstick ovenproof skillet, melt 1 tablespoon of the butter. Add the batter and cook it over medium heat until it begins to set, about 1 minute. Arrange the sautéed pears and their cooking juices attractively over the batter.

6.   Place the skillet in the oven for 8 to 10 minutes. The outside should be set and the inside still a bit runny when the *clafouti* comes out of the oven.

7. Invert the *clafouti* onto a warmed serving platter. It should be light golden brown on the outside. Serve surrounded by raspberry *coulis*.

YIELD: 4 SERVINGS

❧   *In a city of grand hotels, I doubt any are grander than the Crillon, once the mansion of counts, and now the Paris residence of contemporary nobility from the king of Morocco to Elizabeth Taylor. But the service is such that any of us feels noble there. And the food—during a period of bistro re-ascendancy and nagging recession—demonstrates that* haute cuisine *is also still alive and well in many quarters of Paris. The formal dining room of the hotel's Restaurant Les Ambassadeurs is hushed, its walls decorated with gilt mirrors, crystal chandeliers and frescoes overhead. One knows this is an important place, in history as well as cuisine, without bothering to think about it. The paradox is that as opulent as all this is, it does not leave you with a sense of overbearing pretentiousness; it's comfortable. We had a meal that included* Mousseline d'Oeufs Brouillés au Corail et Langues d'Oursin *(sea urchins stuffed with scrambled eggs); a* Suprême de Pintade Fermier Poêle à l'Etouffé *(sautéed breast of guinea hen); and* Feuilletée à la Crème d'Amande et Poires Rôties *(puff pastry with almond cream and roast pears), with* Glace à la Williamine *(ice cream flavored with pear liqueur).*

The terrific chef at Les Ambassadeurs is Christian Constant, who also prepared a seafood risotto, and offered words of encouragement to anyone attempting it at home. Just remember, he said, to keep stirring and add the broth to the rice only when the broth is very hot, otherwise it will lower the temperature of the risotto and diminish its texture.

Risotto aux Fruits de Mer de Christian Constant
(CHRISTIAN CONSTANT'S SEAFOOD RISOTTO)

1 1½-pound lobster
1 tablespoon plus 2 teaspoons
    olive oil
Salt and freshly ground pepper
    to taste

2 cups fresh chicken broth (see
    recipe page 108), or good quality
    canned
4 tablespoons butter
¼ cup onions, finely chopped

½ cup Arborio rice, an imported
    Italian rice available in specialty
    shops
4 tablespoons freshly grated Parmesan
    cheese

⅓ cup heavy cream
⅓ cup fresh lump crabmeat,
    picked over

1.   Kill the lobster by placing it on a cutting board and inserting the tip of a large knife between the eyes. With scissors, carefully cut through the length of the bottom of the tail and remove the meat in one piece. Separate the claws and the legs.

2.   In a nonstick skillet, heat 2 teaspoons of olive oil over medium heat and add the shelled lobster tail, the claws, and the legs. Season with salt and pepper and cook the tail until lightly browned, about 2 minutes on each side. Reduce to a simmer, cover, and cook for an additional 2 minutes. Remove from heat and slice the tail in half lengthwise. Crack the shell of the claws and remove the meat whole. Keep the halves, the claws, and the legs covered and warm.

3.   In a small saucepan, bring the chicken broth to a boil over medium-high heat. Reduce it to a simmer and keep simmering while the rice is cooked.

4.   In a saucepan, melt 1 tablespoon of the butter over medium heat and add the onions and remaining olive oil. Cook, stirring, until just wilted. Add the rice and cook, stirring, until the grains are well coated.

5.   Add ½ cup of the chicken broth and simmer, stirring from time to time until all the liquid has been absorbed.

6.   Add another ½ cup of chicken broth to the rice, stirring from time to time. When all the liquid has been absorbed, add another ½ cup chicken broth. Cook, stirring, until all the liquid has been absorbed. Do not overcook. The rice should be firm, or *al dente.* If the rice is still not sufficiently cooked, add remaining chicken broth.

7.   Stir in the Parmesan cheese and 3 tablespoons butter and blend well. Add the cream and the crabmeat and blend well. Simmer, but do not return to a boil once the cream has been added. Check for seasoning.

8.   Divide the risotto evenly onto 2 warmed plates. Decorate the risotto with the lobster legs and place a half tail along with 1 claw over each serving. Serve with additional Parmesan cheese on the side, if desired.

YIELD: 2 SERVINGS

✣ *Another of the classic dishes that is coming back as diners look for more traditional food is calf's brains in its many forms. It needs to be served with nothing more elaborate than simple boiled potatoes; the browned butter does the rest.*

Cervelle de Veau au Beurre Noir
(CALF'S BRAINS IN BROWN BUTTER)

FOR BLANCHING:

2 calf brains, about 1 pound total
6 peppercorns
Salt to taste
2 tablespoons white wine vinegar

1 bay leaf
2 sprigs fresh thyme, or 1 teaspoon
 dried

FINAL COOKING:

½ cup flour
Salt and freshly ground pepper
 to taste
4 tablespoons butter

2 tablespoons parsley, chopped
2 tablespoons capers, drained
2 tablespoons red wine vinegar

1. Place the brains in a mixing bowl and add cold water to cover. Let stand for several hours, changing the water frequently.

2. Drain and pick over the brains to remove the outer membranes, blood, and other extraneous matter. Place them in a saucepan and add water to cover them completely. Add the peppercorns, salt, vinegar, bay leaf, and thyme. Bring to a boil and simmer for about 3 minutes, no longer. Remove from heat and let cool.

3. Mix the flour with salt and pepper and blend well.

4. Split the brains in half horizontally. Coat them thoroughly with the seasoned flour and shake to remove the excess.

5. Melt half of the butter in a heavy nonstick skillet large enough to hold all the brains at once. Add them and cook on one side over medium-high heat until golden brown, about 5 minutes. Turn and cook for about 3 minutes on the other side, or until lightly browned.

6. Transfer the brains to a warm plate and sprinkle with parsley. Add the remaining butter to the skillet with its drippings and cook until quite brown. Do not burn the butter. Immediately add the capers and red wine vinegar and blend well. Spoon equal portions of the sauce over each serving. Serve with boiled potatoes.

YIELD: 2 SERVINGS

❧ *In my early days as a cook in Paris, a fine roasted veal with tarragon was something to be proud of. It still is. Snap peas with mint make a fine side dish (recipe follows).*

Rôti de Veau à l'Estragon

(ROAST VEAL WITH TARRAGON)

1 3½-pound boneless veal roast cut from the rack, with the bones reserved

Salt and freshly ground pepper to taste

2 tablespoons butter

¼ cup onions, sliced

1 garlic clove, peeled

¼ cup carrots, scraped and cut into thin rounds

1 bay leaf

4 sprigs fresh thyme, or 1 teaspoon dried

4 sprigs fresh tarragon, or 1 teaspoon dried

½ cup dry white wine

½ cup fresh chicken broth, or good quality canned

½ cup heavy cream

1 tablespoon chopped fresh tarragon, or 1 teaspoon dried

1. Preheat the oven to 350°.

2. Sprinkle the roast with salt and pepper. Heat the butter in a heavy skillet and, when hot, add the meat. Turn the meat in the butter to brown it lightly on all sides.

3. Place veal in roasting pan. Scatter the onions, garlic, carrots, bay leaf, and thyme and tarragon sprigs around the veal. Scatter the bones around the meat. Place the meat in the oven and bake for 30 minutes. Turn the meat and add the wine and the chicken broth. Cover loosely with foil and bake for 30 minutes longer, basting occasionally.

4. Turn the meat once more, cover it again, and bake for another 30 minutes.

5. Remove the roast to a tray and discard the bones. Add the cream to the roasting pan and cook over medium heat, stirring to dissolve the browned particles that cling to the bottom. Simmer for 5 minutes and pour the sauce through a sieve.

6. Return the roast to the pan, along with any juices that have accumulated on the tray. Add the strained sauce, sprinkle the chopped fresh tarragon over the meat and bring to a simmer. Slice the veal and serve with the sauce.

YIELD: 6 OR MORE SERVINGS

Mange-Touts à la Menthe
(SNAP PEAS WITH MINT)

1 pound snap peas
Salt and freshly ground pepper
   to taste
4 plum tomatoes, about ¾ pound,
   cored

2 tablespoons butter
1 tablespoon fresh mint, shredded
2 teaspoons lemon juice

1.   Pluck off and discard the end of each pea pod.

2.   Bring enough salted water to boil to cover the peas.

3.   Add the peas. When the water returns to a boil, simmer for 3 to 4 minutes. Do not overcook. Drain.

4.   Meanwhile, drop the tomatoes into boiling water, boil for 10 seconds, drain, and allow to cool. Remove the skins and cut them into ¼-inch cubes.

5.   Heat the butter in a saucepan, add the tomatoes, and stir for 1 minute. Add the peas, mint, and salt and pepper to taste. Stir to blend. Cook for another minute. Add the lemon juice and serve.

YIELD: 4 SERVINGS

⁂   *There's almost nothing more common in Paris than a* crôque monsieur, *a toasted sandwich of ham and cheese. I'm offering you a recipe for only one serving because, in all likelihood, you will find yourself making them individually.*

Crôque Monsieur
(TOASTED HAM AND CHEESE SANDWICH)

2 square slices of firm-textured white
   bread
4 thin slices of Swiss cheese, Comté
   or Gruyère

2 thin slices of baked ham
2 tablespoons butter

1.   For one sandwich, place a slice of bread on a flat surface. Top it neatly with 2 thin slices of cheese cut to fit. Cover with the ham, also trimmed to fit. Cover with the remaining cheese and top with the second bread slice.

2. In a nonstick skillet large enough to hold the sandwich, melt 2 tablespoons butter. Add the sandwich, brush the top with some of the butter, and brown the sandwich over medium-high heat. Turn it over, reduce the heat, and cover and cook until lightly browned. Cut in half and serve piping hot.

YIELD: I SANDWICH

For *Crôque Madame*: Follow the recipe for *Crôque Monsieur*, substituting 2 or 3 thin slices of cooked white chicken meat for the ham.

❧ *A favorite dish of mine that you are likely to find in some of the better Paris restaurants is one made from the finest veal rolled around a delicate stuffing.*

Paupiettes de Veau
(STUFFED VEAL BIRDS)

8 4-ounce boneless slices of veal
6 tablespoons butter
2 tablespoons shallots, finely chopped
½ cup plus 2 tablespoons onions, finely chopped
1 tablespoon plus 1 teaspoon garlic, chopped
½ pound very lean ground pork
½ pound mushrooms, finely chopped
Salt and freshly ground pepper to taste
½ teaspoon chopped fresh thyme, or ¼ teaspoon dried

⅓ cup fine white bread crumbs
1 tablespoon chopped parsley
1 whole egg, lightly beaten
½ cup carrots, finely chopped
1 bay leaf
4 sprigs parsley
1 cup dry white wine
1 cup fresh chicken broth (see recipe page 108), or good quality canned
½ cup canned crushed tomatoes
3 tablespoons finely chopped fresh tarragon (parsley may be substituted)

1. Place the veal slices between pieces of plastic wrap and pound with a mallet or meat pounder until thin.

2. Heat 2 tablespoons of the butter in a skillet and add the shallots, 2 table-

spoons of onions and 1 teaspoon of the garlic. Cook over medium-high heat until wilted, stirring. Add the ground pork and cook, stirring, for 10 minutes, until the sausage is cooked but not browned. Add the mushrooms, salt, and pepper. Stir until the mushroom juices evaporate. Stir in the thyme, bread crumbs, and the tablespoon of parsley. Let the mixture cool slightly, then stir in the egg. Blend well.

3. Preheat the oven to 400°.

4. Rub the bottom and sides of a baking pan with 2 tablespoons of butter; add the carrots and ½ cup onions. Add the bay leaf, remaining chopped garlic, and the parsley sprigs. Set the pan aside.

5. Lay the veal slices on a flat surface and divide the stuffing equally over the center of each slice. Roll each of the slices and seal them with a string or toothpicks.

6. In a skillet, brown the veal rolls lightly in the remaining butter on top of the stove. Arrange them in the baking pan and pour the wine, chicken broth, and the crushed tomatoes around the rolls. On the range top, bring the liquid in the pan to a boil, cover the pan with aluminum foil, and place in the oven. Cook for 35 minutes or until tender, basting occasionally.

7. Remove the foil and string or toothpicks. Bake for 15 minutes more, basting. Remove the bay leaf and parsley sprigs. Serve with the vegetables and the sauce sprinkled with tarragon.

YIELD: 4–8 SERVINGS

Normandy

SPECIALTIES

From the trilogy of normande cooking (cream, Calvados, and apple cider):

Poulet Vallée d'Auge, chicken with cream and apple cider

Matelote à la Normande, a fish stew made with thick slices of saltwater fish, cream, Calvados, and cider

Sole à la Normande, sole cooked in cream and flavored with Calvados

Tripes à la Mode de Caen, tripe baked with Calvados

ALSO

Boudin noir, spicy blood sausage, usually sautéed with apples

Duck, usually roasted or braised, served with a duck liver sauce

Omelette de la Mère Poulard, a sweet souffléed omelette

CHEESES

Pont l'Evêque, Livarot (whose skin is washed in Calvados), and Camembert

DESSERTS

Pommes Bourdaloue, poached apples baked with an almond cream and crumbled almond macaroons

Douillon Normande, apples (or pears) wrapped in a sweet pastry crust and baked

DRINKS

Cider and Calvados; there are no vineyards

AN APPLE A DAY

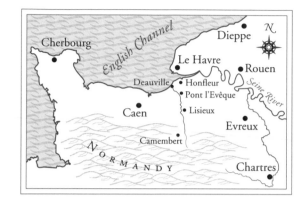

When I was a child, I knew Normandy mostly as some far-off place that would supply my home village in Burgundy with fish during the winter when our rivers and streams were frozen. My parents had a contract with the shipper and every week I would go to the train station to pick up our box of fish—perhaps plaice (a large flounder) or Dover sole. Now the Normandy I know is a much richer place in my mind's eye; it is the font of Atlantic fish, yes, that still come into the port of Dieppe, where the fishing boats dock all along the arc of the town's waterfront, like automobiles parallel-parked. Le Havre is a major port, too. And in the predawn of chilly winter mornings the catch from these ports is shipped off to Paris and beyond, just as it was in the past. But this is also the vibrant wellspring of the best and most varied apples in France, and the apple brandy, Calvados, that comes from them. There are remarkable ducks here, too, the Rouennais, that are half-wild and half-domestic and found nowhere else.

It is the region best known for cuisine built on cream and butter because they both are so undeniably spectacular here. Although heavy cream and butter have fallen on hard times in today's nutritional thinking, the people of Normandy who, in any event, do not march with the times so much as to their own values, do not seem to suffer in health or looks.

Normandy is also a tourist magnet for people fleeing Paris to swim at Deauville in the few weeks of summer that one might call beach weather—most of the year, no matter the season, the region is cool and damp although almost never very cold. Visitors come to see the rejuvenated old industrial city of Rouen, with its dominant cathedral, and its lovely restaurants and *pâtisseries*. Normandy is also so close to England that the English hop over regularly to linger at the seaside or, perhaps, take a ride along the *route de cidre*, a Calvados-tasting adventure

much like the wine tours that must have inspired it.

The port of Honfleur in Normandy

On our way into Normandy, we made an early visit to Beuvron en Auge and by a true coincidence we had the good fortune to arrive just in time for the Marche de Beuvron, a fair that coincides with the apple harvest and the beginning of the cidermaking season. The town is designated officially as a "preserved village," for its historic authenticity, and you can see why. There is a true sense of the genuine here.

The food at the fair couldn't have been more authentic: *boudin noir* (blood sausage) stuffed with apples and cooked over open fires, mussels grilled on open fires, too, and the superb Norman cheeses like Pont l'Evêque and Camembert, with more character by far than anything we experience in the States even though it might be known by the same name. (It is one of the paradoxes of French versus American cheese that although the processes are virtually the same, the differences in tastes are great. This is probably because of the richness of the milk that comes from cows grazing on the fine river-fed grasses of France, the meticulous production of each individual cheese, and the fact that many cheeses are not pasteurized, a procedure that kills some of their life.) Behind the fair was one woman's small, working farm and she had me taste her dandelion jam, rabbit *pâté,* and *confiture de lait,* milk thickened into a spread for toast or crêpes.

At the fair, we were treated to a quick course in making apple cider. The apples are crushed—their flesh turning brown as soon as it comes in contact with the air—and quickly pressed, with the juice forced through several layers of burlap to remove impurities. The next step is to pour it into barrels for fermenting. *Cidre doux,* or sweet cider, is fermented for only one month, whereas the full-flavored cider is fermented for about two and a half months. For the sake of getting into the act, I donned a billowing blue apron and joined a robust, red-cheeked worker in pouring the juice into barrels. I recall those red cheeks of his and assume it was the blustery weather that made his face so flushed but, heaven knows, there was enough cider around to do the trick as well. I don't know how much cider I drank, to tell you the truth, but the fair also presented a group of Burgundian clog dancers to entertain, natives all the way from my home region, and I joined them in song.

An apple orchard bursts into bloom.

It would be another day or two before I got to see

Women inspecting apples, perhaps destined for Calvados, the drink that supplants wine in Normandy

Calvados produced from the apple cider. Denis Lecadre, a chef from Honfleur, took us to an orchard in Pont l'Evêque. There the apple trees are managed much like grapevines that produce wine. The trees look like bushes, planted very close together in long, straight rows, with their branches forced to extend laterally (rather than growing freely about the tree) and joined by wires to the next tree; everything is manipulated to increase the ease of harvest. The apples we saw were Ida Reds, extraordinarily bright and looking for all the world like garlands wrapped around each tree. The most common regional variety is *Reinette de Caux* (*Caux* refers to the *Pays de Caux*, or land of chalk, which describes the limestone plain that is much of Normandy). There are more than a hundred varieties of apples on earth, forty-eight of which are used by brandy producers. The ones they choose are too bitter to eat, but they each possess nuances that are valuable to the brandy-maker, who will blend them the way a winemaker in Bordeaux will blend his Cabernet and Sémillon.

At the Coeur de Leon, a Calvados-maker takes cider that has been fermented for at least six months in wooden barrels and then distills it twice. It is that second distillation, just as with Cognac, that makes the Calvados smooth. When we arrived at the distillery, we saw the still itself immediately, sitting outside the main building; its embers were alight. And the sight of the fires burning and the steam coming out of the top of the still gave me a strange, palpable sense of the alchemy going on inside that big copper caldron as cider was transmuted into brandy.

As for my research into the food of Normandy, I saw two divergent trends: one was an effort to reach back and hang onto tradition with all the tenacity possible in this relentlessly modern time, and another was a willingness to yield a little, mostly for the better. The tenacious tradition could be seen, among other places, in the bakery of Jean François Osmont in Rouen (walk past it at almost any hour—the aroma of the baking bread wafts out and almost physically pulls you into the shop). Osmont, dressed in gray chinos and a sweater, has a tendency to clasp his hands at his lips as he talks, as if he were in prayer. He believes, he says, that the bread is alive until the moment it goes into the wood-burning oven. And during that short life, he always treats it gently, by hand, never by machine. He believes it needs to be coaxed, not rushed, with slow kneading. Bread dough, as he envisions it, is like an athlete's muscles and must be stretched and warmed gently. He talks about proofing as "putting the bread to sleep" for a couple of hours. I like this kind of spirituality; we revered bread in our home in Burgundy, too, never serving it upside down since that seemed irreverent (and to this day, if a roll arrives at my table bottom-up, I reflexively turn it over).

At the same time, in Rouen we met Gilles Tournadre, a chef (Restaurant Gill) who trained in Paris and is known far beyond Normandy. He cooks with a lighter touch than you might expect in this region, and he has an affection for herbs that would have been rare here not too long ago. Herbs, he explained to us, were never that well known in this chilly clime and never widely used, but they can be cultivated with diligent work, and he made a point of taking us up a hill to see a farmer who now grows a wide variety of herbs expressly for Gilles's use.

❧ Here is Gilles's wonderful honeyed duck breasts dish, prepared with cider, of course; Gilles uses it to deglaze the pan the way, more familiarly, one would use wine to create a sauce. He pays particular attention to removing excess fat, even to the extent of parboiling the breasts before they are placed in the skillet for the next step. He believes, as he said, "fat is the enemy of the sauce."

Canard aux Navets et aux Epices

(DUCK WITH TURNIPS AND SPICES)

18 baby white turnips
2 boneless duck breasts, such as
    magrets with skin on, about
    6 ounces each
2 tablespoons coriander seeds
2 whole cloves
2 teaspoons cumin seeds
Salt and freshly ground pepper
    to taste

4 tablespoons natural honey
3 tablespoons white vinegar
1 cup hard cider or ½ cup dry
    white wine
1 cup fresh chicken broth (see
    recipe page 108), or good quality
    canned
2 sprigs flat leaf parsley

1.   Trim the ends of the turnips and peel them. Cut into ¼-inch slices.

2.   Place the duck breasts and the turnips in a large saucepan with boiling salted water to cover. Cook, simmering over low heat for 1 minute. Remove the duck breasts and cook the turnips 2 minutes longer. Remove the turnips and place the duck breasts and the turnips in an ice bath to prevent them from cooking further. When cooled, remove the duck and the turnips, and pat the duck dry with a paper towel. Using a sharp knife, remove most of the skin and fat, leaving only a thin layer of the fatty skin for moistness while cooking. Score the surface of the remaining fat with diagonal slashes.

3.   Grind the coriander, cloves, and cumin coarsely by placing them on a cutting board and crushing them under a heavy saucepan. They can also be ground in a spice mill, but do not grind them too finely. Reserve.

4.   Meanwhile, season the duck breasts with salt and pepper to taste. In a skillet over medium-high heat, cook the breasts skin side down until lightly browned, about 2 minutes. Turn. Add the turnips, turning them from time to time, and con-

tinue cooking another 2 minutes. Remove the duck and turnips from the skillet and pour off the fat. Pat the skin of the duck breasts with paper towels to absorb any excess fat.

5.   In the same skillet, combine the honey and white vinegar. Bring to a boil, stirring constantly until the mixture begins to caramelize lightly and evenly. Add the ground spices while stirring (be careful not to burn). Remove skillet from the heat. Return the duck breasts to the skillet, skin side down, and move them around to coat them with the spice mixture. Remove the duck and keep warm.

6.   Return the skillet to medium-high heat and add the cider or white wine. Cook, scraping the sides and bottom of the pan, until all the brown particles are dissolved. Add the chicken broth and bring to a simmer. Add the duck breasts skin side up and place the turnips around them. Simmer for 3 to 4 minutes. Remove the duck only and keep warm. The meat should be pink inside.

7.   Bring the sauce and the turnips to a boil and cook until reduced by more than half, that is, until the sauce has thickened to a syrupy consistency.

8.   Cut the breasts on the bias into thin slices. Arrange the slices of the breasts in a fan shape in the center of warm serving plates. Garnish with turnips and spoon the sauce around. Decorate with sprigs of flat parsley.

YIELD: 2–4 SERVINGS

Note: You will have to bone the duck breasts yourself or purchase them already boned from a specialty distributor such as D'Artagnan (page 144), which ships overnight.

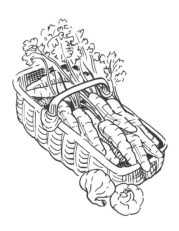

❧   *In the Vallée d'Auge, where the apples grow in profusion, there is nothing like an old-fashioned chicken sautéed in cider and cream, garnished with glazed carrots and, naturally, sautéed apples.*

Poulet Vallée d'Auge

(CHICKEN SAUTÉED WITH APPLE CIDER AND CREAM)

1 whole chicken, about 3½ pounds
Salt and freshly ground pepper to
   taste
2 tablespoons vegetable oil

1 cup hard cider (4% to 5% alcohol)
1½ cups heavy cream
Sautéed apples (see recipe page 33)
Glazed carrots (see recipe page 33)

1.   Cut the chicken into 4 serving portions, and season them with salt and pepper to taste.

2.   In a skillet large enough to hold the chicken pieces in one layer, add the oil over high heat. Add the chicken pieces, skin side down. Cook until browned on first side (about 10 minutes). Turn and cook on second side (about 2 minutes).

3.   Remove the chicken pieces and pour off any excess fat. Then reduce the heat to medium high, return the chicken to the skillet, and add the cider. Cook, simmering, until all the liquid has evaporated. Add the cream and simmer for an additional 5 minutes or until thickened. Check for seasoning.

4.   Place each chicken piece on a warmed serving plate. Divide the glazed carrots onto the plates, placing them in neat stacks with a sautéed apple quarter on each side. Strain the sauce and pour it around the chicken and the vegetables.

YIELD: 4 SERVINGS

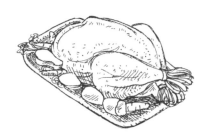

Sauté de Pommes

(SAUTÉED APPLES)

2 Granny Smith apples
2 tablespoons butter

1 tablespoon sugar

1.   Peel, core, and quarter the apples.

2.   Place the apple quarters in a small nonstick skillet over medium heat with the butter and the sugar. Cook, stirring, turning the pieces from time to time, until the juices begin to caramelize and the apples are tender, about 10 minutes. Remove from heat and keep warm.

YIELD: 4 SERVINGS

Carottes Glacées

(GLAZED CARROTS)

2 large carrots, peeled and trimmed
2 tablespoons butter
Pinch of sugar

Salt and freshly ground pepper to
    taste

1.   Cut the carrots into pieces 2 inches long and ¼-inch wide.

2.   Place the carrot pieces in a small saucepan over medium heat with the butter, sugar, and salt and pepper. Add water to barely cover.

3.   Cook, stirring from time to time, until the carrots are tender and the water has evaporated. Check for seasoning.

YIELD: 4 SERVINGS

In Honfleur is the legendary Ferme Saint-Simeon, a Tudoresque hotel and restaurant, built in the seventeenth century but perhaps most famous for its nineteenth-century incarnation as a school for a number of Impressionists, Monet among them. The place has been renovated and expanded so that, surprisingly, behind the Tudor façade there is now an opulent spa. The establishment is run by a large family, the Boellens, with Michelle, the mother, acting as general manager and the others in charge of decoration or personnel or cooking. (The chef, Denis Lecadre, married into this industrious group.) This is the fabulous seafood stew we had there.

Note: The original dish, in addition to the more familiar fish, used daurade, rouget, and John Dory. I have substituted for them; feel free to substitute further yourself—as long as the fish fillets are not too oily and are firm enough to hold up during the cooking.

Matelotte de Poissons

(NORMANDY FISH STEW)

½ cup fennel, trimmed and sliced into pieces 2 inches long and ¼-inch wide each

4 baby carrots, trimmed

8 pearl onions, peeled and trimmed

½ cup knob celery, trimmed and cut into ¼-inch cubes

1 cup string beans, trimmed

1 cup white mushrooms, trimmed and quartered

4 asparagus spears

1 cup snow peas, trimmed

½ pound sole fillets, skinless

½ pound blackfish fillets, skinless

½ pound turbot fillets, skinless

½ pound red snapper fillets

½ pound salmon fillets

4 large shrimp

1 lobster, about 1½ pounds

2 tablespoons olive oil

Salt and freshly ground pepper to taste

¼ cup Calvados

1 cup hard cider

1 cup fish broth (see recipe page 199)

6 tablespoons salted butter, cut into small cubes

¼ cup heavy cream

¼ cup *fines herbes* (chopped herbs such as parsley, chives, tarragon), well blended

1.   In a large pot, bring enough salted water to a boil over high heat to cover all the vegetables. Add the fennel, carrots, and pearl onions. Cook for 5 minutes. Add

the celery, string beans, mushrooms, and asparagus and cook for an additional 3 minutes. Add the snow peas and cook for another minute. Drain the vegetables. Reserve and keep warm.

2.   Cut each of the fish into pieces measuring 2 square inches. Shell and devein the shrimp. Kill the lobster by inserting the point of a sharp knife between its eyes. Place the lobster right side up on a cutting board, detach the claws, and cut the tail into 4 slices (in the shell) using a large heavy knife. Use the back of the knife to crack the claws slightly.

3.   In a saucepan over high heat, heat the olive oil and add the lobster pieces (tail and claws) with salt and pepper to taste. Cook, stirring constantly, until they begin to turn pink. Add the Calvados and ignite it. Once the flames have receded, add the cider and fish broth. Cover and cook for an additional 2 minutes. Remove from heat, reserve and keep warm.

4.   In a nonstick skillet large enough to hold the fish in a single layer, melt 2 tablespoons of the butter over medium-high heat. Add the blanched vegetables and salt and pepper to taste, and cook, tossing, for 2 minutes. Pour the lobster and cooking juices over the vegetables. Bring to a boil and simmer 2 to 3 minutes.

5.   Arrange the pieces of fish in a single layer on top of the vegetables and add salt and pepper to taste. Return to a simmer, cover, and cook for an additional 3 minutes. Add the cream and return the pan to a simmer, then swirl in the remaining butter.

6.   Add the herbs and check for seasoning. Serve immediately on warmed plates.

YIELD: 4 SERVINGS

❧ *Turning to the most notable ingredients available in Normandy (along with a few I just happen to favor), I went on to prepare this pasta dish. A fine side dish is simply steamed broccoli, for which the recipe follows.*

Pasta aux Coquilles Saint-Jacques

(PASTA WITH SCALLOPS)

8 large whole sea scallops (about 1 pound), rinsed to remove sand
1 cup soft goat's milk cheese
1 pound dried tagliatelle or similar pasta
1 cup snow peas
3 tablespoons olive oil
1 tablespoon garlic, finely chopped

4 ripe plum tomatoes, peeled and cut into ½-inch cubes
Salt and freshly ground pepper to taste
1 dash Tabasco sauce
2 tablespoons heavy cream
1 tablespoon basil, coarsely chopped
2 tablespoons pepper vodka

1. Cut each scallop in half horizontally.

2. Remove any crust from the cheese and cut the cheese into ¼-inch cubes.

3. In a large pot, bring enough salted water to a boil to cook the pasta. Cook according to package instructions, about 10 minutes. Do not overcook. One minute before the pasta is done, add the snow peas to the pot. Drain, reserving ¼ cup of the cooking liquid. Reserve the pasta and snow peas and keep warm.

4. In a large saucepan over medium-high heat, add the olive oil and garlic and cook briefly, taking care not to burn. Add the tomatoes, salt and pepper to taste, and the Tabasco and cook, stirring, for about 2 minutes. Add the goat cheese cubes, cream, basil, vodka, and the reserved cooking liquid. Stir until the goat cheese is melted and the ingredients are well-blended.

5. Season the scallops with salt and pepper to taste and add them to the tomato mixture. Cook stirring for about 2 minutes. Add the pasta and toss well until heated through. Check for seasoning and serve immediately on warmed plates.

YIELD: 4 SERVINGS

Broccoli à la Vapeur

(STEAMED BROCCOLI)

1 bunch broccoli
2 tablespoons olive oil
2 teaspoons garlic, minced

Salt and freshly ground pepper to
  taste

1. Using a paring knife, remove and discard the tough bottoms of the stalks. Cut the broccoli into flowerets.
2. Place the broccoli in a steamer and cook for 3 to 4 minutes. Do not overcook.
3. Heat the oil in a skillet, add the garlic, broccoli, and salt and pepper. Sauté briefly, making sure not to burn the garlic. Serve immediately.

YIELD: 4 SERVINGS

❧ *If that steamed broccoli seems too spartan for Normandy, here's a rich vegetable dish more in the creamy spirit.*

Flageolets à la Crème

(GREEN KIDNEY BEANS IN CREAM)

1 pound package dry flageolets
2 quarts water
Salt and freshly ground pepper
  to taste
1 carrot, scraped and quartered
2 cloves garlic, peeled

1 bay leaf
1 onion, stuck with 2 cloves
¾ cup heavy cream
2 tablespoons butter
⅛ teaspoon freshly grated nutmeg
4 tablespoons parsley, finely chopped

1. Place the beans in a large mixing bowl and cover with water to a depth of 2 inches above the top of the beans. Let stand overnight.
2. Drain the beans and place them in a saucepan with 2 quarts of water, salt and pepper, the carrot, garlic, bay leaf, and onion. Bring to a boil and simmer for 45 minutes, or until the beans are tender. Drain. Discard the carrot, garlic, bay leaf, and onion. Reserve ¼ cup of the cooking liquid.
3. Return the beans to the saucepan and add the cream, butter, the reserved cooking liquid, nutmeg, and salt and pepper if necessary. Simmer for 10 to 15 minutes. Sprinkle with chopped parsley and serve.

YIELD: 8–10 SERVINGS

✣ *Here, also, is my version of the classic tripe dish of Normandy.*

Tripe à la Mode de Caen

(BAKED TRIPE WITH CALVADOS)

8 pounds fresh beef tripe, such as
honeycomb, trimmed of all fat
and cut into 2-inch squares
1 calf or beef foot, cut into 2-inch
pieces by the butcher
2 cups onions, coarsely chopped
2 cups leeks, coarsely chopped
1 cup celery, finely chopped
5 garlic cloves, left whole
2 bay leaves
4 sprigs fresh thyme, or 1 teaspoon
dried

3 whole cloves
6 peppercorns
4 whole carrots, trimmed and
scraped
10 cups fresh chicken broth (see
recipe page 108), or good quality
canned
4 cups imported cider from
Normandy
Salt to taste
¼ cup Calvados
2 tablespoons parsley

1.   Preheat the oven to 350°.

2.   Place the tripe and the calf's foot in a kettle with water to cover. Bring to a boil, cook for 5 minutes and drain well.

3.   Place in a cheesecloth the onions, leeks, celery, garlic, bay leaves, thyme, cloves, and peppercorns. Bring the ends of the cloth together and tie with string to make a bundle.

4.   Place the tripe, the calf's foot pieces, carrots, the cheesecloth bundle, the chicken broth, cider, and salt in a kettle and bring to a boil. Then cover it with a tight, ovenproof lid and bake for 5 hours, or until tender.

5.   Skim off and discard most of the fat from the surface of the tripe. Remove and squeeze the cheesecloth bundle to extract all the juices. Discard.

6.   Remove the carrots and cut them into ¼-inch rounds. Return to the kettle.

7.   Remove the calf's foot pieces, cut away the gelatinous skin, and discard the bones. Shred the skin and add it to the tripe. Bring to a boil, add the Calvados, and sprinkle with parsley before serving.

YIELD: 12 SERVINGS

❧ *On one of our days in Normandy we stayed at a little hotel whose charm left us breathless, the Ferme des Poiriers Roses on the road between Pont l'Evêque and Lisieux. When Jacques Lecorneur first brought his wife, Elizabeth, here twenty years ago, it was a dark and rundown farm, and their original optimism dissipated so quickly that Elizabeth cried for fifteen days. It was doubly depressing because the wife of the farmer who sold it to them died just as they moved in and then the farmer, who stayed on for a couple of weeks, cried the whole time, too. Ever since, they have dedicated themselves to cheerfulness, renovating and making this an immaculate and beautiful place to stay. There is now barely an otherwise unused inch anywhere in the little hotel that isn't decorated with fresh flowers or hung with dried ones. The place is lent even more charm and beauty by the presence of the delightful Lecorneur offspring—shyly smiling and outgoing by turns—Florence, twenty-four (and her six-year-old daughter); Fanny, twenty; and Melanie, seventeen. This was a wonderful place to have breakfast before resuming our journey. Here are two of the family's recipes.*

Pain des Anges de Florence

(FLORENCE'S ANGEL FOOD CAKE)

10 egg whites
½ teaspoon cream of tartar
1¼ cups granulated sugar

1⅓ cups sifted flour
1 teaspoon vanilla extract
3 tablespoons melted butter

1.   Preheat the oven to 325°.
2.   Place the egg whites in the clean bowl of an electric mixer. Beat until frothy, add the cream of tartar, and beat until the egg whites reach soft peaks. Add the sugar and continue beating until the whites form stiff peaks.
3.   Using a spatula, gently fold in the flour one spoon at a time. Add the vanilla and the melted butter, blending carefully.
4.   Butter a mold measuring 10 × 5 × 2½ inches. Pour in the batter, smoothing the top, and bake for 25 minutes. Remove from the oven and let cool 2 hours before unmolding.

YIELD: 6–8 SERVINGS

Quatre-Quatre au Chocolat et Vanille de Fanny

(FANNY'S MARBLE CAKE)

10-ounce block of semisweet or milk
   chocolate
1¼ cups sweet butter, softened
1¼ cups sugar
5 eggs, separated

2 cups sifted flour
⅓ cup milk
½ teaspoon cream of tartar
1 teaspoon pure vanilla extract
1 teaspoon grated lemon rind

1. Heat the oven to 375°.

2. Grate the chocolate and set aside.

3. In the bowl of an electric mixer combine the butter and sugar until creamy. Add the egg yolks, flour, and milk and mix at medium speed until well blended.

4. Divide the batter evenly into two mixing bowls.

5. In the clean bowl of the electric mixer add the egg whites and beat until soft peaks form, adding the cream of tartar while beating. Using a rubber spatula divide the whites and fold them gently into each bowl. To the first bowl add the vanilla and lemon rind. Blend well. To the second, add the grated chocolate, blend, and set aside.

6. Butter a pound cake pan measuring 10 × 5 × 2½ inches and pour in the white batter first and the chocolate over it. This will form a marble pattern while baking.

7. Bake approximately 1 hour. Let cool before unmolding.

YIELD: 6–8 SERVINGS

✣ *Because the region is so in love with apples and cream, it is paradise for people who like their desserts; this and the* Pommes Flambées *on page 42 are my own efforts aimed at those sweet teeth.*

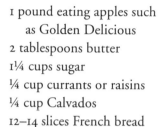

Pouding de Pain aux Pommes

(BREAD PUDDING WITH APPLES)

1 pound eating apples such
    as Golden Delicious
2 tablespoons butter
1¼ cups sugar
¼ cup currants or raisins
¼ cup Calvados
12–14 slices French bread
    (baguette), each slice

about ¼ inch thick
    (recipe follows)
3 egg yolks
2 whole eggs
1 teaspoon pure vanilla extract
1 cup heavy cream
3 cups milk
Confectioners' sugar, for decoration

1.   Preheat the oven to 400°.
2.   Peel the apples, core them, and cut into quarters. Slice very thinly.
3.   Heat the butter in a large nonstick skillet and add the apple slices. Sprinkle with ¼ cup of the sugar and sauté quickly for about 2 minutes over medium-high heat. Add the currants or raisins and the Calvados. Cook briefly and ignite, if desired.
4.   Arrange the bread slices slightly overlapping over the bottom of an 8-×-14-inch oval baking dish. Do not crowd the bread; use only enough to cover the bottom of the pan in one layer.
5.   Spoon the apple mixture evenly over the bread.
6.   Blend the egg yolks and the eggs with the remaining cup of sugar, vanilla, cream, and milk. Beat lightly and pour over the apples and bread slices. Set the baking dish in a larger baking dish and pour boiling water around it. Place carefully in the oven and bake for 40 minutes. Carefully remove from the oven and allow to cool. When the pudding is lukewarm, sprinkle the top with confectioners' sugar brushed through a fine sieve. Heat the pudding under the broiler until the top is nicely glazed.

YIELD: 10 SERVINGS

French Bread

2 envelopes fast-rising active dry yeast
2¼ cups cold water
3 tablespoons olive oil
6 cups bread flour
1 tablespoon salt
6 ice cubes

1.   Place the chopping blade in the food processor bowl. Add the yeast, ¼ cup of the cold water, and the oil. Mix by turning the chopping blade by hand. Add all the flour, turn on the machine, and blend for 10 seconds. Add the salt and blend for 10 more seconds. While the blade rotates, add the remaining 2 cups water. Blend for 30 to 35 seconds, or until the batter begins to form a large ball.

2.   Flour a board and knead the dough on it for about 5 minutes, forming it into a ball. Place the dough into a floured bowl, sprinkle the top with flour and cover with a dish towel. Let the dough rise until it has doubled in size. This should take about 1½ hours.

3.   Remove the dough from the bowl and shape it into 2 loaves about 14 inches long. Place the loaves about 4 inches apart (to leave room for expansion) on a baking sheet. Cover with a towel and let the dough continue to rise to about 50 percent of original volume.

4.   Meanwhile preheat the oven to 400°.

5.   Use a razor blade to score the surface of the loaves several times. Each incision should be about ½ inch deep.

6.   Place the loaves in the oven and throw 2 ice cubes on the oven floor at 2-minute intervals until all 6 ice cubes are used. The ice cubes add steam to produce a thin, crisp crust. Bake for a total of 30 minutes. Then reduce the heat to 375° and bake an additional 10 minutes. Transfer the bread to a rack and let cool.

YIELD: 2 LOAVES

Pommes Flambées au Calvados

(APPLES FLAMED WITH CALVADOS)

3 pounds Golden Delicious or Mac-
  intosh apples
8 tablespoons butter
1 tablespoon lemon juice
¾ cup fresh bread crumbs
8 tablespoons brown sugar
¼ cup Calvados
8–10 servings of vanilla ice cream
  (recipe follows)

1. Preheat the oven to 400°.

2. Peel the apples and cut them in half, then in quarters. Remove the cores and stems. Cut the apples into slices. There should be about 10 cups.

3. Melt 6 tablespoons of the butter and pour it into a large mixing bowl. Add the apples and the lemon juice. Toss and blend well to coat. Sprinkle half of the bread crumbs and 4 tablespoons of the sugar over the apples and toss to coat well.

4. Spoon the mixture into a baking dish measuring 11 × 7 × 1¾ inches deep. Smooth it over, blend the remaining bread crumbs and sugar and sprinkle over the apples. Dot with the remaining butter. Bake for 40 minutes. Sprinkle with the Calvados and ignite if desired. Serve with the ice cream (recipe follows).

YIELD: 8 SERVINGS

Glace à la Vanille

(FRENCH VANILLA ICE CREAM)

¾ cup sugar
6 egg yolks
2 cups milk

2 cups heavy cream
1 split vanilla bean, or 2 teaspoons
   vanilla extract

1. Beat the sugar and yolks with a small whisk in a heavy saucepan until bright yellow. Add one cup of milk and stir.

2. Combine the egg mixture with the cream, the remaining cup of milk, and the vanilla bean in a wide saucepan. Stirring constantly, bring the mixture to 180° using a rapid reading thermometer. Do not boil or the mixture will take on an undesirable cooked flavor. Strain the mixture in a fine sieve into a stainless bowl. Return the vanilla bean and cool.

3. Remove the vanilla bean and place the mixture in an ice-cream machine and freeze according to the manufacturer's instructions.

YIELD: 1 QUART

Brittany

SPECIALTIES

Galettes, slightly thicker crêpes, made with buckwheat flour and typically filled with savory fillings (white-flour crêpes are generally filled with sweet ones)

Agneau de pré-salé, lamb that has fed on the salty marshes and meadows

Artichokes stuffed and baked, boiled and sauced, or whittled to their hearts and sautéed

Raw or steamed clams and oysters

Mussels in soups or omelettes

Cotriade Bretonne, the Breton *bouillabaisse,* a creamy fish soup made with conger eel, sardines, mackerel, and hake

DESSERT

Kouigh-Amann, a thick butter cake made with yeast and sometimes flavored with honey, more often served with tea than as a dessert

CIDERS

Apple and pear cider are the beverages of choice

Mead, a rough liquor fermented from honey, is offered on some occasions

SALT TO TASTE

Much of Brittany is a peninsula reaching out into the Atlantic from the rest of France as if it were trying to get away and strike out for independence, and for much of its history it has had only the most uneasy sort of relationship with the French. Like Alsace, it has its own language and its distinct approach to life. Here the wild terrain—stark cliffs towering above the unruly ocean and vast salt marshes where the wind comes up past the rocks so powerfully it feels like an opponent—is the home of a rough-hewn, determined people. Many of them make their living on the water. Shellfish, in particular, are a staple. All along the coastal roads, hut-like structures sell oysters, almost always raw, fresh and plump beyond belief, served with a bit of lemon and bread, and that's it.

Here, there is a fondness for buckwheat crêpes, called *galettes,* less refined than other crêpes, perhaps, but perfectly suited to the people. The seaweed is eaten in Brittany as well, often sold pickled. The coffee is bitter, as it is in England, and the fermented honey, mead, the ancient drink that the people of Brittany hold on to, does not go down smooth.

Saltiness permeates Brittany. It is in the air; it is in the best-known food export of the region, the *pré-salé* lamb, which feeds on the salt marsh; and the people even enjoy their butter salted.

As it happens, all French cooks swear by sea salt, and here we were at the source. On an early day in Brittany we drove to the Ile de Noirmoutier (officially, just outside Brittany on the southern side of the border), where salt is mined in great quantity for export to the rest of France. But the most prized salt, five times more expensive than standard sea salt, is collected in what the people describe as a harvesting, scraping it from the surface of the salt marsh. It is called *fleur de sel.*

The island is connected to the coast by a road that is under water at high tide and

A common sight in Brittany: briny oysters for sale in an open-air stall

has been known to be the death of more than a few drivers. (To reduce the risk of drowning, the government has erected a series of poles with ladders so people can climb to safety if they have to.) At low tide, when the road is bared, the fishing boats are stuck in mud. It is these small local boats that are famous for the line-caught fish they bring to market; the island is also known for its potatoes—the fields are fertilized with seaweed and the potatoes have a naturally salty taste that gives them character, fairly shouting in Breton, the language of Brittany.

Back on the Breton mainland we were headquartered in La Roche-Bernard, a town settled by the Vikings. It overlooks a river called La Vilaine, which translates

as "ugly" and is so named because of its muddiness. In fact, the name is too self-effacing; the river and town are striking, in the shadow of a huge rock formation. In the

A fisherman tends his net in the chilly waters off Brittany.

old quarter on a narrow street we found the *crêperie* of Madame Christianne Gatin. Both species of crêpe, white flour (usually for desserts) and buckwheat (more often than not for main courses), are turned out by Madame Gatin and her two daughters. Buckwheat, in French, is *blé noir,* or black flour, which is sometimes also called *sarrasin,* in a reference to the historical Moorish invasion. It is only the buckwheat crêpe that is known as a *galette.* Madame Gatin was not entirely sure she wanted to share her buckwheat recipe with me—she said she never had given it to anybody before—but she finally acquiesced and we entered her tiny white-tiled kitchen, most of it taken up by three large crêpe griddles.

To spread the batter on her griddles she uses a little rubber scraper, shaped something like a windshield wiper, and she wields it with grace and speed. When I tried it, the batter flew around and finally settled into an unattractive, shapeless form. Madame Gatin, with great patience, showed me how it was necessary to just barely graze the surface of the batter as you draw it into a circle. When it came time

to cook for the customers, Christianne and her daughter, Catherine, worked side by side. Christianne would begin each crêpe, cooking it until brown on the first side. Then she would pass it to Catherine at the next griddle where the fillings would be added and the crêpe would be formed into a neat, square package. One more flip and the crêpe was atop the stack of plates ready to go out to the diners.

Pré-salé lamb are raised on the salt marshes and often exported, one of the region's best-known delicacies.

Out in the rustic dining room I discovered that thirteen young women had arrived to celebrate a labor victory: they had won long-term contracts at a nearby food-processing plant. I joined them; we were all drinking Calvados (a reflection of Brittany's proximity to Normandy) and getting giddier by the minute. I think these young women sang every drinking song they had ever heard, and certainly some that were new to me.

✣ To make the crêpe batter, Christianne insisted on using a wooden spoon and did a lot better than I might have imagined (although I don't know why I had any doubt, really; my grandmother used to beat mayonnaise with a spoon). Anyway, you can try it with a spoon or take the easy way out and turn to a whisk or an electric mixer. The crêpes will work well as a main course or a dessert, depending on the filling you choose. See the fillings listed below the recipe.

Galettes de Sarrasin
(BUCKWHEAT CRÊPES)

2 cups buckwheat flour
1 cup all-purpose flour
3 eggs, well beaten
2 cups milk

1½ tablespoons sea salt
3 cups water
1 tablespoon vegetable oil
3 tablespoons melted butter

1. In a mixing bowl combine the flours, eggs, milk, and salt, using a wire whisk and scraping the bottom and sides of the bowl to blend the ingredients until the batter is very smooth.

2. Add the water ½ cup at a time, blending after each addition; then add the oil and blend well.

3. Heat a 9-inch nonstick skillet over medium heat. Brush it lightly with melted butter and add about ¼ cup of the batter. Immediately after pouring, rotate the pan to spread the batter so that it coats the pan evenly. Cook until golden brown. Turn and cook on the other side until done. Remove and keep on a warm platter. Cook as many crêpes as needed. Leftover batter can be refrigerated covered.

4. Fill with the desired filling (see lists below), fold over in fourths, and serve.

YIELD: 16–18 CRÊPES

Fillings for main course (singly or in some combination): thinly sliced ham, grated cheese, diced tomato, sautéed mushrooms, sautéed onions, bacon, scrambled eggs, smoked salmon

For dessert: jam, apple sauce, chocolate sauce, ice cream, fresh fruits or berries, lemon juice, butter and sugar

✤ *At Domaine d'Orvault, just outside Nantes, I cooked with the chef Jean-Yves Bernard. The dish in question was artichokes and clams. Like shellfish, artichokes are produced here in considerable quantity, and they grow to a great size in Brittany.*

Artichauts aux Palourdes

(ARTICHOKE BOTTOMS WITH CLAMS)

4 medium-sized artichokes
1 lemon, cut in half
2 tablespoons olive oil
¼ cup onions, finely chopped
1 tablespoon finely chopped garlic
8 plum tomatoes, cored, peeled, and finely chopped—about 2 cups
½ teaspoon sugar
4 sprigs fresh thyme, or 1 teaspoon dried
2 tablespoons fresh basil or parsley, chopped

1 cup fresh chicken broth (see recipe page 108), or good quality canned
Salt and freshly ground pepper to taste
¼ teaspoon red pepper flakes, or to taste
24 littleneck clams in the shell, thoroughly cleaned
Sprigs of parsley or chervil, for garnish

1. Prepare the artichoke bottoms. Using a sharp knife, cut off the stems of the artichokes to produce a neat flat base. Rub any surface with lemon to prevent discoloration. Trim all around the sides and base until the base is smooth and white with the green exterior pared away.

2. Place the artichoke on its side on a flat surface. Slice off the top, leaving a base about 1½ inches deep. Using a paring knife, trim around the sides and bottom to remove the green exterior that remains. Remove the fuzzy choke with a melon ball scoop. Cut each bottom into 8 wedges. Make sure to rub them with lemon juice.

3. In a saucepan or skillet heat the olive oil. Add the onions and garlic and cook, stirring, until wilted.

4. Add the tomatoes, sugar, thyme, artichokes, basil or parsley, chicken broth, salt and pepper, and red pepper flakes. Bring to a boil and simmer, covered, for 15 minutes.

5. Spread the clams over the top of the cooking liquid. Cover and cook until the shells open. Do not overcook. Check for seasoning.

6. Serve immediately, dividing the clams evenly among warm soup plates. Garnish with parsley or chervil.

YIELD: 4 SERVINGS

❧ *On our way to La Roche-Bernard, we stopped in a sleepy seaside town called Sables d'Olonne, where the chef-owner Joseph Drapeau prepared a sea scallop and leek dish that was both simple and beautiful.*

Coquilles Saint-Jacques à la Fondue de Poireaux Saffranés

(SCALLOPS WITH SAUTÉED LEEKS AND SAFFRON)

1½ pounds sea or bay scallops
3 tablespoons butter
2 cups leeks, white part only, cleaned, trimmed, and thinly sliced
Salt and freshly ground pepper to taste

¾ cup cream
½ teaspoon saffron threads
4 tablespoons chopped chives for garnish

1. Rinse the scallops under running water to remove any sand. If using sea scallops, cut them in half crosswise. If using bay scallops, leave them whole.

2. In a small saucepan over medium heat, melt 1 teaspoon of the butter. Add the leeks and salt to taste. Cook, stirring, until wilted, about 5 minutes. Remove from the burner and keep warm.

3. In another small saucepan, add the cream, 1 teaspoon butter, and salt and pepper to taste. Cook, stirring, until the sauce comes to a slow boil. Add the saffron, check for seasoning, remove, and keep warm. Avoid using a wire whisk once the saffron has been added.

4. Season the scallops with salt and pepper to taste.

5. In a small nonstick skillet melt the remaining butter over high heat. Add scal-

lops and cook until lightly browned. Turn and brown on second side. Be careful not to overcook or the scallops will become tough. The total cooking time should be about 3 minutes.

6. To serve, spoon the leeks into the middle of a warmed serving plate. (Use a circular form to shape them, if desired.) Pour the sauce around the bed of leeks. Arrange the scallops decoratively over the sauce in a circle around the leeks. Garnish with chopped chives.

YIELD: 4 SERVINGS

꽃 *Another fine chef in the region with a natural enough penchant for scallops is Jacques Thorel, a mercurial man who swings from high good humor to ruminative, almost brooding moments, like a painter approaching a difficult creation. He served us beautifully sautéed lobster one day, and then filled the lobster shell with mashed potatoes, his way of making a little joke by replacing the noble lobster meat with the more mundane potatoes. He and his wife, Solange, have operated the Auberge Bretonne La Roche-Bernard since 1980. The dining room is built around a glass-enclosed courtyard that contains an immaculate vegetable garden. The lovely garden becomes the centerpiece for the room. Jacques went to the market for fresh scallops, which are sold live in Brittany, still in the shell and with their roe.*

This recipe calls for small tart molds, 3 inches in diameter, preferably of the nonstick variety. I know many home kitchens may not have them, but the dish is so simple to prepare and the results so attractive that I think it isn't a bad idea to purchase a set for this and other little tarts.

Coquilles Saint-Jacques en Chemise à la Vinaigrette d'Herbes

(ZUCCHINI-WRAPPED SCALLOPS WITH HERB VINAIGRETTE)

4 small tart molds, preferably non-stick, 3 inches in diameter and ½ inch deep
¾ pound small zucchini, trimmed
2 tablespoons olive oil

Salt and pepper to taste
1 pound large sea scallops
Vinaigrette aux Herbes (recipe follows)
4 sprigs of flat leaf parsley

1. Preheat the oven to 425°.

2. Using a mandoline or vegetable slicer, slice the zucchini into very thin rounds. Place the slices in a small mixing bowl and toss them with the olive oil and salt and pepper to taste. Line the bottom of each mold with about 12 zucchini slices overlapping in a spiral pattern.

3. Cut each scallop horizontally into 3 slices. Arrange the scallop slices overlapping in a spiral pattern on top of the zucchini. Season with salt and pepper to taste. Top with the remaining zucchini slices arranged in the spiral pattern, and using your hands gently pack it down so that each tart is more compact.

4. Place molds on a cookie sheet and bake in oven for about 10 minutes.

5. Unmold onto separate serving plates. Spoon 2 tablespoons of the vinaigrette (recipe follows) around and over each serving. Garnish each with a sprig of flat leaf parsley.

YIELD: 4 APPETIZER SERVINGS

Vinaigrette aux Herbes
(HERB VINAIGRETTE)

1 tablespoon sherry vinegar
1 teaspoon aged balsamic vinegar
Salt and freshly ground white pepper
    to taste

3 tablespoons extra-virgin olive oil
2 tablespoons flat leaf parsley, finely
    chopped
2 tablespoons chives, finely chopped

1. In a small bowl, using a wire whisk, combine the sherry vinegar, balsamic vinegar, and salt and pepper to taste. Mix until all the salt has dissolved.

2. Slowly whisk in the olive oil.

3. Add herbs and combine well. Check for seasoning.

YIELD: ABOUT ½ CUP

❧ *Dessert in Jacques's restaurant was an apple soufflé prepared by his pastry chef of twelve years, Yvette. Here is my modified version. I include the orange-flavored liqueur Grand Marnier, partly because it complements apples so well and also because our visit to the Grand Marnier bottling plant and distillery near Paris was still fresh in my mind. (At the plant—housed almost inconspicuously in what once was a villa—orange skins from the West Indies are macerated in alcohol, which is then joined with cognac and filtered to produce the liqueur, an invaluable culinary asset.)*

Soufflé aux Pommes

(APPLE SOUFFLÉ)

5 apples, such as Golden Delicious
4 tablespoons butter
¾ cup sugar
1 teaspoon grated lemon rind

3 tablespoons Grand Marnier
8 egg whites
Confectioners' sugar, to sprinkle
  over the top

1. Chill 6 1¼-cup soufflé dishes.

2. Preheat the oven to 450°.

3. Peel, core, and quarter the apples, and then cut them into thin slices. You should have about 4 cups.

4. Heat 2 tablespoons of butter in a skillet and then add the apple slices, ½ cup sugar, and the lemon rind. Cook, stirring, over high heat until the liquid evaporates, about 10 minutes. Continue cooking until the apples have browned only slightly, then mix in the Grand Marnier.

5. Purée the apple slices and their cooking juices in a food processor for about 1 minute, then transfer them to a large mixing bowl and set aside.

6. Using a pastry brush, thoroughly coat the insides of the soufflé dishes with the remaining butter and return them to the refrigerator.

7. In a large and well-cleaned mixing bowl, use a flexible wire whisk to beat the egg whites until they are stiff but still moist. Gradually add the remaining ¼ cup sugar.

8. Use a rubber spatula to fold the egg whites into the apple purée.

9. Spoon the mixture into the soufflé dishes. They should be filled to about ¼ inch over the rim. Scrape around the top inside edge of the mold with your thumb

to leave a narrow space between the soufflé mixture and the edge of the mold, which will allow for expansion and cause the soufflé to rise evenly.

10.   Place the dishes on a cookie sheet and bake on middle rack for 7 minutes. Reduce the heat to 425° and bake for 7 minutes longer. Sprinkle with confectioners' sugar and serve immediately.

YIELD: 6 SERVINGS

✣   *The profusion of crêpes here in Brittany leads me to offer this recipe of my own.*

Crêpes Soufflées
(WARM ORANGE CRÊPES)

4 eggs, separated
¼ cup plus 3 tablespoons
    granulated sugar
2 tablespoons finely grated
    orange rind
¼ cup fresh orange juice with
    the pulp

2 teaspoons cornstarch
1 tablespoon Grand Marnier
8 crêpes (recipe follows)
2 tablespoons melted butter
1 tablespoon confectioners'
    sugar   .

1.   Preheat the oven to 425°.
2.   Put the egg yolks in a mixing bowl and add ¼ cup sugar, orange rind, orange juice, cornstarch, and Grand Marnier. Beat briskly with a wire whisk until very smooth.
3.   Beat the egg whites until stiff. Toward the end, beat in the remaining sugar, continuing to beat until peaks form.
4.   Add about ¼ of the egg whites to the orange mixture and beat quickly with a wire whisk to blend. Add the remaining egg whites and fold them in with a rubber spatula.
5.   Butter a baking dish large enough to hold the 8 filled crêpes in one layer.
6.   Using a flat work surface, spread the crêpes out, fill them evenly with the orange mixture, and roll up.
7.   Arrange the filled crêpes in the baking dish. Brush them with the melted butter.

8. Place the baking pan in the oven and bake for 10 minutes or until slightly brown on top. Sprinkle with the confectioners' sugar and serve.

YIELD: 4 SERVINGS OF 2 CRÊPES EACH

❧ *The basic crêpe batter below is about the minimum feasible amount you can prepare. Even so, it will produce a few more crêpes than needed for the Crêpes Soufflées. Don't hesitate to freeze the extras, or just wrap and refrigerate them for a snack at another time.*

Basic Crêpes

½ cup all-purpose flour
1 large egg
1 teaspoon sugar
Pinch of salt

¾ cup milk
3 tablespoons butter
½ teaspoon pure vanilla
    extract

1. In a large mixing bowl, blend the flour, egg, sugar, and salt with a wooden spatula. Gradually add the milk, stirring constantly.

2. In a nonstick crêpe pan, about 5 or 6 inches in diameter, melt the butter, and add it and the vanilla extract to the crêpe batter, stirring constantly. Strain through a fine sieve.

3. In the same crêpe pan over medium heat, add about 2 tablespoons of the batter, rotating the pan to make sure that the bottom is fully covered with a thin layer of batter. Cook for 45 seconds to 1 minute (the crêpe should be lightly browned). Turn over and cook about 30 seconds more. Transfer to a flat surface. Add more batter and repeat until finished.

YIELD: 12–14 CRÊPES

Charente

SPECIALTIES

Snails in the traditional garlic and parsley butter sauce, also
in many other dishes (wrapped in pastries and baked,
snail stews, etc.)

Eels—fried; grilled; in a soup called *bouilliture*

Baby eels, known as *pibales,* are sautéed until sizzling with
garlic, olive oil, and sometimes hot peppers

CHEESES

Over fifty types of Cabécou, a goat's milk cheese

DESSERTS

Nuts in countless confections—almonds in both the
macaroons and *nougatines* of Poitiers; chestnuts boiled in
sugar syrup, known as *marrons glacés*

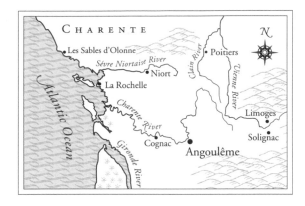

COGNAC COUNTRY

One of the peculiarities of dining out in France is that on the tables of some of the finest restaurants are little containers of butter with the brand name still attached. In the United States this would seem silly, of course (can you imagine Land O Lakes served in its own tub at some $100-a-person establishment?), but here it makes sense. The butter is Echiré, a butter so highly regarded that it has its own governmental Appellation d'Origine Contrôlée, just as wine does. (Like other fine French butters, it is available in some specialty shops in the United States and is well worth the search.) Surprisingly, Echiré is produced not in Normandy, where cream and butter are so renowned, but in a region called the Charente, an area from just above the city of Bordeaux, including La Rochelle on the Atlantic and reaching nearly to Limoges in the interior. Although the Charente is perhaps relatively little known among American tourists, the appeal of its products and its wealth of other attractions cannot be denied. It is the nation's producer of Cognac, for instance; it has its share of charming towns—gorgeous La Rochelle on the seaside is chock-a-block with strolling visitors on a sunny spring day—and superb restaurants, and it is the source of some of the finest mussels on earth.

The butter made in this area is like butter made nowhere else, although it is hard to find the words that express the distinction. It is rich and smooth and, well, buttery (the producers of butter have not developed a vocabulary for their product the way vintners have). The locals, like the French everywhere else, give most of the credit for the remarkable quality to *le terroir,* that is, the climate and the land. Beyond that, the milk is kept as fresh as human beings can manage. It is collected from farms twice a day, and then the cream is immediately extracted by centrifugal force. The churning of the cream in huge vats creates an almost surreal blob of butter that is packaged in dainty, distinctive little baskets. But I am sure the taste, wher-

ever else it may come from, is due in large measure to the fact that Echiré butter is high in fat, even by French standards. French law maintains that butter must be 82 percent fat. Echiré is 83.5 percent (by comparison, American butter is 78 percent fat).

Richard Coutanceau, in the kitchen of his restaurant in La Rochelle

When we traveled to visit the source of that other resource of the Charente, mussels, we chose as our destination a farm not far from La Rochelle, which provided an astonishing vista. The mussels there are raised on poles that stretch for 12 miles or so along the coastline and extend ½ mile into the sea at intervals of about 12 yards. When you go out into the water among them, as I did, all you see anywhere is poles laden with mussels. This particular spot was chosen for development of the industry because the rivers that empty out near La Rochelle come laden with nutrients that mussels evidently thrive on. The farmers seed the poles by wrapping them with nets filled with tiny juvenile mussels. Then, in a year or two, when the harvest is ready, flat-bottomed boats, equipped with crane-like devices, cruise out among the poles and lower long cylinders over each one, hauling the cylinder up laden with mussels and dumping the harvest in the boat until the bottom is wall-to-wall mollusks, perhaps a thousand pounds per boat in one trip.

The mussels themselves, small compared to those we are used to in the States, are worth all the effort—and more—because they are so plump (I thought they did look well fed) and sweet. One of the most inspired chefs we met on this trip was Richard Coutanceau, who runs a restaurant that bears his name in La Rochelle, and he offered some mussel advice I hadn't heard before. I always knew enough not to debeard a mussel until the last minute since, once you pull the beard away, the mussel starts to die, but he maintains that you can keep the mussel alive if you remember to pull the beard directly upward toward the rounded edge of the shell, presumably because it tears less of the body.

Cognac is a brandy that comes only from the area of that name, just north of Bordeaux in a region known as Poitou Charente. As with many another splendid food or drink, the development of Cognac was born of necessity. Four hundred years ago, when the French winemakers realized that their wine was deteriorating on long sea voyages, they tried to find a way to stabilize

Constructing barrels for a Cognac cave

it, and distilling the wine to remove impurities turned out to be the answer; double distillation was still better, yielding an even more delicate flavor. Our guide in Cognac, Jean-Marie Beulque-Schaub of the Château de Bourg-Charente, made sure we noticed one of the more

A lesson on Cognac at Château de Bourg-Charente: double distillation is the secret

interesting by-products of the process, the black foam on the roofs of buildings in the area. That foam, he explained, is a mold whose growth is encouraged by the vapors released by the Cognac barrels (certainly this is the mellowest mold on earth). Cognac makers think of the vapor as Cognac lost to the air and call it *la part des anges,* the angels' share.

Among the region's truly superb chefs is Dominique Bouchet, who had been chef at the prestigious Jamin in Paris and at the Tour d'Argent before opening his own sensational establishment, Le Moulin de Marcouze, in his hometown of Mosnac. When he returned from Paris in 1988 he bought the ruins of a flour mill and used that as the beginnings of the house he would build for himself and his wife. Then he added a restaurant and finally some hotel rooms. He is a restless, animated man who wastes little time when he goes anywhere: testimony to his energetic personality is the helicopter pad outside the restaurant.

For the sardines in this recipe, however, he could drive rather than fly, just twenty-five minutes away to the port of Royan where the sardines are brought in by fishermen in small boats. He emphasized that the sardines should be cooked under a very hot broiler so that they are done quickly, before they have a chance to dry out. Dominique also has a nice touch with desserts, two of which follow the sardine recipe.

Note: Sardines are always better if filleted just before using them. But it is a delicate procedure and you may prefer to persuade the fish shop to do it.

Sardines de Royan sur Fondue de Tomates de Dominique Bouchet

(BROILED SARDINES ON A BED OF TOMATOES DOMINIQUE BOUCHET)

12 whole fresh sardines (about ¼ pound each), cleaned
2 tablespoons olive oil
1 cup canned crushed tomatoes
1 garlic clove, peeled
Salt and freshly ground pepper to taste

5 tablespoons butter, softened
2 tablespoons shallots, finely chopped
½ cup dry white wine
¼ cup heavy cream
1 tablespoon chives, finely chopped

1.   Preheat the oven broiler until it is very hot.

2.   To fillet the sardines, make a vertical incision below the head and slice down toward the bone. Then start from the tail end and insert the knife between the flesh and bones. Using a back-and-forth motion and staying as close to the bone as possible, cut until the entire fillet has been removed. Repeat on other side to remove sec-

ond fillet. Trim away any dark portions around the edges of the fillets and remove any remaining bones with kitchen tweezers.

3.   Brush a broiler pan with a little of the olive oil. Place the sardines on the pan in 4 bunches of 6 fillets each. Form each bunch by slightly overlapping the fillets in a fan shape. Brush sardines with more of the olive oil. Set aside until sauces are prepared.

4.   In a small saucepan over medium heat, add the remaining olive oil, tomatoes, garlic clove, and salt and pepper to taste. Cook, stirring, until heated through. Keep warm.

5.   In another small saucepan, melt 2 tablespoons of the butter over low heat. When it begins to bubble, add the shallots and cook, stirring, until wilted, but not brown. Add the white wine and stir from time to time until it reaches a syrupy consistency (about 2 minutes). Add the cream and bring to a boil. Remove from heat and whisk in the remaining butter, 1 teaspoon at a time. Do not return the sauce to a boil once butter has been added. Season with salt and freshly ground pepper, keeping in mind that very little salt is required, as the sardines themselves (even these fresh ones) are naturally quite salty. Stir chives into the sauce and check for seasoning. Keep warm.

6.   Season the fillets with salt and pepper to taste and place them under the broiler, about 3 inches from the heat source. Rotate the broiler pan from time to time to assure even cooking. The total broiling time should be about 3 minutes. The fish are done when the skin begins to bubble and is lightly browned.

7.   Divide the tomato mixture evenly onto 4 warmed serving plates. Spoon it into the center of the plates, flattening slightly to make a bed for the sardines. Using a wide spatula, place each fan of sardines over its tomato base. Spoon the sauce around and serve.

YIELD: 4 SERVINGS

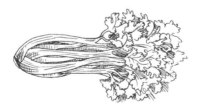

❧ *Grand Marnier has always been one of the most interesting and pervasive ingredients in my cooking, using its orange essence to infuse everything from sauces to soufflées. Just try this cookie and you'll see what I mean. This recipe results in thin, crisp cookies layered with Grand Marnier–flavored whipped cream. The batter for the cookies is best when prepared the day before, or at least two hours before.*

Croustillants à la Crème de Grand Marnier

(CRISP COOKIES WITH GRAND-MARNIER CREAM)

3½ tablespoons butter, very soft
3 tablespoons granulated white sugar
3½ tablespoons granulated light
   brown sugar (strained through a
   fine sieve to remove any lumps)
¼ cup all-purpose flour

3 tablespoons freshly squeezed orange
   juice
¾ cup heavy cream
2 tablespoons Crème de Grand
   Marnier
1 cup raspberry *coulis* (recipe follows)

1.   In a mixing bowl, use a wire whisk to combine the butter and the sugars. Whisk the ingredients together briskly, scraping the sides and bottom of the bowl. When well mixed, incorporate the flour and combine well. Add the orange juice and whisk, again scraping the sides and bottom of the bowl, until the mixture is smooth. Chill overnight, or for at least 2 hours.

2.   Preheat the oven to 375°.

3.   To form the *croustillants,* dip your fingertips in cold water and then, using your second and third fingers, dip into the dough, gathering about 1 teaspoon from the bowl. Spread the batter onto a nonstick cookie sheet using a circular motion. Each cookie should be about 3 inches in diameter and as thin as possible (almost transparent). It will be necessary to dip more than once into the dough for each 3-inch round. Repeat the dipping and spreading, making sure the dough-circles are at least 1 inch apart, as they will spread slightly during cooking. For 4 portions bake 20 *croustillants.*

4.   Bake for 6 to 8 minutes, or until crisp and caramel-colored.

5.   Use a spatula to remove the *croustillants* from the cookie sheet immediately after they are taken from the oven, and place them on a flat surface to cool.

6. Meanwhile, in a mixing bowl beat the cream with a wire whisk. When it has reached soft-peak consistency, add the Crème de Grand Marnier and continue to beat to stiff peaks. Do not overbeat or the cream will become grainy and turn to butter.

7. Transfer the whipped cream to a pastry bag with a fluted tip. Pipe out a circle of cream onto the center of each dessert plate, and gently press one of the *croustillants* on top of it. This first bit of cream is meant only to glue the dessert into place. Pipe a decorative circle of cream in the center of the *croustillant* and cover it gently with another *croustillant*. Repeat until 5 croustillants are layered on top of each other with cream between on each plate. On top of the fifth one, pipe some more cream in a decorative fashion.

8. Pour 2 tablespoons of raspberry *coulis* (recipe follows) around each portion and serve, with the remaining *coulis* on the side.

YIELD: 4 SERVINGS

Coulis de Framboise

(RASPBERRY SAUCE)

1 cup fresh raspberries
2 tablespoons Crème de Grand
　　Marnier

1. Place the raspberries in the container of a food processor or blender and blend until smooth.

2. Strain through a fine sieve to remove the seeds.

3. Add Crème de Grand Marnier and blend well.

YIELD: 1 CUP

❧ *Here in the Cognac region, at the Moulin de Marcouze, I prepared a steak with Cognac and peppercorn sauce. It goes well with sautéed zucchini and potatoes (recipe follows).*

Steak aux Poivres

(STEAK IN A COGNAC AND PEPPERCORN SAUCE)

4 tablespoons crushed white pepper-
    corns, or to taste

4 12-ounce boneless rib steaks, about
    1 inch thick, trimmed of excess fat

2 tablespoons olive oil

4 tablespoons butter

¼ cup shallots, finely chopped

3 tablespoons Cognac

½ cup red wine

¼ cup fresh chicken broth (see recipe
    page 108), or good quality canned

1 tablespoon Dijon mustard

Salt to taste

2 tablespoons parsley, finely chopped

1.   Place the peppercorns on a cutting board and crush them to a fine texture using the bottom of a heavy skillet. Sprinkle both sides of the steaks with the crushed pepper, pressing it into the meat.

2.   In a large, heavy skillet, over high heat, heat the olive oil and then add the steaks. Cook the first sides until lightly browned (about 2 minutes), then turn and cook for 2 minutes more for rare, or to desired doneness. Remove the steaks to a plate and keep warm.

3.   Drain all the fat from the skillet and melt 1 tablespoon of the butter over medium heat. Add the shallots and cook, stirring, until wilted, but not brown. Add the Cognac and ignite by tipping the skillet to bring the liquor into contact with the flames from the gas burner, or, if you do not have a gas stove, ignite the Cognac with a match. Add red wine to deglaze the pan. Cook, scraping the bottom and sides of the pan to loosen and dissolve any brown particles. Continue to cook the sauce over high heat until reduced by more than half. Add the chicken broth, the mustard, and any juices that have accumulated around the steaks, and combine well. Swirl in the remaining butter and season with salt to taste. Do not return the sauce to a boil once butter has been added.

4.   Transfer the steaks to heated serving plates and garnish with zucchini and potatoes (recipe follows). Spoon the sauce over and around the meat and sprinkle with chopped parsley.

YIELD: 4 SERVINGS

Garni de Courgettes et Pommes de Terre

(SAUTÉED ZUCCHINI AND POTATO GARNISH)

2 cups red waxy potatoes, cut into
½-inch cubes

2 tablespoons olive oil

1½ cups zucchini, trimmed and cut
into ⅛-inch slices

Salt and freshly ground pepper
to taste

2 teaspoons garlic, finely chopped

1 tablespoon chives, finely chopped

1.   Place the potatoes in a saucepan with salt to taste and water to cover. Bring to
a boil and cook for about 3 minutes. Drain and reserve.

2.   In a large nonstick skillet, heat the olive oil and add the potatoes. Cook, stirring, until lightly browned. Add the zucchini and salt and pepper, and continue to
stir. Add the garlic and continue to cook the vegetables until the zucchini is tender.

3.   Sprinkle with chives and check for seasoning.

YIELD: 4 SERVINGS

⚜   *When we traveled to Limoges to witness the craftsmanship in the capital of the
French porcelain industry, we also arranged to meet Gil Dudognon at the hotel-restaurant
Chapelle Saint-Martin, not far from Limoges and set in a park of rolling green lawns
dotted with hundred-year-old pines. Gil has impressive restaurant experience on his
résumé but prefers classic home-style cooking. For this dish, he used the veal known as* veau
sous la mère, *literally "calf under its mother." What it actually means is that the calves
have been reared only on their mothers' milk—and they are said to be the very best. He
serves it with mashed potatoes that are extraordinarily rich and liquid, like a sauce. To
accomplish that, he employs a lot of butter, milk, and cream.*

Côtes de Veau Chapelle Saint-Martin

(VEAL CHOPS SAUTÉED WITH VEGETABLES)

2 tablespoons vegetable oil

3 tablespoons butter

1 1¼-pound rib veal chop (2 to 3
inches thick)

Salt and freshly ground pepper to
taste

1 cup onions, coarsely chopped

1 cup carrots, cut into ¼-inch dice

1 cup knob celery, cut into ¼-inch
    dice
4 sprigs thyme, or ½ teaspoon dried
1 bay leaf

1 cup fresh chicken broth (see recipe
    page 108), or good quality canned
1 tablespoon freshly squeezed lemon
    juice

1.   In a large, heavy skillet, heat the oil over medium-high heat and add 2 table-spoons butter. Season the veal with salt and pepper to taste and cook until lightly brown on the first side, moving it around from time to time to prevent it from sticking to the bottom of the pan. This should take about 3 minutes. Turn and repeat on second side.

2.   Add the onions, carrots, celery, thyme, and bay leaf. Cook for about 2 minutes, stirring the vegetables around the veal chop so that they do not burn. Pour off any excess fat and add the chicken broth. Reduce the heat, cover tightly, and cook at a simmer for about 20 minutes. There should be enough stock to cover the vegetables surrounding the veal chop.

3.   Remove the chop from the skillet and keep warm. Remove and discard thyme sprigs and bay leaf. Continue to cook the sauce until reduced by half.

4.   Swirl the remaining tablespoon of butter into the sauce, 1 small piece at a time. Add the lemon juice and check for seasoning.

5.   Remove the veal from the bone and cut it into thin slices. Arrange the sliced meat on a warmed serving platter along with the vegetables and sauce and mashed potatoes (recipe follows).

YIELD: 2 SERVINGS

Purée de Pommes de Terre de Gil Dudognon

(SAUCE-LIKE MASHED POTATOES)

1½ pounds Idaho or Washington
    State potatoes, skin on
Salt and freshly ground pepper to
    taste

1 cup milk
½ cup heavy cream
4 tablespoons butter

1.   Place the potatoes in a large saucepan with salt to taste and water to cover. Bring to a boil and simmer for about 20 minutes, or until tender. Drain and peel the

potatoes and return them to the saucepan. Leave in a warm place for about 20 minutes to allow excess moisture remaining in the potatoes to dry out.

2. Press potatoes through a fine sieve or potato ricer.

3. In a small saucepan, bring milk and cream to a simmer.

4. In a large saucepan melt 2 tablespoons of the butter and add the crushed potatoes, stirring with a wooden spoon. Add the milk and cream mixture little by little, stirring well after each addition. Blend in the remaining butter. Season with salt and pepper to taste.

YIELD: 4 SERVINGS

❧ *At La Belle Etoile, in Niort, we dined with Claude Guignard, who arrived at the restaurant as an apprentice, rose through the ranks, and bought the place in 1979; he and his wife, Laure, have run the establishment together ever since. The sea bass dish was cooked by Guignard's chef, Jean-Michel. The bass was caught just off the Charente coast and the butter in the sauce was none other than Echiré. The white butter sauce with tomatoes is a classic known as* sauce Dugléré.

Filets de Bar au Beurre Blanc et Tomates de La Belle Etoile

(FILLETS OF SEA BASS WITH TOMATO AND BUTTER SAUCE)

12 ounces sea bass fillets with skin on, cut into 2 equal portions
Salt and freshly ground pepper to taste
6 tablespoons butter
2 tablespoons shallots, finely chopped

½ cup tomatoes, peeled, seeded, finely diced
1 tablespoon aged white wine vinegar
¼ cup dry white wine
1 tablespoon chives

1. Season the fish on both sides with salt and pepper to taste.

2. In a large skillet, cook 2 tablespoons of the butter over medium heat. When the butter becomes a hazelnut color, add the fish, skin side down, shallots, tomatoes, vinegar, and white wine. Cover and cook for about 2 minutes. Turn the fillets over, cover again, and cook for an additional 2 to 3 minutes. Do not overcook. Remove the fish from the skillet and keep warm.

3.   Reduce the heat under the skillet to low, and use a wire whisk to blend the remaining butter with the vegetables and cooking liquid, adding it 1 teaspoon at a time. Whisk until the sauce thickens slightly. Add the chives, combine well, and check for seasoning. Do not allow the sauce to boil once the butter has been added.

4.   Place each portion of bass on a warmed serving plate. Divide the sauce evenly over the 2 portions, pouring it over and around the fish. Arrange sautéed cabbage leaves (recipe follows) decoratively alongside the fillets and serve.

YIELD: 2 SERVINGS

Chou de Milan Sauté

(SAUTÉED SAVOY CABBAGE)

1½ cups leaves of savoy cabbage   Salt and pepper to taste
1 tablespoon butter

1.   Core the cabbage and remove the ribs from each leaf. Tear the leaves into bite-sized pieces.

2.   In a small skillet, melt the butter over medium heat and add the cabbage. Season with salt and pepper to taste, and cook, stirring, until wilted and tender. Remove and keep warm.

YIELD: 2 SERVINGS

✤   *In the coastal areas of the Charente, around La Rochelle, shellfish of all sorts are favored. As for the oysters, there are none better.*

Huîtres au Chou et Beurre Rouge

(OYSTERS WITH CABBAGE AND RED WINE SAUCE)

24 oysters
3 cups savoy cabbage, cored
   and shredded
Salt to taste
½ cup butter

¼ cup shallots, finely chopped
1 cup dry red wine
2 tablespoons red wine vinegar
4 sprigs parsley, for decoration

1.   Open the oysters and remove them from their shells into a dish. Reserve the liquor as well. Keep cool.

2.   Place the cabbage in a steamer with salt to taste and cook for 2 minutes. Keep warm.

3.   Place the oysters, with their liquid, in a saucepan and bring to a simmer. Remove from heat and keep warm.

4.   In a small saucepan, melt 1 tablespoon of the butter. Add the shallots, cook briefly, add the wine and vinegar, and reduce by half. Add the remaining butter and 1 tablespoon of the oyster cooking liquid and beat briskly with a wire whisk until smooth.

5.   To serve, warm 4 serving plates and spoon the cabbage in the center of each plate. Place 6 drained oysters around each serving of cabbage and cover each oyster with some of the sauce. Garnish with a sprig of parsley.

YIELD: 4 SERVINGS

❧ *When we stayed in La Rochelle it was at the seventeenth-century Hôtel de la Monnaie, just inside the ramparts that follow the lines of the city and a few steps away from Richard Coutanceau's restaurant. The sea is so close to the restaurant that it seems to be nearly part of it, an engulfing aesthetic experience as you look out over the muted colors, changing and blending until the sun sets.*

Richard, who is slighter of build than most of the chefs we met, is soft-spoken, with sandy curly hair that lends him an even gentler appearance. Nevertheless, he is certainly one of the most demanding chefs in France when it comes to the quality of his ingredients (he attributes his reverence for freshness and quality to his parents; his mother was a fine cook and his father a knowing gourmet).

His mussel dish turns to curry powder for some zest and also as an echo of the city's past. Richard explains that, by using it, he is recalling La Rochelle's history as a spice port on the route to India.

La Mouclade Rochelaise de Richard Coutanceau

(CREAMY CURRIED MUSSEL SOUP OF RICHARD COUTANCEAU)

1 cup heavy cream
1 tablespoon mild curry powder
1 tablespoon freshly squeezed lemon
  juice
3 tablespoons butter
¼ cup shallots, thinly sliced
4 sprigs thyme

1 bay leaf
1 cup dry white wine
9 cups mussels in the shell, cleaned
  (about 3 pounds)
4 tablespoons flour
Salt to taste

1. Combine the cream, curry powder, and lemon juice in a small bowl and mix well. This step enables the curry flavor to develop.

2. Melt 1 tablespoon of the butter in a large pot over high heat and add the shallots, thyme, and bay leaf. Stir until wilted. Add the white wine and bring to a simmer. Add the mussels, cover, and cook for 2 to 3 minutes, or just until the mussels open. Stir from time to time to assure even cooking. As soon as the mussels open, remove them from the heat and strain the liquid through a fine sieve. Reserve 2 cups of the cooking juices.

3. Remove the top shell from each mussel and discard it, leaving the mussel meat attached to its bottom shell. Arrange on a serving platter and keep warm.

4.   In a large saucepan, melt the remaining butter over medium heat and whisk in the flour, stirring until the mixture is smooth. Cook briefly and do not brown. Slowly add the 2 cups reserved cooking juices, whisking constantly as you pour. Bring to a rolling boil. Add the cream and curry mixture and combine well. Strain the sauce through a fine sieve. Add salt to taste and check for seasoning. Ladle the sauce over the mussels and serve immediately.

YIELD: 4 SERVINGS

✣   *This dish—the recipe is from the Coutanceau restaurant—is usually refrigerated overnight and served cold.*

Gratin Charentais

(GRATIN OF BACON AND VEGETABLES)

½ pound spinach, washed and dried
3 cups Swiss chard, cut into julienne
  strips
3 cups cabbage, coarsely chopped
Salt and pepper to taste
¼ pound smoked pork, finely

chopped
1 pound fresh pork shoulder, diced
4 cups leeks, sliced
4 cups onions, sliced
1 cup flat parsley, coarsely chopped
3 large eggs, beaten

1.   Preheat the oven to 375°.

2.   In a large kettle, combine the spinach, Swiss chard, cabbage, and salt and pepper to taste, adding enough water to cover. Bring just to a boil, simmer 5 minutes, and drain well.

3.   Place a cast-iron skillet over medium heat, add the smoked pork and the pork shoulder and cook, stirring, until lightly browned, about 8 minutes.

4.   Add the leeks and onions and cook, stirring, until all the moisture is evaporated. Add the parsley and the drained vegetables and cook for 2 minutes more, continuing to stir. Check seasonings and remove from heat.

5.   Add the eggs and blend well. Place the mixture in a baking dish and bake for 30 minutes. Allow to cool before eating.

6.   Serve with crusty French bread (see recipe page 42).

YIELD: 6 SERVINGS

✣ *Cognac gives this veal and mushroom dish its final bit of refinement.*

Côtes de Veau aux Champignons Sauvages
(VEAL CHOPS WITH WILD MUSHROOMS)

4 veal loin chops, about ½ pound
   each, with excess fat removed
Salt and freshly ground pepper
   to taste
¼ cup flour
2 tablespoons butter
¾ pound fresh wild mushrooms,

such as morels, chanterelles, cèpes,
   or boletes
2 tablespoons shallots, finely chopped
½ cup dry white wine
½ cup heavy cream
1 tablespoon Cognac

1.   Sprinkle the veal with salt and pepper. Dredge lightly in the flour and shake to remove the excess.

2.   Heat the butter in a nonstick skillet large enough to hold the chops in one layer. Cook over medium heat for 10 minutes on one side, then turn and cook for about 10 minutes on the other side. Transfer the chops to a warm platter and cover with foil to keep warm.

3.   In the same skillet, without removing the butter, add the mushrooms and salt and pepper to taste. Cook over high heat, stirring constantly, for 2 minutes. Add the shallots and cook for another minute, stirring. Add the wine and cook over high heat until the wine is almost evaporated. Add the cream and simmer for 5 minutes, or until the sauce is thickened and golden.

4.   Pour the juices that have accumulated on the platter under the veal into the sauce and add the Cognac. Place the chops on warm serving plates and divide the sauce and the mushrooms equally over them. Serve immediately.

YIELD: 4 SERVINGS

Loire Valley

SPECIALTIES

Fresh vegetables include asparagus, green beans, Swiss chard, mushrooms, pumpkins

Fruit such as plums and pears

Freshwater fish (*sandre* and trout), prepared variously

Friture, bite-sized fried fish, served with vinegar, lemon juice, or tartar sauce

Game such as roasted pheasant, boar (*sanglier*), and rabbit cooked with prunes

Charcuterie, such as *rillettes* (soft *pâtés* of pork), and *rillons* (crisply fried pork bellies), *andouilles* and *andouillettes* (tripe sausages)

Chicken cooked in its own blood with onions

Meat roasted with red wine

Fricassée of chicken with vegetables

Cerneaux, green walnuts served as *hors d'oeuvres*

CHEESES

Chèvre (goat cheese), including *crottins* of *Chavignol*

DESSERTS

Pithiviers gâteau, made from puff pastry filled with almond paste; almond macaroons

Stuffed prunes or cakes made with prunes

Fouace, a sweet brioche pastry

WINES

Crisp, marvelous whites, including Sancerre and Vouvray

THE GARDEN OF FRANCE

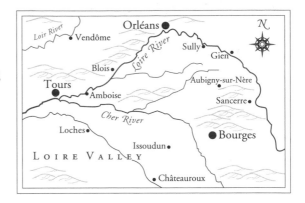

The people of the Loire Valley don't point to one particular cuisine that is theirs. Rather they like to think of themselves as occupying the garden of France, where all things are possible. Fresh vegetables, fish, and game seem to appear effortlessly and in profusion here.

They talk about the woods along the river so thick with game that if you drive through during the night you must be constantly vigilant not to hit something live. As a result, of course, the restaurants are extraordi-

The town of Sancerre gives its name to one of France's best white wines.

The goats of the Loire Valley can be thanked for the region's memorable cheese, usually produced as crottins.

narily blessed—and capable—with pheasant, partridge, quail, and boar. When they talk about the wonderful freshwater fish hereabouts, they mention especially the delicate and sweet white-fleshed *sandre,* as well as the plentiful trout.

An indication of the wild riches is that a kind of snack food, like potato chips, is the *friture,* or bite-sized fried fish, that you find at many a little restaurant along the wide, shallow Loire River. The tiny fish, such as *ablettes* and gudgeon, are eaten whole. You sprinkle the fish with lemon and hold it by the tail—a quick crunch and it's gone. *Friture,* it is said, must be prepared only from the very freshest fish, caught that day. As for the vegetables, the tenderest asparagus is in plentiful supply in the late spring. Then come Swiss chard and the tender beans called *haricots verts.*

As in so many French regions, individuality matters here. In the Val de Loire, when the people express wariness about European unity, it isn't a political stance so much as a concern that unification, and the additional regulation that could come with it, will smooth out the nuances that make for uniqueness. We heard this concern particularly among the goat-cheese makers (there is no cow cheese in the area, only the world-admired *chèvre*). Every farmer seems to have his own approach, some more rustic and primitive and some more modern. So the differences from farm to farm can be distinctly noticeable.

One cheesemaker we met, a young woman named Christine, was particularly adamant about the need to adhere to the old ways. When I asked her about pas-

A cheesemaker discusses the crottins *of* chèvre *aging on racks behind her.*

teurization, her face lit up and she exclaimed that pasteurization was out of the question. She said the unpasteurized cheese lingered on the palate longer, like a good wine. (Although the French do take extraordinary steps to be hygienic in their production of food, more than one observed to us, in an intended distinction with America, that food producers here were obsessed less with sanitation than taste—an irony in this, the homeland of Pasteur.)

Depending on aging and other factors, the small rounds of *chèvre* (called *crottins*) might be mild or strong, so creamy they resemble a custard or so brittle it's difficult to bite through them.

As for the wines of the Loire, while not as lofty as those of Bordeaux or Burgundy, they are a serious matter, too. The sensual Vouvray and the smoky Sancerre are both magnificent in their own right. One brilliant day we visited a winemaker of high repute, the Château de Sancerre; we strolled about the palace and its tower, a vestige of a thirteenth-century fortress. From the windy perch of the tower's peak, you overlook all the villages of Sancerre down in the valley and the vine-covered slopes reaching up from them. Here as elsewhere the picking of the grapes does not happen at a precise time, but is dependent on the particular weather of a particular year. Our guide at the château told us that he always used the lilies as a harbinger of the grapes: the harvest, he said, would begin one hundred days after the lilies bloomed.

The Loire Valley's huge châteaux are perhaps unparalleled for their size and drama, and they are often surrounded by smaller, equally beautiful châteaux, some of which have been converted to hotels. One of these, exquisite in every respect—but especially in its immaculate formal gardens—is the Hostellerie Château de Pray in Amboise. We got the opportunity to work in the kitchen there and turned out these langoustine *(crayfish) tartlets. The recipe calls for several separately prepared elements, but don't be put off by that. The assembly is relatively simple. It will require that you have on hand small tart forms.*

Note: Although we used langoustines, *prawns are close in character and more available, so I suggest those in this recipe merely for pragmatic reasons.*

Tartelettes du Château de Pray

(PRAWN AND TOMATO TARTLETS)

Pastry dough (recipe follows)
Tomato compote (see recipe page 80)
1 tablespoon olive oil
16 prawns, shelled
¼ teaspoon curry powder
Salt and freshly ground pepper
   to taste

2 cups *mâche* (lamb's lettuce),
   washed
1 cup chanterelles (or other wild
   mushrooms), washed, trimmed,
   and cut into bite-sized pieces
Lemon vinaigrette (see recipe
   page 81)

1.   Heat the oven to 400°.

2.   Transfer the ball of dough to a floured surface and flatten it slightly with the palm of your hand before beginning to roll. Sprinkle with flour and roll the dough evenly, giving it quarter-turns after every few rolls. The dough should be rolled to about ⅛-inch thickness. Using a 3- to 3½-inch cookie cutter, cut out circles to fit individual tart molds. Lift the dough circles carefully with a spatula and place them in the individual tartlet molds, pressing the dough into the mold.

3.   Fill each tart shell with about 3 tablespoons of the tomato compote. Bake for about 10 minutes.

4.   Meanwhile, in a nonstick skillet heat the olive oil and add prawns. Sprinkle

with curry powder and salt and pepper to taste. Cook, stirring, for 2 to 3 minutes over high heat. Do not overcook. Set aside.

5. In a mixing bowl, toss the lettuce and mushrooms in lemon vinaigrette.

6. To assemble, unmold the tartlets and place each one in the middle of a plate. Top each tartlet with 4 prawns. Arrange the salad decoratively around each tartlet.

YIELD: 4 SERVINGS

Pastry Dough

1 cup all-purpose flour
8 tablespoons butter, chilled
   and cubed

½ cup Gruyère cheese,
   grated
¼ teaspoon salt

1. Place the flour, butter, cheese, and ¼ teaspoon salt in the container of a food processor and blend until a ball is formed.

2. Remove the dough and chill in refrigerator for half an hour. Note: This dough can be used for almost any nondessert tart—quiches and the like.

Farce aux Tomates

(TOMATO COMPOTE FILLING)

2 tablespoons olive oil
¼ cup onions, finely chopped
1 sprig thyme
1 sprig tarragon
1 garlic clove, peeled

2 cups of tomatoes, peeled,
   seeded, and diced
2 tablespoons tomato paste
Salt and freshly ground pepper
   to taste

1. In a saucepan heat the olive oil and add onions, thyme, tarragon, and garlic. Cook, stirring, over medium heat until wilted. Add tomatoes, tomato paste, and salt and pepper and combine well.

2. Cover, reduce heat, and simmer for about 10 minutes or until all the liquid has disappeared.

3. Remove garlic clove and herb sprigs before use.

Vinaigrette au Citron

(LEMON VINAIGRETTE)

Salt and freshly ground pepper
    to taste
1 tablespoon freshly squeezed
    lemon juice

3 tablespoons virgin olive oil

1.   In a small mixing bowl combine salt and pepper to taste with the lemon juice until the salt is completely dissolved.

2.   Whisk the olive oil in slowly. Check for seasoning.

✤   *Any section on the food of the Loire needs to include a recipe for* friture, *and here's one I put together. In the United States the most appropriate substitute fish is whitebait. Tartar sauce is a fine accompaniment, and a recipe follows.*

Friture de la Loire

(DEEP FRIED BITE-SIZED FISH)

4 cups vegetable oil
2 pounds whitebait
½ cup milk
2 cups all-purpose flour

Salt to taste
Lemon wedges
Tartar sauce (recipe follows)

1.   Preheat the oil to 375° in a deep-fryer or wok.

2.   Rinse the fish in cool water and drain. Then pat them dry with paper towels.

3.   Place the fish in a bowl and toss with the milk until the fish are coated.

4.   Pour the flour into a dish. Dredge the whitebait in the flour to coat it well. Shake off any excess flour.

5.   Place ¼ of the fish in the basket of the deep-fryer or in the wok and cook, shaking the basket, for about 2 minutes, or until the fish are crisp. Drain on paper towels. Continue until all the fish are cooked. Drain on paper towels and season with salt to taste. Serve hot with the lemon wedges and Tartar sauce.

YIELD: 6–8 SERVINGS

Sauce Tartare

(TARTAR SAUCE)

1 egg yolk
1 tablespoon white wine vinegar
2 tablespoons Dijon mustard
Salt and freshly ground white pepper
   to taste
1 cup vegetable oil
2 tablespoons fresh lemon juice

4 tablespoons onion, finely minced
2 tablespoons capers, drained and
   chopped
¼ cup cornichons or sour pickles,
   chopped
¼ cup parsley, finely chopped

1.   Put the egg yolk in a mixing bowl and add the vinegar, mustard, and salt and pepper. Beat with a wire whisk for 10 seconds.

2.   Add the oil gradually, stirring with the whisk until all the oil is incorporated. Add the lemon juice.

3.   Add the remaining ingredients and blend well. Cover and chill.

YIELD: 1½ CUPS

＊   *In Sancerre, I took advantage of the Loire River salmon and, of course, the superb white wine of the region in cooking for a television segment at the Château de Sancerre, which is one of several properties belonging to the Lapostle-Marnier family of Grand Marnier fame. I was happy to have my grandson Nicolas along and, for the show, he pitched in when it came time to prepare this dish.*

Tranches de Saumon à la Sauce Vinaigrette

(POACHED SALMON STEAKS WITH CHERVIL VINAIGRETTE SAUCE)

2 quarts water
1 cup dry white wine, preferably
   Sancerre
3 tablespoons white wine vinegar
½ cup onions, thinly sliced
¼ cup carrots, thinly sliced

½ cup celery, chopped
4 black peppercorns
2 sprigs of fresh thyme, or 1 teaspoon
   dried
1 bay leaf
1 garlic clove, peeled

1 pinch cayenne pepper, or to taste
2 parsley sprigs
Salt to taste

4 boneless salmon steaks with skin
    attached, 4–6 ounces each
Chervil vinaigrette (recipe follows)

1.   Make a *court bouillon,* an aromatic poaching liquid, by placing all the ingredients except the fish in a large skillet or small fish poacher. Bring to a boil, cover, and simmer for 10 minutes. Let cool.

2.   When the *court bouillon* is ready, submerge the fish entirely. If there is not enough liquid to cover the fish by at least 1 inch, add water to cover. Return the liquid to a boil, lower the heat to a simmer, and poach for about 5 minutes. Let stand about 5 minutes longer before serving. Do not overcook.

3.   Serve the fish warm or cold over the vinaigrette, saving a little of the sauce to drizzle on top (recipe follows).

Vinaigrette au Cerfeuil
(CHERVIL VINAIGRETTE)

1 tablespoon Dijon mustard
Salt and pepper to taste
2 tablespoons red wine vinegar
1 tablespoon shallots, finely sliced
1 small garlic clove, peeled

3 tablespoons chervil (parsley
    can be substituted), coarsely
    chopped
⅓ cup olive or other vegetable oil
2 tablespoons water

1.   Place the mustard, salt, pepper, vinegar, shallots, garlic, and chervil in a blender or very fast food processor. Blend well.

2.   As it blends, pour the oil through the opening in the cover. If the vinaigrette is too thick, add the water and blend. Check for seasoning.

YIELD: 4 SERVINGS

✼   *A splendid accompaniment to the preceding poached salmon, especially given the goat cheese to be sampled everywhere in the Loire, is quite obviously a goat cheese salad.*

Salade de Concombres et Chèvre

(CUCUMBER AND GOAT CHEESE SALAD)

2 cucumbers, peeled and thinly sliced
1 large tomato, cored and coarsely
    cubed
¼ pound goat cheese, crumbled
1 teaspoon Dijon mustard
1 tablespoon red wine vinegar

2 tablespoons water
Salt and freshly ground pepper
    to taste
2 tablespoons olive oil
2 tablespoons parsley, finely
    chopped

1.   In a salad bowl, combine the cucumbers, tomato, and goat cheese.

2.   In the container of a food processor, blend mustard, vinegar, water, and salt and pepper to taste. Add olive oil slowly while the machine is still turning. (The vinaigrette can also be prepared in a mixing bowl, in which case all ingredients should be combined well before whisking olive oil in slowly.)

3.   Pour the vinaigrette over the salad and toss well. Sprinkle with parsley and serve.

YIELD: 4 SERVINGS, AS A SIDE DISH

✤ *Since the Loire is so justly proud of its vegetables, the idea of a hearty vegetable soup is unavoidable.*

Potage Garbure

(FRESH VEGETABLE SOUP)

4 tablespoons butter

1 cup onions, coarsely chopped

2 whole garlic cloves

2 cups fresh carrots, peeled and diced into ½-inch cubes

4 cups white turnips, peeled and diced into ½-inch cubes

2 cups celery ribs, diced into ½-inch cubes

2 cups fresh green beans, cut into 1-inch lengths

2 cups peeled potatoes, cut into ½-inch cubes

2 cups ripe tomatoes, cored and cut into ½-inch cubes

Salt and freshly ground pepper to taste

4 cups fresh chicken broth (see recipe page 108), or good quality canned

4 cups water

⅓ cup heavy cream

1. Heat half of the butter in a heavy soup kettle, add the onions and garlic. Cook, stirring, until the onions are wilted but not brown. Add the remaining vegetables and stir. Add salt and pepper to taste and cook, stirring, for about 3 minutes.

2. Add the broth and the water and simmer, stirring occasionally, for 1 hour.

3. Pour ⅓ of the mixture at a time in the container of a food processor and blend until smooth. Return the mixture to the kettle, bring to a boil, check for seasoning, add the remaining butter, and stir in the cream. Simmer for 2 minutes. Serve with crusty bread.

YIELD: 8–10 SERVINGS

Bordeaux

SPECIALTIES

Most of the cuisine revolves around the wine, employed in
stewing or braising fish, meat, and vegetables. It is reduced into
rich sauces (including the famed *Sauce Bordelaise*), acts as the
base of marinades, or is used to poach fruit for dessert.

ALSO

Mussels, steamed with a cream and wine sauce, or
grilled on a bed of pine needles, a dish known as *éclade de moules*

Oysters served on the half shell with small fried sausages

Locally caught salmon prepared in countless ways

Foie gras is enjoyed in *pâtés,* or simply sautéed

Magrets de canard, or fresh duck breasts, are sautéed or
grilled and served rare

WINES

Big, round, complex reds of Pauillac, Pomerol, Margaux,
and St. Julien (often bearing the name of a renowned château)

The sophisticated whites of Graves, and the syrupy dessert
wines of Sauternes

GRANDEUR IN A GLASS

L
ike no other area in France—not even Burgundy—Bordeaux is known for its wine.
The city of Bordeaux is charming enough,
draped along the Garonne River, and the cook-
ing here is of high caliber. But of course the wine matters at least as much, particularly the red, which is of inestimable value standing alongside the food as well as in
its use as part of the preparation of many dishes. The white (Graves and Sauternes, especially) has always been notable but the red, a blend that leans heavily on
the remarkable Cabernet Sauvignon grape, has led to Bordeaux's reputation as perhaps the greatest wine growing area in the world.

Bordeaux is not far from the Atlantic, but the locals say it is the river they have to
thank most—for its ability to moderate the weather in its immediate environs and
invigorate the soil (the soil, in fact, is rather gravelly and forces the roots of the vines
to dig deep and struggle for their survival, a bit of adversity that is said to build character). Some vintners believe that to produce a great wine, you have to be able to see
the river from the vineyard.

In the size of its land area alone, 250,000 acres stretching out from the city and
through the towns, the Bordelais region is remarkable in France and the world. Just
listen to the names: St. Estèphe, St. Julien, Pauillac, Margaux, each a village with
its own Appellation d'Origine Contrôllée, or AOC. This is the home of Lafite-
Rothschild and Latour and Haut-Brion. It is big enough and generous enough to
embrace producers of wine who rigorously hold to the old ways and those who swear
by more modern, scientific approaches. When we visited, it was our intention to see
winemakers who inclined toward one end of the spectrum as well as the other, but
we also hoped to introduce Americans to châteaux of great quality that may be less

An artist takes his inspiration from the sprawling Château Langoa, the home of Anthony and Eva Barton.

familiar to them than, say, Château Margaux. (All of the finer wines of Bordeaux can grace any meal and, personally, I always like to get out of the rut of using the same wine over and over again.)

It is in Bordeaux, to take one gleaming example, where you will find Anthony Barton and his wife, Eva, a handsome and debonair family, steeped in history and in love with it. It is a family that knows how to pose with a dog the way comfortable gentry are supposed to. The Bartons' home, the sprawling yet immaculately symmetrical eighteenth-century Château Langoa et Leoville Barton, also conveys a sense that theirs is a life of ease indeed.

But the leisurely air is deceptive. There is an earthiness here, too, and a stubbornness that has transcended the centuries. The family has fought frosts and bad years. It has refused to yield the land bought by Hugh Barton in 1821, even during the most blighted times. And it has kept up the quality of wines, Leoville-Barton and Langoa-Barton, that critics have long hailed as among the best of the St. Juliens. When they are sold in the United States, they are so reasonably priced for wines of this caliber that they are a true bargain.

The Barton wines age well—in fact they cry out for aging. When we were there, the wry Anthony Barton said that, if people ask him when his wine is ready to drink, he would like to say, "in about twenty years," but it will be fine enough in five and that seems the more practical recommendation. (The wine writer Robert M. Parker, Jr., after noting that the Barton wines are now more widely available in the United States than they had been, thanks to improved distribution, describes them as seeming "to combine the savory, complex, graceful fruitiness of St. Julien with the cedary toughness and virility of Pauillac." For our part, we simply found them delicious, every one.)

The Bartons are almost as famous for their idiosyncratic family history as for their wines. The first Barton to arrive in France was Thomas, an Irishman, and the

Wine aged in the traditional fashion, in oak barrels

Bordeaux bottles on a conveyor belt, ready for labeling

family has resolutely maintained its Irish citizenship ever since—although the name is most familiarly pronounced BAR-tone—"We're proud to be Irish," Eva Barton says. (In any case, pride is no sin in Bordeaux, where the vintners like to stock local restaurants with their very own wines just to be sure they will be available for them when they dine out.)

When it comes to the *vendange* (the harvest) in the early fall, pride in the French as well as the Irish quickly comes to the fore in the Barton household. The French students who travel here to work know that the *vendange* is an important time indeed, but some foreign students, Eva Barton says, too often "think it's a party and they drink too much—the best you can hope is that they will fall asleep and stay out of the way." When the grapes are finally and successfully harvested, it is cause for celebration—indeed, a grand party: fresh tomato soup, avocados and crab, roast lamb with beans, cheeses and salads and tarts—five hours of eating and drinking, all of it culminating in a bouquet for the lady of the house presented by the grape pickers.

After spending time with the Bartons we went on to make good friends with the people of the Château Lynch-Bages, winemakers with centuries of history here, too, but in many ways now swept up in expansion and modernization. (They have no fear of holding some of their wine in metal barrels rather than wood, for instance, or picking the grapes by machine rather than by hand.) The whole enterprise—the vineyards, as well as the beautiful new hotel rooms—has about it the paradoxical air of modern energy in a slow dance with the languorous past. Jean-Michel Cazes, the proprietor of his family's own Lynch-Bages land, also supervises vineyards owned by AXA, one of France's large insurance companies. That big-big-business connection aside, I don't want to make Jean-Michel sound like anything other than a true wine-maker. Despite his impressive recent business triumphs he maintains a common-man sense about him; he is the sort of boss who enjoys sitting at the long table in a mess hall to join the pickers for lunch. No matter where Jean-Michel puts his energies on any given day, no matter how much he may diverge from the old ways, his wines are glowingly praised, widely regarded as substantial and rich, deserving the reputation that has led to their ever wider popularity.

The warm and generous proprietors welcome visitors at Lynch-Bages, but if you take it in your mind to drive along the D2 and visit this as well as other vineyards on the *route des vins*, it's best to call ahead at least to let the winemakers know you are coming and also to verify visiting hours. Whatever you do, don't let the grandeur of Bordeaux scare you. As forbidding as some of these astonishing estates may seem from the road, the people who run them are almost unfailingly gracious and even flattered when guests arrive. Some travelers have observed, and I think it is generally true, that the wine regions are the most hospitable of all the areas of France.

❦ *The grape pickers at Lynch-Bages eat in a hall dominated by a large fireplace, where many of the meals are prepared; the day I joined them we had some wonderful grilled lamb.*

Gigot d'Agneau Grillé
(CHARCOAL-GRILLED LEG OF LAMB STEAKS)

12 lamb steaks, about 6 ounces each, cut from the leg

4 tablespoons fresh rosemary, or 2 tablespoons dried

Salt and freshly ground pepper to taste

2 tablespoons olive oil

1. Heat the charcoal grill.
2. Sprinkle the steaks evenly with the rosemary and salt and pepper to taste.
3. Brush the steaks with olive oil.
4. Place the steaks on the hot grill and cook each side for 2 to 3 minutes, depending on the desired degree of doneness.
5. Serve with Gracieuse's white beans (recipe follows).

YIELD: 12 SERVINGS

❦ *A Portuguese woman named Gracieuse is the head cook of the château, and this is the recipe she shared with me.*

Haricots Blancs à la Gracieuse
(GRACIEUSE'S WHITE BEANS)

4 tablespoons butter

2 cups onions, cut into small cubes

6 tablespoons garlic, minced

2 pounds white navy or kidney beans, soaked overnight and drained

4 quarts water

6 sprigs fresh thyme, or 1 tablespoon dried

2 bay leaves

4 whole cloves

Salt and freshly ground white pepper to taste

1. In a large kettle or saucepan melt the butter over medium heat. Add the onions and garlic and cook until wilted. Then add the beans and 4 quarts of water,

along with the thyme, bay leaves, cloves, and salt and pepper to taste. Bring to a boil and simmer for 1 hour, or until the beans are tender but not mushy.

2.   Check for seasoning. Serve with the lamb steaks (see recipe above).

YIELD: 12 SERVINGS

❧   *At another of the great vintners of Bordeaux, Château Haut-Brion, we met the vineyard manager, Jean-Bernard Delmas, a robust man in his mid-fifties with a full head of salt-and-pepper hair whose avocation is cooking. He has strong feelings about it. For instance, he prefers to cook with young wine, right out of the barrel, to give his dishes a vigorous boost. He chose to prepare a striped bass for us in red Bordeaux. Jean-Bernard likes to flambé the wine when it first comes to a boil to be sure all of the alcohol has burned off. And he also believes in adding a bit of oil to the butter in the roux so the butter will be less likely to burn: a man full of solid tips.*

Note: The bass he prepared for us was quite large; a similar approach can easily be adapted at home by using two 4-pound striped bass or red snappers, then marinating and roasting them together in a large roasting pan.

Bar au Vin Rouge

(BASS IN RED WINE SAUCE)

6- to 8-pound striped bass, cleaned
  and scaled, gills removed
2 bottles red Bordeaux
2 cups leeks, cubed
1 cup carrots, cubed
1 cup celery, cubed
3 small onions stuck with 1 clove each
1 cup white turnips, cubed
6 parsley sprigs

2 bay leaves
4 sprigs thyme
1 tablespoon whole peppercorns
Salt and freshly ground pepper
  to taste
4 tablespoons vegetable oil
4 tablespoons butter
4 tablespoons flour
¾ cup heavy cream

1.   In a fish poacher or some other noncorrosive container large enough to hold the bass, prepare the marinade by pouring in the wine and adding the leeks, carrots, celery, onions, turnips, parsley, bay leaves, thyme, peppercorns, and salt and pepper

to taste. Add the fish and let it marinate overnight, or about 12 hours, turning it from time to time.

2. Preheat the oven to 400°.

3. Remove the fish from the marinade, brush it on both sides with 2 tablespoons of the vegetable oil, and place it in a roasting pan. Roast the fish for about 30 to 45 minutes depending on size. Baste it from time to time with the marinade. To check for doneness, gently pull on a spine of the dorsal fin; when it comes out clean the fish is done.

4. Meanwhile, place the marinade in a large saucepan and bring to a boil. Continue to cook until reduced by half.

5. Prepare a *roux* in a small saucepan by adding the remaining oil and the butter and cooking over low heat until the butter melts. Add the flour, stirring with a whisk until well blended. Do not brown.

6. Pouring only 1 cup at a time through a fine strainer, add 4 cups of the reduced marinade to the roux. After each addition, blend with a whisk until smooth. Add cream and blend well. Bring to a simmer but do not allow sauce to return to a boil. Check for seasoning and keep warm.

7. Remove the fish from the oven. With a paring knife, starting on the dorsal side, loosen the skin at the edges and then pull it back along the whole length of the fish. Transfer the fish to a warmed serving platter and spoon sauce over it. Serve remaining sauce on the side. Serve with boiled parsley potatoes.

YIELD: 6–8 SERVINGS

✤ *While Jean-Bernard cooks as an avocation, the château's professional cook is a woman named Christine, who prepared a buttery apple tart for lunch that had delightful overtones of vanilla.*

Tarte aux Pommes à la Christine
(CHRISTINE'S APPLE TART)

1½ cups all-purpose flour
8 tablespoons cold butter, cut into
   small cubes

¼ teaspoon salt
7 tablespoons plus 1 teaspoon sugar
3 to 4 tablespoons cold water

| 6 Granny Smith apples | ¾ cup heavy cream |
| 1 whole egg | 1 teaspoon vanilla extract |

1. Preheat the oven to 400°.

2. In the container of a food processor, add flour, butter, salt, and 1 teaspoon of sugar. Pulse the machine briefly. While the machine is turning, add 3 tablespoons of water slowly until a ball is formed. Add more water if necessary.

3. Sprinkle a work surface lightly with flour and roll the dough into a 12-inch circle. Drape the circle over the rolling pin and transfer it to a 10-inch fluted tart pan. Prick the dough with a fork and chill it in the refrigerator for 15 minutes.

4. Peel and core the apples. Quarter them and slice the quarters lengthwise, into slices about ¼-inch thick. Beginning at the edges and working toward the center, arrange the apple slices in concentric circles until the tart is completely full. Sprinkle with 4 tablespoons of sugar.

5. Place the tart pan on a cookie sheet and bake on the bottom rack of the oven for 15 minutes.

6. Meanwhile, in a small mixing bowl beat the egg. Add the cream, remaining sugar, and vanilla. Mix until well blended.

7. Remove the tart from the oven and pour the cream mixture over it evenly.

8. Reduce oven temperature to 375°, and return tart to the oven for about 30 minutes or until pastry is golden-brown and baked thoroughly.

YIELD: 8–10 SERVINGS

✤ *After we left Château Haut-Brion, we drove to see the fine chef Jean-Marie Amat at his startlingly modern restaurant-hotel, Le Saint James. Jean-Marie, forty-five years old, is so soft-spoken he seems almost shy at first, but he is capable of sarcasm and humor and likes to make outlandish statements in a completely deadpan way. Beneath the*

columns that lead to the entrance of the restaurant is the inscription "Changer la face du monde" (Change the face of the world), a bit grandiose but evidence of a real desire to challenge himself and others. From this restaurant, if you look across the river, you can watch the lights of Bordeaux come up in the evening: the old city and the new restaurant juxtaposed in the soft air. The cooking here is one of contrasts, too. Often Japanese or Chinese touches mingle with the French. Oysters are a favorite in the Bordeaux region and here is Jean-Marie's salmon tartare with oysters.

Tartare de Saumon aux Huîtres et au Caviar de Jean-Marie Amat

(JEAN-MARIE AMAT'S SALMON TARTARE WITH OYSTERS AND CAVIAR)

8 ounces skinless salmon fillet
8 to 12 oysters (depending on the size)
Salt to taste
1 tablespoon chives, chopped
¼ cup heavy cream

2 teaspoons fresh lemon juice
½ teaspoon Absolut Citron, or other lemon vodka
2 heaping teaspoons Sevruga caviar (or salmon caviar)

1.   Slice the salmon into thin strips and then cut the strips crosswise into small cubes. Chop the cubes coarsely with a sharp, heavy knife, working quickly so as to be able to return the chopped fish to the refrigerator as soon as possible.

2.   Meanwhile, open and shell the oysters, making sure to reserve their liquor in a small bowl. Chop the oysters coarsely and add them to the salmon, along with 1 teaspoon of the oyster liquor. Add salt to taste and 1 teaspoon of the chives and mix well.

3.   Make a sauce by combining the cream, lemon juice, vodka, salt to taste, 2 teaspoons of the oyster liquor, and the remaining chives in a small mixing bowl.

4.   Place a 2½-inch ring form in the center of a chilled serving plate and fill it evenly with the *tartare*, smoothing the top before removing the ring. Alternatively, shape the salmon *tartare* into a circle with a serving spoon. Top the *tartare* with the dollop of caviar. Spoon the sauce around the *tartare* and serve.

YIELD: 2 SERVINGS

❧ *For my own effort in Bordeaux, I turned to a local fish*, rouget, *but I suggest you substitute red snapper, the closest American ingredient. And I decided on a white Bordeaux, a Graves, which often has a nutty, smoky flavor that marries beautifully with fish.*

Filet de Rouget à la Bordelaise

(FILLET OF RED SNAPPER WITH BORDEAUX WINE)

½ pound small red potatoes, peeled and cut into ¼-inch cubes

4 red snapper fillets, skin on, about 6 ounces each

Salt and freshly ground pepper to taste

¼ cup flour

2 tablespoons olive oil or vegetable oil

¼ pound mushrooms, cut into 1¼-inch cubes

1 large sweet red pepper, cored and cut into ¼-inch cubes

⅓ cup shallots, minced

½ cup dry white Bordeaux wine, such as a Graves

1 tablespoon lemon juice

3 tablespoons butter

2 tablespoons chives, chopped

1.   Place the potatoes in a small saucepan with salted water to cover. Bring to a boil and simmer for 4 minutes. Drain and set aside.

2.   Sprinkle the fillets with salt and pepper to taste. Dredge them in flour, shaking to remove the excess.

3.   Heat the oil over high heat in a nonstick skillet large enough to hold the fish in one layer. Place the fillets skin side down in the hot skillet and cook for about 2 minutes. Turn them skin side up and cook for about 2 minutes more, or until lightly browned. Remove and keep warm.

4.   Leaving the fat in the skillet, add the potatoes, mushrooms, and red peppers. Sprinkle with salt and pepper to taste. Cook, stirring, for 1 minute. Add the shallots and cook briefly. Add the wine and simmer until reduced by a little more than half. Swirl in the lemon juice and the butter over low heat. Check for seasoning and add the chives. Keep warm.

5.   To serve, place each fillet in the center of a warm plate and spoon the vegetables and sauce over it.

YIELD: 4 SERVINGS

Périgord/Dordogne Valley

SPECIALTIES

Truffles in omelettes, sauces, and many other preparations (*Périgourdine* refers to a garnish of truffles)

Sauce Périgueux, a sauce of Madeira, truffles, and truffle juice, traditionally served with steak

Walnut oil in sautés of vegetables or fish, as well as in salad dressings (the salads often containing walnuts, too)

Goose and duck *foie gras*

Confit of goose, preserved goose served with crisp skin and moist inside

Goose *rillettes,* the coarse *pâté* more familiarly prepared from pork *mique,* pork with dumplings

Tourain, garlic soup, traditionally finished by drinking the dregs mixed with a dash of red wine

Magret de canard, duck breast usually cooked rare

Wild mushrooms, some of the best in France, including morels, cèpes, and the delicate *mousserons,* or fairy-ring mushrooms

Friture, bite-sized fried freshwater fish such as gudgeon

CHEESES

Cabécou, a zesty soft goat cheese

DESSERTS

Prunes stuffed with prune butter
Prune flan
Almond sponge cake
Fresh strawberries; strawberries with *sabayon*

WINES

Excellent reds of the Côtes de Duras and Buzet and of Bergerac; often fine reds of Cahors
The whites of Bergerac
The sweet wines of Monbazillac

BLACK DIAMONDS

I f you visit this ancient region, the Périgord, especially along the Dordogne River—where we chose to do almost all of our cooking and eating for the region's segment in the "Cooking in France" series—you will find yourself in an area of breathtaking surrounding drama. The Dordogne winds through a valley of sheer cliffs (the very place where Cro-Magnon man was discovered) pierced by caves adorned with prehistoric art. A later era (much later) is represented by the splendid châteaux, so staggering in number that local storytellers have come up with a ready explanation. They say this excessive splendor is the result of divine predicament: one day God found himself with too many castles and impatiently chose to solve the problem by dropping them on the Dordogne.

But it would be a mistake to allow the great beauty of the area to distract you from the food—rich, satisfying, homey but frequently, by American standards, opulent, too. It is here that the truffles (so costly back home) are at their best and are plentiful. It is here that walnut oil, a relatively expensive product in America, is part of the everyday cooking.

If you have never tried it, walnut oil is an adventure in itself. The flavor is very strong and more nutty, more pungent than any other oil I can think of. (Walnut oil spoils faster than some others, perhaps within several weeks—and that is critical; to be at its remarkable best it must be very fresh.) The ubiquitous walnuts of the Périgord are not just for oil. They will become the pronounced ingredient in salads (*salade aux noix*), cakes, and even ice creams. And they will be macerated in brandy to produce a walnut liqueur. But it is as an oil that the walnut is most fascinating, partly because of the production process. A splendid place to see it produced—as well as to drink in the Périgord's reverence for the past—is the mill, Moulin de la Tour, at Ste. Nathalène, about five miles from Sarlat. The mill is still powered by water drawn from a pond and stream out back; it still generates heat through the burning of wood.

In this small, dark, Dickensian place the oil is extracted from the nuts by brute force: the room is dominated by a stone grinding wheel that crushes the walnuts into a mash that is then cooked in a caldron for half an hour before it is shoveled into a pressing machine. The mill can turn out 300 quarts of oil a week, much of it during visiting hours, when the owners find the time to entertain tourists with grace and friendliness (and gain a good deal of their income from immediate sales of oil on the premises).

As for the truffles, the "black diamonds" of Périgord, they are such a signature ingredient in dishes of the region that anything you see described as *Périgourdine* is supposed to include them in some way to earn the name. They bring a musky, rich sense to any dish they touch. The Périgord truffle is extraordinarily adaptable, unlike the white truffles from Italy, for instance, which blend in less well with a wide variety of food and are primarily useful for pastas. I particularly like the way truffles of the Périgord look: the blackness is conspicuous, shouting out its presence.

A stone wheel crushes walnuts for oil at Moulin de la Tour.

For many years now, the search for truffles has been

evolving and becoming more efficient. Once the only
guides the truffle hunters employed were pigs, discrim-
inating animals, evidently driven to rapture by the

*Dogs are trained to sniff out
truffles for the harvest.*

buried fungi. A pig would be led to the vicinity of an oak or chestnut tree (truffles
have an affinity for their roots and grow near them) and there it would sniff one out,
only to be yanked away before it had a chance to actually get at the truffle. Today,
dogs are increasingly used instead of pigs; they are easy to transport, quick working,
and reliable—and will not damage the truffles.

In fact, a dog doesn't normally have any use for a truffle, but, thanks to cleverly
devised training that would be familiar to any Skinnerian behaviorist, scientists
found they could simulate the aroma of the fungi in a lab and then train dogs to follow that aroma to its underground source if they rewarded them with a tidbit. When
we went into a field with skilled people from one of the big truffle producers,
Pebeyre of Cahors, we looked on as the three trained dogs leaped out of a car (a feat
not so easy for pigs, if you can even get them into the car in the first place) to begin
the hunt. As a trainer called out *"Cherchez! Cherchez!"* the dogs went off rapidly in
search of the source of that alluring aroma, found it, and received a little snack as

recompense, a pathetic morsel compared to the valuable treat that now belonged to the human hunter.

The garden near the outdoor dining area at Le Vieux Logis

And as if truffles and walnuts weren't enough, the mushrooms of the Périgord are among the best in France. The cèpes are unparalleled. These big, meaty mushrooms (occasionally available in the United States) are sensational in sautés; I love them in omelettes or as a garnish for poultry and meat; I can eat cèpes constantly and with almost anything. (Like any kind of mushroom, these must be young; when they get old, their texture diminishes as they grow limp and spongy.)

The young ducks and geese here are among the tenderest, but when they grow old they must be braised to soften them. The reason the *magret de canard,* the duck breast that is now so popular, can be served rare is that it is from a young duck and still tender. With goose that would be impossible at any time; even the youngest goose's breast is never tender enough for this sort of cooking.

Our temporary headquarters along the Dordogne was the town of La Roque-Gageac, a lovely, small port squeezed between the elm-capped cliffs and the green, tranquil river. Huddled there, with its houses, hotels, and castles, the town makes the most of what the land will provide, and as you climb to visit the caves, you pass home after home, clinging to the cliff sides like orchids on a tree trunk.

At the bottom of the cliff is a hotel and restaurant called La Belle Etoile, and it was there that we met the young couple who run the restaurant, Regis and Fabienne Ongaro. We spoke to them in a small lobby in front of the fireplace—all that remains of the original sixteenth-century room that was gutted by fire—after both had experienced a withering day of work. Regis, hair mussed and eyes weary, but his smile, incredibly, still quick, said that although he was the cook, Fabienne was the critic and they developed their menus together. Was she hard on him? "Oh, yes," he said, as Fabienne laughed. The food here, as it is throughout most of the Périgord, is basic, marked by only the freshest produce: roast chicken, *friture* (the fried tiny fish that you eat whole, common on this river as it is on the Loire), and desserts like *sabayon* and strawberries browned under a broiler.

Here, as elsewhere in the Périgord, one can expect to find preserved goose or duck, crisp and moist. To prepare this dish, called a *confit,* the meat is slow-baked and then placed in a crock, sealed with fat, and stored for at least a month to allow the flavor to develop. It can be savored alone or added to other dishes, and is often employed as an embellishment to a *cassoulet,* for instance, to add finesse and variation.

Less typical variations on the local cuisine, in part because of the elegance of the cooking and the restaurant itself, are to be found at the Vieux Logis in Tremolat. Its chef is Pierre-Jean Duribreux, somebody with whom I felt an immediate kinship. He is a classically trained forty-year-old who began cooking when he was sixteen. I watched him shape his vegetables so that each piece of knob celery, each piece of carrot had exactly seven facets—and that is precisely what I had to learn to do as an apprentice half a century ago. At the same time, his cooking is not fossilized; he continually incorporates new elements. He was unafraid, for instance, to employ Asian ingredients in a dressing intended to accompany beef he had delicately simmered in broth.

The restaurant-hotel's grounds are meticulous in layout. A square swimming pool sits in a perfect lawn, lined by evenly spaced trees. A stream divides the swimming area from the outdoor dining patio, which is protected by linden trees; if proof were ever required that food is enhanced by its environment, one finds it here. Vines cling to the hotel's stone walls and, on a brilliant day, the grounds are all shades of green harmonizing in the sunshine. The waiters stride out to the dining patio through the dappled light.

❧   *Garlic soup can be found all over France, but it is one of the most prevalent dishes in the Périgord. This one was prepared for us at the Château de Cazenac near Sarlat by Armelle Constant. The French take advantage of the last few spoonfuls of soup by pouring some red wine into their plates and then drinking it with great relish. The custom is known as* faire chabrol.

Tradition has it that a wedding party would show up en masse early on the morning after to surprise the newlywed couple, all in good humor but not necessarily so welcome. To compensate for the intrusion, the visitors would come bearing a tourain.

Tourain à l'Ail

(GARLIC SOUP)

2 tablespoons lard or olive oil
⅓ cup garlic, peeled and finely
   chopped
¼ cup flour
8 cups water, boiling (or 4 cups water
   and 4 cups red wine)

Salt and freshly ground pepper to taste
3 tablespoons red wine vinegar
2 whole eggs, separated
2 cups French baguette (see recipe
   page 42), thinly sliced and lightly
   toasted

1.   In a large saucepan, melt the lard over low heat and add the garlic, stirring constantly until wilted. Do not brown.

2.   Add the flour, whisking until smooth. Stir continuously, scraping the sides and bottom of pot to make sure all the flour is incorporated. Cook over low heat, stirring constantly for a few minutes.

3.   Add the boiling water or water-and-wine combination, one cup at a time, and salt and pepper to taste. Stir well with a wire whisk after each addition to eliminate any lumps.

4.   Add the vinegar and blend well. Bring to a boil, then reduce the heat, cover, and simmer for 10 minutes.

5.   In a small mixing bowl, blend the egg whites with 1 cup of the soup. Pour this mixture back into the saucepan, stirring briskly with a whisk. Partially cover and simmer for 10 minutes longer.

6.   In another small mixing bowl, blend the egg yolks with 1 cup of the soup. Pour the mixture back into the soup, stirring briskly with a whisk. Do not allow the

soup to boil again once the yolks have been added. Check for seasoning and keep warm.

7.   To serve, place bread pieces in a heated soup tureen or in individual soup plates and pour the hot soup over them. Serve with additional bread on the side.

YIELD: 4 SERVINGS

✢   *On the night of our arrival at the Château de Cazenac, Philippe Constant, Armelle's husband, served a dessert of simple but lovely baked apples.*

Pommes Philippe Constant
(PHILIPPE CONSTANT'S BAKED APPLES)

4 large Golden Delicious apples   4 tablespoons butter
½ cup apple jelly

1.   Preheat the oven to 375°.
2.   Peel the apples and, using an apple corer, remove the seeds, leaving the apple whole.
3.   Place apples in an ovenproof baking dish just large enough to hold them snugly. Fill each apple with 2 tablespoons apple jelly and top them with 1 tablespoon butter.
4.   Bake for 30 minutes, or until the apples are soft. Do not overcook.

YIELD: 4 SERVINGS

❧ *Jean-Marie Miquel, whose restaurant in Najac is near enough to Périgord to show-case that region's influences, employs walnut oil in this chicken and cabbage dish as the crowning touch. The lengthy ingredient list makes it look harder than it is.*

Suprêmes de Volaille Jean-Marie

(JEAN-MARIE'S CHICKEN BREAST WRAPPED IN CABBAGE LEAVES)

3 chicken livers

3 chicken hearts

4 ounces salt pork, skin removed
  and cut into pieces

3 tablespoons sliced shallots

1 whole egg

½ cup dried French bread, cubed
  and soaked in ⅓ cup milk

1 tablespoon flour

½ cup parsley or chervil

Salt and freshly ground pepper
  to taste

4 boneless, skinless breasts of chicken

4 large cabbage leaves, blanched for
  4 minutes and drained

4 cups fresh chicken broth (see
  recipe page 108), or good quality
  canned

4 whole small leeks, trimmed
  and cleaned

2 large carrots, peeled, quartered
  lengthwise, and cut into 3-inch
  strips

2 medium-sized white turnips,
  peeled and cut into quarters

8 celery pieces, about 3 inches in
  length

1 whole onion, peeled

6 peppercorns

4 whole cloves

1 bay leaf

1 country ham bone (if available),
  cut into 2 pieces

4 teaspoons walnut oil

4 sprigs of chervil or parsley

Coarse salt

1.   Combine the chicken livers and hearts, salt pork, shallots, egg, bread and milk, flour, parsley, and salt and pepper in the container of a food processor and pulse until the ingredients are coarsely chopped. Check the seasoning. Divide the mixture into 4 portions.

2.   Cut each chicken breast in half lengthwise and sprinkle with salt and pepper.

3.   Place the cabbage leaves on a flat surface and lay ½ chicken breast in the center of each. Spoon a portion of the stuffing mixture over each chicken piece and cover with the remaining chicken breast piece.

4.   Lift the outer edges of the cabbage leaves to form a packet and tie them together with a string.

5.   Place the cabbage packets in a large saucepan, add the chicken broth, bring to a boil, and simmer for 5 minutes. Check for seasoning.

6.   Add the leeks, carrots, turnips, celery, onion, peppercorns, cloves, bay leaf, and ham bone. Return the liquid to a boil and reduce the heat to simmer for 20 to 25 minutes, or until done.

7.   To serve, remove the strings from the packets and place each on a warm serving plate with the vegetables around it. Sprinkle 1 teaspoon walnut oil over each packet and garnish with sprigs of chervil or parsley. Serve with coarse salt on the side. The cooking broth may be served on the side in a cup.

YIELD: 4 SERVINGS

✻   *Duck breast, not surprisingly in an area known for its goose and duck* foie gras, *is also a regional specialty. I headed off to the market in Sarlat to buy the duck breasts for this recipe. The whimsical touch is to serve them with orange baskets, filled with orange segments; to produce baskets the cook must carefully remove the skin of each orange so that it remains intact.*

Magret de Canard à l'Orange
(DUCK BREAST WITH ORANGES)

4 whole oranges
2 6- to 8-ounce duck breasts, boned
Salt and freshly ground pepper to
   taste
1 tablespoon shallots, finely chopped

1 teaspoon sugar
1 tablespoon red wine vinegar
1 tablespoon Grand Marnier
1 cup chicken broth (recipe follows)
1½ tablespoons butter

1.   To make baskets from the orange peel, cut around the equator of 2 of the oranges, inserting the knife just deep enough to cut through the skin but not the flesh. Insert a narrow spoon handle between peel and flesh and, working carefully, loosen one from the other. Pull the skin away in halves, being careful to leave the orange flesh in one piece. The 4 emptied halves of orange peel will serve as the baskets. Decorate them by cutting triangles out along their rims to create spiked edges.

2.   Remove any remaining white membrane from the whole oranges with a sharp

paring knife. Remove segments from the peeled orange by inserting a paring knife alongside each segment and cutting the flesh away from the membrane. Pluck the segments out. Squeeze the remains of the orange to extract the juice and reserve.

3. With the remaining whole oranges, use a zester to obtain 2 tablespoons of orange zest. Cleanly remove the remaining peel and cut the fruit into segments, as above. Divide all the segments into the 4 baskets and keep warm.

4. To prepare the duck, trim the excess fat from the duck breasts, leaving a ⅛-inch layer. Sprinkle them with salt and pepper to taste.

5. Heat a skillet large enough to hold the breasts in one layer and add them, skin side down, over medium-high heat. Cook until golden-brown and then turn and cook on second side. The total cooking time is about 10 minutes for medium rare, although cooking time will vary according to thickness of the duck breasts. Baste with cooking juices occasionally. Remove and keep warm.

6. Pour off the duck fat, leaving only the brown particles in the skillet and add shallots and sugar, stirring constantly until the mixture caramelizes. Be careful not to let it burn.

7. Add the vinegar, Grand Marnier, fresh orange juice, chicken broth, and any juices that have accumulated around the cooked duck breasts. Cook, stirring, until the liquid is reduced by more than half. Strain the sauce through a fine strainer into a small saucepan and swirl in the butter. Add the orange zest. Check for seasoning and keep warm.

8. Cut the duck breasts on the bias into thin slices about ⅛-inch thick. Separate the slices and arrange them in a fan shape on each of 4 heated serving plates. Place an orange basket on each plate and pour sauce around the meat and over the baskets. Serve with sautéed potatoes and sautéed mushrooms (recipes follow).

YIELD: 4 SERVINGS

Soupe Volaille
(CHICKEN BROTH)

5 pounds chicken bones, with most
 of the fat removed
2 cups coarsely chopped onions
1 cup coarsely chopped carrots
1 cup coarsely chopped celery

2 garlic cloves, peeled
6 sprigs parsley
2 bay leaves
4 sprigs thyme or 1 teaspoon
 dried thyme

6 peppercorns
2 whole cloves

4 whole fresh allspice
4 quarts water

1. Place the bones in a 6-quart stockpot, cover them with water, and bring to a boil. Discard the water at once and rinse the bones thoroughly with cold water. Return the bones to the stockpot.

2. Combine the other ingredients along with 4 quarts of water. Bring to a boil.

3. Reduce the broth to a slow simmer. As fat and particles rise to the surface, skim thoroughly, using a ladle for fat and a perforated metal skimmer for the tiny particles. Simmer for 2 hours, skimming every half hour.

4. Strain the broth through a fine sieve into a stainless-steel bowl (this allows rapid cooling).

5. Let the broth reach room temperature before placing it in the refrigerator. When it is cool, remove the fat that solidified on top.

Note: This broth can be frozen and kept for about a month.

YIELD: 10 CUPS

✳ *Duck or goose fat is used to sauté just about everything in the Périgord, and it will add immeasurable flavor to a dish, most especially potatoes. But if you can't find any, or don't wish to use it, substitute vegetable oil, as I have done here.*

Sauté de Pommes de Terre à l'Ail
(SAUTÉED POTATOES)

1½ pounds red waxy potatoes, peeled
2 tablespoons vegetable oil
Salt and freshly ground pepper
   to taste

1 whole garlic clove, peeled
1 tablespoon parsley, finely chopped

1. Using a knife or mandoline, slice the potatoes to about ⅛-inch thickness. Wash the potato slices and dry well.

2. In a large nonstick skillet, heat the oil over medium-high heat. Add the pota-

toes and salt and pepper to taste. Cook the potatoes, tossing them constantly, until lightly browned.

3. After the first 5 minutes, add the garlic clove and continue to toss the potatoes. When potatoes are done they should be tender in the middle and slightly crisp at the edges.

4. Add the parsley and toss. Remove the garlic clove, check for seasoning, and serve.

YIELD: 4 SERVINGS

❧ *The wild mushrooms of the region, particularly cèpes, are famous the world over. That inspires me to suggest this wild mushroom* sauté.

Sauté des Champignons Sauvages

(SAUTÉED WILD MUSHROOMS)

2 cups chanterelles or cèpes (or other
   wild mushrooms)
1 tablespoon butter

1 tablespoon shallots, finely chopped
Salt and freshly ground pepper to
   taste

1. To clean the mushrooms, cut away the very end of the stem that has been in contact with the earth. Scrape away any remaining dirt with a paring knife or brush it away with a basting brush. Do not submerge the mushrooms in water.

2. In a large nonstick skillet, melt the butter over high heat and add the mushrooms, shallots, and salt and pepper. Cook, stirring, until no moisture remains and the mushrooms begin to brown slightly.

3. Check for seasoning and serve.

YIELD: 4 SERVINGS

❧ *This is a beef dish that we had prepared for us at Le Vieux Logis. The dressing over the vegetables is supposed to seep into the beef juices once the dish is served; the combination of flavors will pleasantly surprise you.*

Pot-au-Feu de Filet de Boeuf

(STEWED BEEF AND VEGETABLES)

2 large carrots, peeled and trimmed
1 knob celery, peeled
4 leeks, cleaned and trimmed, white only
Salt to taste
4 cups fresh beef broth, or good quality canned

Freshly ground pepper to taste
12 ounces fillet of beef, trimmed of all fat and gristle, cut into ½-inch slices
Dressing (recipe follows)
Sprigs of fresh parsley, thyme, or coriander, for decoration

1. Cut the carrots, the knob celery, and the leeks into pieces about 2 inches long and ¼ inch wide. There should be about ¾ cup of each. The pieces should be the same size so that they will cook at the same rate.

2. Place the carrots, celery, and leeks in a large saucepan with salt to taste and water to cover. Bring to a boil and drain immediately.

3. In another large saucepan, bring the beef broth to a boil over medium-high heat and add salt and pepper to taste. Add the carrots, celery, and leeks and simmer for 15 to 20 minutes. Do not boil.

4. Meanwhile, season the fillet on both sides with salt and pepper to taste. Add the slices to the vegetables and continue to simmer over low heat for an additional 2 to 3 minutes. Do not allow to boil.

5. Divide the vegetables between 2 warmed serving plates, placing them decoratively over the center. Arrange beef slices around the vegetables in a fan. Spoon the dressing (see recipe below) over the meat and vegetables and sprinkle with salt and pepper to taste. Decorate with a bouquet of fresh herbs.

6. Broth can be served on the side in a consommé cup.

YIELD: 2 SERVINGS

Périgord/Dordogne Valley ❧ III

Dressing for Pot-au-Feu

¼ teaspoon garlic, finely chopped
¾ teaspoon lemon juice, freshly
  squeezed
½ teaspoon Nuoc Nam, also known
  as Vietnamese fish sauce*

½ teaspoon soy sauce
Freshly ground white pepper to taste
⅓ cup virgin olive oil
½ teaspoon whole coriander seeds

1. Combine the garlic, lemon juice, Nuoc Nam, soy sauce, and pepper in a mixing bowl.

2. Add the olive oil slowly, whisking briskly to emulsify the dressing.

3. Add the coriander seeds and mix well.

YIELD: ABOUT ⅓ CUP

*Available in Asian stores

Toulouse and Languedoc

SPECIALTIES

Eel, served jellied, grilled, or braised
Cassoulet, made with the famous white beans, *confit* of
duck and pork
Magret de canard, rare-cooked duck breast
Aligot, mashed potatoes with cheese and garlic
Truffade, a dish of sliced potatoes with melted cheese on top
Tripoux, stuffed lamb tripe braised in white wine
Charcuterie in wide variety—hams, sausages, and *fricandeau,*
a pork *pâté* wrapped in pork fat or salt pork

CHEESE

Cabécou, a creamy goat cheese often used in salads or baked
with potatoes

DESSERT

Raisine, a thick fruit preserve

HIGH-KICKING GAIETY

O n our way out of the Périgord and heading southeast—from the land of the goose to the land of the olive—we managed to find our way to some of the most pleasant culinary experiences we had in all of France. The first was in Najac, a mountainous area not too far from Toulouse. There the first surprise was the absolutely lonely beauty of the area surrounding the city. We slept the night and breakfasted in the morning at the Hôtel Longcol, a rambling farmhouse renovated by Fabienne Luyckx, once an antiques dealer, who left her business behind to dedicate herself to this stunning hotel that barely peeks through the woods. As my eyes searched the distance out over the mountains, it was hard to believe that there was any civilization—which is to say any great cooking—within hailing distance.

Just a short ride away, however, we came to L'Oustal del Barry, a hotel overlooking Najac, a town that has seen its troubles, historically speaking. Once it was a bastion of the Counts of Toulouse, but it was destroyed in an early war—nevertheless, a feudal castle of stunning beauty remains. From the restaurant at L'Oustal del Barry, run by Catherine and Jean-Marie Miquel, you can see this brilliant castle off in the distance as you dine, an unexpected touch. But not nearly so unexpected as the adventurous cooking here.

Jean-Marie, forty-three, has never worked anywhere else. He began cooking with his mother, and for years was content to transform the lovely produce and the beautiful herbs of his gardens into more or less traditional dishes. It is worth noting how often great French chefs learn to cook in the early years with their mothers. More than simply teaching a skill, this kind of experience surrounds childhood with the aromas, the tastes, the rewards of cooking, and you never forget it. It seems to me that Americans would do well to heed this message from abroad; I see very few youngsters in the United States who are integral parts of their parents' kitchens.

The town of Roquefort,
source of the pungent cheese

As much as Jean-Marie loved the cooking of his mother, he did ultimately get bored and wanted to break out. Now, he says, his mother thinks he's crazy. But I don't. As I go to restaurants around France, I always mark up the menus to remind me of the experience, and at this one, the menu is full of my chicken scratch, switching from French to English. "*Très bien*" I wrote next to the roasted salmon with sorrel, "*originale*" next to the poached sweetbreads with a meat glaze, and "very good, *très léger*" next to the thin-crusted apricot tart with a syrupy muscat sauce. I don't ever fall for cooking that employs invention for its own sake, but here when you have something as unusual as a green tomato sorbet—and it works so well!—there is nothing to do but admire, and enjoy.

Our next adventure was in the town of Albi, a commercial center of the area, but far too quaint and peaceful to be thought of for its business alone. It is the birthplace

A master cheesemaker describes how the mold that creates blue veins in Roquefort cheese is borne by an underground breeze through the cave where it is aged.

of Henri de Toulouse-Lautrec, and there is a lavish museum to honor him. (Among the paintings and posters you get to see one of the artifacts of his dissolute life, a cane hollowed out to hold his liquor.) The city is the sort of place that would be fun to visit even if it didn't have some pretty good places to eat besides. At the Hôtel Altea, I was greeted by a touring folkloric group that does the can-can just as it must have been done in Toulouse-Lautrec's days, kicking high and swirling their skirts (at one point, instead of maintaining the familiar can-can line, they surrounded me in a moment of pure gaiety I will not soon forget). And it is stunningly beautiful here: as you stand on a hillside above the Tarn River and let your gaze go across the rooftops, you are engulfed by a striking harmony, the dark river blending into the shades of red and brown of the city's houses.

Just outside Albi, on the bank of the Tarn, I cooked with a twenty-five-year-old chef at a hotel called La Reserve. His name is Sylvain Martin and he made a point of using the fabulous local goat cheese, Cabécou, a specialty of the medieval religious center and town of Rocamadour. We were joined in the cooking by Jean-François Rieux (who is the ultimate supervisor of this kitchen as well as one in another hotel owned by the same company), a more seasoned chef. He trained with André Daguin, among others, and, just like Toulouse-Lautrec, he happened to have a cane

in which was secreted some brandy. It was an amusing authentic touch.

From Albi, we trekked on to the south and Carcassonne, a city known for its astonishingly intact medieval walled fortifications. There I found another chef who pleased me enormously, just as my new friend Jean-Marie Miquel had. The chef this time was Bernard Rigaudis, whose establishment, Domaine d'Auriac, was once nothing more than ruins dating back to the days of Charlemagne. His family rebuilt the place, creating the handsome hotel-restaurant that he now runs so well. We hit it off immediately; he's a hunter and fisherman just like me, and can talk about his exploits endlessly.

He looks a little like George Burns, and when he smiles his eyes really do twinkle. He, like me, has been modernizing his food over the years, cutting out fats where they seem unnecessary and cutting down on them when they are excessive. "I respect the spirit of tradition," he says, "but if it means being extreme in the use of fat, I just eliminate the fat." Even his *cassoulet* is relatively light. But the lightness of it isn't all that matters here; the fact is that beans were once a major crop in the Toulouse region, but they were abandoned for more profitable cereal crops. The good cooks of the area still hold on to their culinary history, but they have to import the beans from the north—or try to generate a decent crop in their private gardens.

As we continued on our way, driving from Carcassonne toward the southeast and the sea, through the vineyards and the villages, the sense of the Mediterranean was almost palpable and then, suddenly, we were there, a place so different from anything we had seen in several days that it left us with a tangible sense of France's diversity. There, for instance, were the warm estuaries where the sea life of Mediterranean cuisine is born and nurtured. There you find refined hotels like the Château de Villefalse and also ruddy, rough-and-tumble fishermen like Didier Marty, the fellow we met in the town of Bages.

The first time we saw this burly man with tousled black hair, he was wearing a suit, but clearly he wasn't comfortable with such formality. He is, after all, a young man of the sea, happier in the yellow waterproof garments that are the uniform of his work. Didier fishes mostly for the eel that grow in the estuaries, as well as bar, sole, and *daurade.* He (along with his wife, Rosemary) also runs a small, rustic restaurant, Le Portanel, where the seafood is nothing if not the freshest anyone could hope for. From Le Portanel, there is a view across a bay of the city of Narbonne and its famous cathedral.

In the village of Bages, the houses are smack up against each other in a jumble of winding streets. Didier smokes his own fish and, like all self-sufficient people, he tends to be inventive. Since the eels need to be cleaned of their viscous coating with some abrasive substance, Didier, believe it or not, does that in a cement mixer in which he has placed some sand.

❧ *When we were in Najac, Jean-Marie Miquel took us to a charcuterie where ham was smoked to perfection. He purchased the meat that had come from a mature female pig; this meant it would have a stronger flavor, he said. I took all this talk of ham as an inspiration to use smoked ham in a curried lentil soup of my own devising.*

Potage de Lentilles et Jambon à l'Indienne

(CURRIED LENTIL SOUP WITH HAM)

½ pound lean country smoked ham
3 medium-sized carrots
½ pound green lentils
2 tablespoons butter
1 cup onions, finely chopped
1 tablespoon garlic, minced
2 tablespoons curry powder
5 cups fresh chicken broth (see recipe page 108), or good quality canned

2 cups water
1 bay leaf
3 sprigs fresh thyme, or 1 teaspoon dried
Salt to taste
1 tablespoon red wine vinegar
2 tablespoons coriander, finely chopped

1.   Remove most of the fat from the ham and cut it into ½-inch cubes.

2.   Trim and scrape the carrots and cut them into ¼-inch cubes.

3.   Pick over the lentils, wash them, and drain into a colander.

4.   Heat 1 tablespoon of the butter in a soup kettle or saucepan. Add the ham, carrots, onions, garlic, and curry powder. Cook briefly over medium heat, stirring until the onions have wilted.

5.   Add the lentils, 4 cups of the chicken broth, water, bay leaf, thyme, and salt. Bring to a boil and simmer for 24 to 30 minutes, stirring occasionally.

6.   Remove 1 cup of the soup with more lentils than liquid and set it aside. Discard the bay leaf and thyme sprigs.

7.   With a potato masher or wire whisk, stir the soup briskly to mash the lentils. Then return the soup to a boil and add the remaining cup of chicken broth, along with the reserved lentils, the vinegar, and the remaining butter. Check for seasoning and serve sprinkled with coriander.

YIELD: 4 SERVINGS

❧ *Jean-Marie prepared this stew with beef cheeks, which are extraordinarily flavorful, tender, and lean with a gelatinous texture, but feel free to substitute shank or shoulder meat.*

La Daube de Joux de Boeuf au Vin Rouge

(BEEF CHEEKS SIMMERED IN RED WINE)

2 tablespoons vegetable oil
2 pounds lean beef cheek meat,
    trimmed of all fat and gristle
    and cut into 2-inch cubes (or
    substitute shank or shoulder)
Salt and freshly ground pepper to
    taste
½ cup smoked country ham, coarsely
    chopped
1 cup onions, thinly sliced
1 cup carrots, trimmed and sliced

1 bottle dry red wine
10 peppercorns
4 whole cloves
Bouquet garni tied with string and
    consisting of:
    1 leek
    1 celery branch with leaves
    1 bay leaf
    1 sprig thyme
Vegetable garnish (recipe follows)

1.   Heat the oil in a skillet large enough to hold the beef in one layer. Brown the meat on all sides over high heat so that it is seared quickly.

2.   Sprinkle the beef with salt and pepper to taste. Transfer to a Dutch oven.

3.   To the original skillet add the ham, onions, and carrots and cook, stirring, until wilted. Deglaze the pan by adding red wine, scraping the bottom of the skillet to loosen and dissolve brown particles. Simmer over medium heat for 5 minutes.

4.   Pour the contents of the skillet over the meat in the Dutch oven. Add peppercorns, cloves, and the *bouquet garni.* Bring to a boil, cover, and simmer about 2 hours or until meat is tender. Stir from time to time to assure even cooking.

5.   Remove and discard *bouquet garni.* Transfer the pieces of meat to a platter and keep warm.

6.   To prepare a sauce, purée the cooking juices and vegetables with a food mill or in a blender or food processor. This will thicken the sauce and eliminate the need

for flour. Pour the sauce back into the Dutch oven. Bring to a boil and simmer for 5 minutes. Check for seasoning. Just before serving, add the meat and heat through.

7.   Serve with vegetable garnish (recipe follows).

YIELD: 6 SERVINGS

Mélange de Légumes
(VEGETABLE GARNISH FOR DAUBE)

8 small red potatoes, peeled
Salt to taste
2 tablespoons butter
1 cup carrots, cleaned, trimmed, and
    cut into ⅛-inch slices
1 cup turnips, cleaned, trimmed, and
    cut into ⅛-inch slices

1 teaspoon sugar
Freshly ground pepper to taste
⅓ cup water
2 tablespoons parsley, finely chopped

1.   Place the potatoes, with salt to taste and water to cover, in a large saucepan. Bring to a boil and cook for 15 minutes, or until done. Drain and keep warm.

2.   In a large skillet, melt the butter over medium heat and add the carrots and turnips, stirring from time to time. Sprinkle with sugar and salt and pepper to taste and cook, stirring, until the vegetables are wilted and the sugar has begun to caramelize.

3.   Add ⅓ cup water to deglaze the caramel and cook until almost all the moisture has disappeared. Add the cooked potatoes and check for seasoning. Sprinkle with parsley to garnish.

YIELD: 6 SERVINGS

✤   *In Albi, at La Reserve, this is the potato dish we prepared with the goat cheese called* Cabécou. *The young chef used duck fat, which really does impart a fine flavor to the potatoes, but vegetable oil will suffice as a substitute and I have stipulated it here. The* tourtes *were assembled in four individual 3-inch nonstick tart pans, each about ½ inch in depth. The recipe can also be accomplished in one 9-inch ovenproof nonstick sauté pan. It makes a fine lunch with a simple green salad tossed with oil and vinegar on the side.*

Tourtes de Pomme de Terre au Lard et au Fromage de Chèvre

(POTATO, BACON, AND GOAT CHEESE TARTLETS)

1 pound Idaho or Washington State
  potatoes, peeled
1 cup vegetable oil
4 ounces salted slab bacon
8 sheets phyllo dough
⅓ cup melted butter

4 tablespoons goat cheese, softened
1 tablespoon parsley, finely chopped
Salt and freshly ground pepper to
  taste
4 tablespoons heavy cream

1.   Preheat the oven to 400°.

2.   Use a mandoline or vegetable slicer to obtain thin, uniform slices of potato, about ⅛ inch thick.

3.   Heat the oil in a large skillet. Place 1 potato slice in the oil to see if it bubbles. When it does bubble, the oil is hot enough to fry the disks. Cook the potatoes until tender, but do not brown. They should remain limp. Drain potatoes on paper towels and sprinkle with salt to taste.

4.   Meanwhile, cut the bacon into ⅛-inch slices and then into matchstick-shaped strips. Place them in boiling water to cover, return to a boil, drain, and dry well. Transfer to a heated skillet and cook, stirring, until just barely browned, but still soft.

5.   On a clean work surface, unroll one sheet of phyllo dough for each tart and brush them with melted butter. Cover each with a second sheet and brush once again with butter.

6.   Cut 8-inch circles from the layered phyllo and place them in the tart pans,

allowing the excess to overlap. For each tartlet, arrange potato slices of roughly the same diameter in overlapping rings on top of the dough, starting from the outside, so the cover is complete and has a neat design. Every space should be filled. Sprinkle 2 teaspoons bacon pieces over the potatoes. Spread 1 tablespoon goat cheese on top and sprinkle with chopped parsley. Arrange a second layer of potatoes in a fan over the mixture, leaving a tiny opening in the center. Sprinkle with salt and pepper to taste. Fold the overlapped dough up over the filling.

7.   Brush the surface of each tartlet with butter and bake for 7 to 8 minutes. Pour 1 tablespoon cream through the opening in the tart and bake for an additional 5 minutes, or until the cream has set.

8.   Unmold the tarts and serve hot.

YIELD: 4 SERVINGS

⚜   *I don't think anything as good as a* crème brûlee *will ever go out of style. Here's the one we cooked at La Reserve in Albi. It's a good idea to buy the type of brown sugar that pours easily and then force it through a strainer to make doubly sure you eliminate any lumps.*

Crème Brûlee au Grand Marnier

(BURNT-CREAM CUSTARD WITH GRAND MARNIER)

6 egg yolks	½ cup milk
½ cup sugar	⅓ cup Crème de Grand Marnier
2⅓ cups cream	¼ cup brown sugar

1.   Preheat oven to 350°.

2.   In a large mixing bowl, whisk together the egg yolks and sugar and beat until the mixture turns a light lemony color. Add the cream, the milk, and the Crème de Grand Marnier and combine well.

3.   Arrange 6 individual-serving-size ramekins (preferably ¾ inch deep by 4½ inches in diameter) side by side in a large roasting pan. Fill each with ⅔ cup of the

mixture. Pour hot water to the depth of ¼ inch into the roasting pan around them.

4. Bake for 20 to 25 minutes, or until the mixture has set but is still creamy. Do not overcook.

5. Allow the ramekins to cool at room temperature until they are no longer steaming. Chill the ramekins.

6. About 1 hour before serving, remove ramekins from refrigerator to take off the chill. Just before serving, preheat the broiler to the highest setting.

7. Sprinkle each ramekin evenly with 2 teaspoons brown sugar. Place them under the broiler until the sugar is caramelized and has turned dark brown. Rotate them as necessary to brown the sugar evenly.

YIELD: 6 SERVINGS

❧ *A* bourride *refers to a seafood preparation that is bound by the garlicky mayonnaise called* aïoli. *This is one prepared for us by the chef Didier Faugeras at Restaurant Le Languedoc in Carcassonne. It goes well with rice pilaf or rice with mushrooms and pistachios (recipes follow).*

Bourride de Baudroie à la Vraie Setoise

(BOURRIDE OF MONKFISH WITH VEGETABLES)

1 monkfish liver, if available (you can request that your fishmonger save the liver); optional
½ cup olive oil
1½ cups carrots, peeled and cut into ¼-inch cubes
1½ cups Swiss chard, stalks cut into ¼-inch cubes and leaves shredded
1½ cups celery, cut into ¼-inch cubes

1½ cups leeks, white only, cut into ¼-inch cubes
Salt and freshly ground pepper to taste
2 egg yolks
⅛ teaspoon cayenne pepper
1 garlic clove, peeled
1½ pounds boneless, skinless monkfish fillets cut into 1½-inch cubes

1. Place half of the liver in salted water to cover and discard the remainder. Bring to a boil and simmer for 10 minutes. Drain and cool.

2. In a heavy saucepan or large skillet, add 2 tablespoons of the oil. Over

medium heat, add the carrots, Swiss chard, celery, leeks, and salt and pepper. Cook, stirring, until wilted. Cover and cook over low heat, stirring occasionally, for about 10 minutes.

3. Meanwhile, make *aïoli* using a mortar and pestle or a blender. Thoroughly pound or blend the egg yolks, liver, cayenne, salt and pepper, and garlic into a smooth-textured paste. Continue pounding and slowly add the remaining oil until the mixture is thick and smooth, similar to mayonnaise.

4. Place the fish pieces over the vegetables in one layer and add salt and pepper to taste. Cover and cook for 5 to 7 minutes or until tender. Transfer the fish carefully to a platter and keep warm.

5. Over very low heat add the *aïoli* to the vegetables, mixing thoroughly with a wire whisk until the mixture thickens but the egg yolks do not begin to cook and congeal as they would in scrambled eggs. Remove from the heat and continue stirring.

6. Divide the vegetables onto 4 warmed serving plates, place the fish pieces on top and serve immediately, with rice pilaf or rice with mushrooms and pistachios, if desired (recipes follow).

YIELD: 4 SERVINGS

Riz Pilau

(BASIC RICE PILAF)

2 tablespoons butter
2 tablespoons finely chopped onions
½ teaspoon minced garlic
1 cup parboiled (converted) rice
1½ cups fresh chicken broth (see recipe page 108), or good quality canned, or water

3 parsley sprigs
1 sprig fresh thyme, or ¼ teaspoon dried
1 bay leaf
Salt and freshly ground pepper to taste

1. Melt 1 tablespoon of the butter in a saucepan and add the onions and garlic. Cook, stirring, until wilted. Add the rice and stir briefly over low heat until the grains are coated with butter.

2. Stir in the broth, making sure there are no lumps in the rice. Add the parsley,

thyme, bay leaf, and salt and pepper to taste. Bring to a boil, cover with a close-fitting lid, and simmer for 17 minutes.

3.   Remove the cover and discard the parsley, thyme, and bay leaf. Using a fork, stir in the remaining butter. If the rice is not to be served immediately, keep covered in a warm place.

YIELD: 4 SERVINGS

❊   *If you feel a desire to make the rice a little more exotic, here's a satisfying alternate.*

Riz aux Champignons et Pistaches

(RICE WITH MUSHROOMS AND PISTACHIOS)

2 tablespoons butter	1 cup parboiled (converted) rice
½ cup onions, finely chopped	1½ cups water
¼ pound mushrooms, diced	Salt and freshly ground pepper to
¼ cup shelled pistachio nuts	taste

1.   Heat 1 tablespoon of the butter in a saucepan. Add the onions and cook briefly, stirring, until wilted. Add the mushrooms and continue stirring for about 2 minutes.

2.   Add the pistachios and the rice and stir to blend. Add the water and salt and pepper to taste. Stir and bring to a boil. Cover tightly and simmer for 17 minutes.

3.   Uncover and stir in the remaining butter. Keep warm and serve.

YIELD: 4 SERVINGS

✢   *Also in Carcassonne we stopped in to see Jean-Claude Rodriguez at the Restaurant Château St. Martin Trencavel, known for its* cassoulet.

Cassoulet

(WHITE BEAN STEW)

1½ pounds dried white beans
3 quarts water
1 onion stuck with 2 cloves
1 bay leaf
1 carrot, trimmed and scraped
Salt and freshly ground black pepper
½ pound lean salt pork with rind
1 garlic sausage (*cotechine*)
2 tablespoons duck fat (or vegetable oil)

1 tablespoon garlic, minced
1½ cups onions, chopped
2 cups canned crushed tomatoes
Lamb stew (recipe follows)
Duck *confit* (see recipe page 129)
Roast pork (see recipe page 130)
3 tablespoons bread crumbs made from toasted bread
3 tablespoons melted butter

1.   Pick over the beans and wash them well. Place them in a soup kettle or large saucepan with the water, onion with cloves, bay leaf, carrot, salt and pepper, and salt pork. Prick the garlic sausage in several places with a fork and add it to the pot. Simmer for 30 minutes.

2.   Remove the sausage and set aside. Continue cooking for 30 minutes, or until the beans are tender. Remove the salt pork.

3.   Slice off and reserve the salt pork rind, then return the salt pork to the kettle. Cut the rind into ¼-inch pieces and set aside.

4.   Heat the duck fat in a saucepan and add the garlic, the diced pork rind, and the onions. Cook for about 5 minutes without browning. Add the tomatoes and let simmer for 15 minutes, stirring often.

5.   When the beans are tender, drain and reserve the beans, salt pork, and the cooking liquid. Discard the onion and the bay leaf. Place the beans in a large soup kettle and add the tomato mixture and the lamb stew (recipe follows), including the meat and the sauce. Stir to blend and check for seasoning. Cover and simmer for 10 minutes.

6.   Preheat the oven to 400°. Cut the salt pork into 10 to 12 slices and set aside.

Skin the garlic sausage and cut it into 10 to 12 slices and set aside. Heat the duck *confit* (see recipe page 129), remove the pieces, and cut or pull the meat from the bones. Slice the meat as neatly as possible. Slice the roast pork (see recipe page 130) into 10 to 12 slices.

7.   Spoon about ⅓ of the beans into a large casserole and arrange the pork slices over them. Spoon half of the remaining beans over the pork. Arrange the duck meat over the beans. Spread the remaining beans over the duck and arrange the salt pork and the garlic sausage over all. Sprinkle with the bread crumbs and dribble butter over the top.

8.   Bake for 30 minutes. Check on the casserole as it cooks. If it seems to be getting too dry, add a little of the bean liquid. When ready to serve, the *cassoulet* should be piping hot and bubbling and lightly browned.

YIELD: 10 SERVINGS OR MORE

Ragoût d'Agneau

(LAMB STEW FOR CASSOULET)

2 tablespoons vegetable oil or duck fat
2½ pounds shoulder of lamb, cut into 2-inch cubes
Salt and freshly ground pepper to taste
1 cup onions, finely chopped
1 tablespoon garlic, minced
1 cup dry white wine

2 cups fresh chicken broth (see recipe page 108), or good quality canned, or water
3 tablespoons tomato paste
4 sprigs fresh thyme, or 1 teaspoon dried
1 bay leaf
4 sprigs parsley

1.   Heat the oil in a heavy skillet over medium-high heat. Add the lamb and salt and pepper to taste. Stir until lightly browned, about 10 minutes. Add the onions and garlic.

2.   Remove all the fat, then add the wine, broth or water, tomato paste, thyme, bay leaf, and parsley. Cover tightly, bring to a boil, and simmer for an hour, or until the lamb is fork-tender.

3.   Remove from the heat and serve or use for cassoulet.

YIELD: 6 SERVINGS, OR ENOUGH FOR A 10-12–PORTION *CASSOULET*

Confit de Canard

(DUCK CONFIT FOR CASSOULET)

1 large duck, about 5½ pounds,
   cleaned
Salt and freshly ground black pepper
   to taste
2 bay leaves, crumbled

4 sprigs fresh thyme, or 1 teaspoon
   dried
2 garlic cloves, peeled
1 pound lard or duck fat

1.   Using a butcher's knife, remove the breasts and the neck of the duck, leaving the skin on. Reserve the gizzard and all the fat and skin from the carcass of the duck.

2.   Sprinkle the duck with a generous amount of salt and pepper, the chopped bay leaves, and the thyme. Rub on all sides. Pack the pieces, including the gizzard, into a bowl, cover closely, and refrigerate for at least 12 hours.

3.   Heat a Dutch oven or cast-iron pot and place the duck pieces in it skin side down. Add the gizzard, skin, duck fat, garlic cloves, and the lard. Bring to a boil and cover. Simmer for 1¼ hours, or until the duck is tender.

4.   Arrange the duck pieces in a terrine or earthenware pot. Strain all the fat over the duck. The duck pieces should be completely covered. Let stand until thoroughly cold. Cover closely and refrigerate. This can be kept for weeks.

YIELD: ENOUGH FOR A 10-12–PORTION *CASSOULET*

Carré de Porc Rôti
(ROAST PORK)

1 2½-pound boneless, center-cut pork
    loin, with most of the fat removed

Salt and freshly ground black pepper
    to taste

1.   Preheat the oven to 400°.
2.   Sprinkle the pork all over with salt and pepper.
3.   Place the pork, fat side down, in a roasting pan and bake for 20 minutes.
4.   Turn the pork and continue cooking for 20 minutes. Cover loosely with a
sheet of aluminum foil. Continue baking for 20 minutes or until thoroughly cooked
and tender.

YIELD: 6 SERVINGS, OR ENOUGH FOR A 10-12–PORTION *CASSOULET*

❧   *Despite all the cooking we did in this area, there was none more impressive than the
work of Bernard Rigaudis at Domaine d'Auriac. In this dish, he used Loire River salmon
and Chardonnay from nearby Limou.*

Note: The vegetables should be uniformly sliced, and the best tool to do that is
either a mandoline or a vegetable slicer.

Saumon à la Crème de Ciboulette
(SALMON STEAKS WITH CHIVE SAUCE)

1 cup carrots, trimmed, peeled, and
    sliced in ⅛-inch rounds
1 cup daikon, trimmed, peeled, and
    sliced in ⅛-inch rounds

1 cup zucchini, trimmed and sliced in
    ⅛-inch rounds
2 tablespoons butter

4 6-ounce salmon steaks, cleaned,
with skin and bones, about ¾ inch
thick
Salt and freshly ground pepper to
taste

¾ cup Chardonnay wine
¾ cup cream
2 tablespoons chopped chives
2 limes, cut in half

1. Place the carrots in a saucepan with salted water to cover. Bring to a boil and simmer for 3 minutes. Add daikon and simmer for 1 minute more. Add zucchini and cook an additional minute. Drain and keep warm.

2. In a nonstick skillet large enough to hold the fish in a single layer, melt the butter and cook over medium heat until bubbling. Add the fish and cook until one side is lightly browned (about 1 minute or a little more) and turn. Season the cooked side with salt and pepper to taste.

3. Cook the second side also until lightly browned. Turn again, to season the second side. The salmon should remain pink in the center. When the central bone can be removed easily, the fish is done. Remove and keep warm.

4. Drain any excess fat and pour the wine into the skillet over high heat, scraping the bottom and sides of the pan to loosen any solids. Cook until little liquid remains. Add cream and bring to a boil. Swirl to combine with cooking juices and cook until the sauce starts to thicken. This should take place very quickly. Add chives, combine well, and check for seasoning.

5. If desired, remove the skin and remaining bones carefully so that the salmon steak does not break apart.

6. Arrange the carrot, daikon, and zucchini slices alternately around the edge of 4 warmed serving plates. Place a salmon steak in the center and spoon sauce over the fish only. Garnish each with half a lime.

YIELD: 4 SERVINGS

❧ *Since Bernard had sturgeon available, I used it to make this fish soup. Monkfish or mako shark is a good substitute.*

Soupe d'Esturgeon et de Coquilles Saint-Jacques
(STURGEON AND SCALLOP SOUP)

3 tablespoons olive oil
1 cup onions, finely chopped
1 tablespoon garlic, minced
½ cup leeks, finely chopped
½ cup fennel, finely chopped
1 teaspoon saffron threads
1 jalapeño pepper, cored, seeded, and finely chopped
2 cups plum tomatoes, peeled, seeded, chopped, and cut into 1-inch cubes
1 cup dry white wine

4 cups water
1 bay leaf
2 sprigs fresh thyme, or 1 teaspoon dried
Salt and freshly ground pepper to taste
1 pound skinless, boneless sturgeon fillets, cut into 1-inch cubes (or substitute other firm fish such as monkfish or mako shark)
1 pound bay scallops
3 tablespoons parsley, chopped

1.   Heat 2 tablespoons of the oil in a large soup kettle or saucepan. Add the onions, garlic, leeks, and fennel and cook, stirring, until wilted. Add saffron, jalapeño pepper, and tomatoes. Cook, stirring, over high heat for about 2 minutes.

2.   Add the wine, water, bay leaf, thyme, and salt and pepper to taste. Bring to a boil and then simmer for 10 minutes, stirring often.

3.   Add the fish, return the broth to a boil, and simmer for 2 minutes. Add the scallops and cook for another 3 minutes. Stir in parsley. Swirl in the remaining olive oil and check for seasoning.

4.   Serve with a platter of garlic *croûtons* (recipe follows).

YIELD: 4 SERVINGS

Garlic Croûtons with Parmesan Cheese

1 loaf French baguette (see recipe page 42)
2 garlic cloves, peeled
2 tablespoons olive oil

Freshly ground black pepper to taste
4 tablespoons Parmesan cheese, grated

1. Preheat the oven to 450°.

2. Rub the crust of the bread all over with the garlic cloves. Cut the bread into ½-inch-thick slices and brush the slices with olive oil. Grind some black pepper over the oiled side and sprinkle with Parmesan cheese.

3. Place the bread slices on a baking sheet and bake until golden brown (about 10 minutes).

❧ *Traditionally, the following dish is produced in a cast-iron pot—a cocotte noire—a vessel known for its remarkable ability to convey heat evenly. The recipe is another from Domaine d'Auriac.*

Poulette Louragaise en Cocotte Noire

(CHICKEN STEWED IN RED WINE SAUCE)

1 3½-pound chicken, cut into serving pieces, with the liver removed and cut into 4 pieces
Salt and freshly ground pepper to taste
2 tablespoons olive oil
½ cup onions, sliced
1 tablespoon garlic, minced

4 ripe plum tomatoes with skin removed, cut into ½-inch cubes
2 sprigs fresh thyme, or 1 teaspoon dried
1 bay leaf
1 cup dry red wine
2 tablespoons parsley, chopped

1. Season the chicken pieces with salt and pepper. In a cast-iron skillet large enough to hold the pieces in one layer, heat the olive oil and add the chicken (reserv-

ing the liver). Cook until lightly browned, then add the onions and garlic and cook briefly.

2. Add the chicken liver, tomatoes, thyme, and bay leaf. Cook, stirring, for 1 minute.

3. Add the wine and bring to a boil, stirring frequently. Cover and simmer for 25 minutes.

4. Remove the chicken pieces and keep warm. Continue cooking the liquid until it is reduced by half. Remove bay leaf and thyme sprigs. Check for seasoning. Return the chicken pieces to the sauce. Sprinkle with parsley.

5. Serve with green mashed potatoes (see recipe page 236), or buttered noodles (see recipe page 293).

YIELD: 4 SERVINGS

❧ *At the Restaurant Le Portanel in Bages, it was my pleasure to grill some beautifully fresh fish, before heading off to a hotel-spa, the nearby Château Villefalse in Sigean, for a respite. It was* loup de mer, *for which I usually substitute striped bass and eel in the United States.*

Loup de Mer et Anguille Grillée
(GRILLED STRIPED BASS AND EEL)

2 striped bass, about 1½ pounds each, cleaned but with heads and tails intact (substitutes: red snapper or sea bass)
2 small eels, about ½ pound each, cleaned

Salt and freshly ground pepper to taste
4 sprigs thyme, or 2 teaspoons dried
4 sprigs fresh rosemary, or 2 teaspoons dried
4 tablespoons olive oil

1. Preheat the broiler or heat the grill to high.

2. Sprinkle the fish and the eels with salt and pepper both inside and out. Place a sprig or teaspoon of thyme and rosemary inside each. Brush with 2 tablespoons of the olive oil.

3. Place the fish and eels under the broiler or on the grill, about 3 inches from the heat source. Cook them on 1 side for about 3 minutes, then brush with some of the remaining olive oil and turn again. Brush fish and eels with more olive oil, and continue to turn and brush them until done. Total cooking time should be about 10 minutes.

4. Remove the skin and bones from the fish and serve with lemon wedges and melted butter.

YIELD: 4 SERVINGS

❧ *In the Albi region—it's called Albigeois—is the town of Roquefort, where the cheeses are impregnated with a mold that creates a quality and taste that are utterly distinctive (the fact that blue cheese tastes just like Roquefort does not contradict that observation; it's the same mold but the cheese can't be called Roquefort because it isn't from there). I thought it would be interesting to do a cheese soufflé using this pungent cheese, and was rewarded with this result.*

Soufflé de Fromage de Roquefort
(ROQUEFORT SOUFFLÉ)

4 tablespoons butter
3 tablespoons flour
1½ cups milk
¼ teaspoon freshly grated nutmeg
Salt and freshly ground pepper
   to taste
1 tablespoon cornstarch

2 tablespoons water
6 large eggs, separated
2 teaspoons Dijon mustard
2 teaspoons Worcestershire sauce
⅓ pound Roquefort cheese, cut
   into ¼-inch cubes

1. Preheat the oven to 400°.

2. Using 1 tablespoon of the butter, coat the insides of 4 soufflé dishes, 1½-cup capacity each, and place them in refrigerator.

3. Melt the remaining butter in a saucepan and add the flour, stirring with a wire whisk. When blended, add the milk and continue stirring rapidly with the whisk.

Bring to a boil and simmer. Add the nutmeg and salt and pepper to taste. Cook, stirring, for 30 seconds.

4. Blend the cornstarch and water and add to the bubbling sauce. Cook for 1 minute. Add the egg yolks and stir vigorously. Cook, stirring, for about 2 minutes.

5. Spoon and scrape the mixture into a large mixing bowl. Add the mustard and Worcestershire sauce and the Roquefort cheese. Blend until smooth.

6. Beat the egg whites until they reach soft peaks. Add ⅓ of the whites to the soufflé mixture and beat thoroughly. Add the remaining whites and fold them in quickly but gently with a rubber spatula.

7. Spoon and scrape the mixture into the soufflé molds, filling them to the rim. Place them on a baking sheet and run your thumb around the rim of each mold to remove any overflow that could prevent the soufflé from rising. Bake them in the oven for 15 minutes, rotating them if necessary to ensure even cooking.

YIELD: 4 SERVINGS

Gascony and the Basque Country

SPECIALTIES

Rôtis à l'ail, garlic toasts
Brandade de morue, a purée of salt cod with potatoes
Jambon de Bayonne, dry cured hams
Pâtés of many types
Gasconnade, a roast leg of lamb with garlic and anchovies
Foie gras of both duck and goose, and truffled *pâté* of *foie gras*
Confit of goose or duck (preserved in its own fat)
Axoa, a dish of ground veal cooked with onions, and sweet and hot red peppers
Sauce Basquaise, which includes tomatoes, onions, and garlic, along with hot and sweet peppers
Piments d'Espelette, the red and green peppers of Espelette
Piquillos, sweet red peppers marinated and served in olive oil
Garbure, a thick green vegetable soup
Matelote, a fish stew with wine

CHEESE

Ardi Gasna, a type of ewe's cheese

DESSERTS

Touron, an almond paste candy
Flagnarde, an egg-and-butter cake filled with fruit and served hot
Gâteau Basque, cookie-dough cake made with pastry cream, whipped cream, or cherries
Fromage de brebis, ewe's milk cheese served with cherry jam

BRANDY

Armagnac

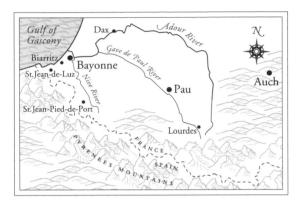

FOIE GRAS FESTIVAL

The southwest of France, an area generously described as reaching along the Atlantic coast from near the Spanish border at Biarritz, up to La Rochelle and eastward as far as Carcassonne and Albi, is now largely seen as one of the most active producers of chefs and the evolving French cuisine. In one of the cities in that large area, Auch, in Gascony, we found my friend André Daguin at the Hôtel de France, where he reigns not only over his own property but is a respected presence for miles around. Daguin carries the role well; he is a big man with a robust personality. As for his passions, he cares about *foie gras* with an intensity it would be hard to find elsewhere, even among other devotées.

Gascony is one of the major *foie gras*–producing regions of France, where fatted goose and duck livers have, if anything, gained in popularity in recent years. You now find them everywhere. At its best the liver is lightly cooked, still pink at the center. It comes in delicately grilled slices or beautifully poached, or—more familiar to Americans—as the main component of a variety of *pâtés*. Daguin may well be the *foie gras* king of the southwest. (His daughter Arianne oversees an American company, D'Artagnan, that imports *foie gras* and other French specialties to restaurants, individual consumers, and specialty shops in the United States. See address page 144.) The season for *foie gras* is supposed to be September through the winter, but nowadays the delicacy seems available almost year-round. At the height of the season, the big raw livers—one weighing between a pound and a pound and a half is considered to be just right for tenderness and flavor—can be found at markets throughout the major goose and duck regions.

When we sat down to one of a number of leisurely meals at Daguin's restaurant he treated *foie gras* with the sort of formality and ritual often reserved for wine: we were offered a sensational tasting that included terrines of different flavors. There

was the subtle truffle *foie gras,* then the equally distinc- tive terrines of prunes and of chives. In between we were instructed to taste the raw *foie gras* macerated in salt. The idea is that the salted *foie gras* works as a palate

Free-range geese wander down to the Gers River.

cleanser to allow a purer tasting of the next offering. I had never had such an expe- rience before in France—an edifying display of *foie gras*'s versatility as well as Daguin's showmanship—and doubt that I will experience it anywhere else. But it did make the point about the dedication to *foie gras* around here.

The claims for *foie gras* even reach into the arena of health. Some preliminary and hotly disputed reports have it that goose fat, rather than harming the heart, is in fact good for it (look at how little heart disease there is in the southwest, the proponents argue), and one can only hope it is true: on the table at Daguin, in addition to all that *foie gras,* is a little pot of melted goose fat blended with shallots and wine to spread on bread.

Because the prevailing image abroad is one of ducks and geese being painfully force-fed, the French frequently try to alter that image by describing scenes where the animals willingly come forward to be fed huge quantities of grain. I guess that's

André Daguin, one of the region's most accomplished chefs, likes to lead friends to the farms and fields around Auch.

true in some farms, but my own experience is that the animals tolerate the feeding more than they actually seek it out. The movement toward fattening ducks as well as geese began only in the 1950s; that led not just to big duck livers but to big everything and the most notable culinary result is the *magret de canard,* or duck breast, as a delicacy to be cooked lightly, as one would a steak. Some people credit Daguin with launching the popularity of this dish.

Paradoxically, perhaps, in a region known for the unnatural overfeeding of geese and ducks, there is a vigorous environmental movement that Daguin was eager to show us. On one busy day, as we followed the fast-driving André over dirt roads and through the hills and woods, he showed us how some farmers were absolutely dedicated to raising free-range animals in as natural a state as possible. One deer farmer, for instance, raises venison with so little restriction that as we stood on a hilltop looking off at the deer running through the meadow, we were sure they felt as wild as any deer ever did. Like flocks of birds swerving to move in unison with a leader, we saw a single deer lurch off to the left and the whole herd move with him, as one.

Similar free-range farms are the habitats of chickens whose range seemed much larger than those, also referred to as "free," that I had seen in the United States. We even visited a goose farm where the geese seemed to remain voluntarily: a tranquil, winding stream called the Gers River ran beneath a 1,800-year-old Roman footbridge in the woods, and there, at a bend of the stream were the farmer's geese, simply going about life.

More to the south and to the west are Biarritz and Bayonne. Here, virtually on the Spanish border, the Spanish influence on the food is, as you might expect, pervasive. (The recreation has a Spanish feel to it as well: one of our diversions was to attend a pelota match, the men playing a game that resembles jai alai.) The primary culinary difference between the Basque country and

In the Basque country seafood moves to the fore.

Biarritz is known for the fishing as well as for the recreation.

Gascony, even though they are adjoining, is that seafood plays a major role in Basque cooking, whereas in much of Gascony, just a bit to the interior, you hardly ever see it. The Basques produce one of the most famous dry-cured hams in France, the Bayonne ham.

But it is the peppers of the area that take star billing. *Piquillos,* sweet red peppers marinated and served in olive oil, show up in just about every dining room. *Piments d'Espelette* (peppers grown in Espelette, often seen as the hot red variety, used dried or fresh) are a major cooking ingredient and so are a variety of sweet red peppers. A preparation that combines both hot and sweet is *axoa,* a ground veal dish sautéed with onions and lots of those peppers. *Sauce Basquaise,* in fact, generally means a sauce that includes tomatoes, onions, and garlic, along with hot and sweet peppers.

Biarritz is where André Daguin's son, Arnaud, moved to open his own restaurant, Les Platanes, after a period of working with his father in Auch. Arnaud is slighter in build than André but his personality is just as large, as his impressive curled mustache attests. His wife, Véronique, is a former gym teacher who, these days, is grateful for the stamina she developed as an athlete: running a restaurant can be exhausting. She also chooses the wine, and for the lunch we had, she served nothing but the local product—which was terrific with pigeon stuffed with *foie gras* and served alongside glazed turnips. The restaurant is small, about forty seats, and the kitchen is only about ten by ten. But, limited as the establishment may be in space, the young Daguins have already won their first Michelin star. Besides the pigeon there were slices of fried salsify garnished with Bayonne ham, artichoke soup flavored with tarragon, a roulade of spinach stuffed with sea bass and sweet peppers, and apples in caramel with ice cream. Arnaud likes to say how much the people of this area enjoy themselves. No doubt.

One of the most enjoyable activities around here, in addition to eating, is fishing, and Arnaud took us to the Port Vieux, the tiny old fishing port at the southern end of Biarritz. It is straight out of a tourist's dream: one end of the port is lined with small restaurants and the other with tiny two-story storage shacks called *crampotes*. The area is so small and beautiful that the few dock slips available for fishing boats are prized indeed. We met Arnaud's friend Jean Commariec, who actually lives in one of those *crampotes,* which he has renovated and upgraded; this former shack is immaculate and bright now, its shutters painted light blue and its windows hung with checkered curtains. Jean goes out to fish from five to eight every morning and brings back squid, tuna, sole, and the French fish called *loup* (a sea bass) and *daurade* (a porgy). He believes the colder, cleaner water of the Atlantic provides firmer, more flavorful fish than the Mediterranean. Competitive pride aside, the seafood here is first-rate, for sure.

❧ Simple preparations of foie gras *are often the most appealing, and here's one from André Daguin that I especially liked.*

Foie Gras Poché à l'Ail

(POACHED FOIE GRAS WITH GARLIC)

10 garlic cloves, peeled
1 whole duck *foie gras* (about
    1½ pounds)*
Salt and pepper to taste

1 cup dry white wine
1½ cups fresh chicken broth
    (see recipe page 108), or
    good quality canned

1.   Place the peeled garlic cloves in a small saucepan with water to cover. Bring to a boil and simmer for 1 minute and drain.

2.   Pry the lobe of the *foie gras* open slightly, without breaking it, to reveal the connecting veins. Carefully remove the veins and any surrounding green liquid or stains.

3.   Season with salt and pepper to taste and press the 2 sides firmly back together.

4.   Place an oblong casserole just large enough to hold the *foie gras* over medium-high heat. Add the *foie gras* and cook until lightly brown on one side. Turn and cook on second side and add the garlic, stirring so that the cloves do not burn. Brown lightly.

5.   Add the wine, bring to a simmer, and cook partially covered for 10 minutes. Turn the *foie gras* carefully. Add the chicken broth and salt and pepper to taste, return to a simmer, and cook, partially covered, for 10 minutes more.

6.   Remove the *foie gras* carefully and keep it warm while you reduce the cooking liquid by half. Transfer the liquid, along with the garlic cloves, to a blender and blend to a fine texture. Check for seasoning.

7.   Slice the *foie gras* on the bias and pour sauce around the slices. Serve with sliced and toasted French bread (see recipe page 42).

YIELD: 6 SERVINGS

*Fresh *foie gras* is available in the United States in some specialty shops and by mail from D'Artagnan:

D'Artagnan
399 St. Paul Avenue
Jersey City, NJ 07306

❧ *When Arnaud served this dish of lamb and mushrooms, I commented that it was a bit on the ample side. He responded that in this part of the country hearty eating hadn't gone out of style.*

Sauté d'Agneau aux Cèpes

(LAMB SAUTÉED WITH CÈPES)

10 ounces boneless loin of baby lamb, cut into 1½-inch cubes
Salt and freshly ground pepper to taste
1 tablespoon duck fat (lard or olive oil can be substituted)

3 cups cèpes, sliced (other wild mushrooms can be substituted)
1 tablespoon garlic, chopped
1 tablespoon flat leaf parsley, finely chopped

1. Preheat the oven to 400°.
2. Sprinkle lamb with salt and pepper to taste.
3. In a skillet large enough to hold the lamb pieces in a single layer, melt the duck fat over high heat. Quickly brown the lamb pieces on all sides. Transfer the lamb to an ovenproof dish and roast it in the oven for about 5 minutes, for medium rare.
4. In the same skillet over high heat, add the mushrooms and cook, stirring, until lightly browned. Add garlic and parsley and cook briefly. Do not burn the garlic. Add salt and pepper to taste and any juices that have accumulated around the lamb pieces.
5. Spoon the mushrooms onto two warmed serving plates and place the pieces of lamb over them.

YIELD: 2 SERVINGS

✹ *Not too far from Biarritz was our next main destination, St.-Jean-Pied-de-Port, and the Hôtel les Pyrénées. Along the way, we visited the port of St.-Jean-de-Luz, a constant source of fine tuna. I bought some of that incredibly fresh tuna, which I employed in this dish.*

Thon Frais Grillé à la Sauce Niçoise

(MARINATED BROILED TUNA STEAKS WITH SAUCE NIÇOISE)

4 center-cut tuna steaks, about
   1 inch thick and 6 ounces each
Salt and freshly ground pepper
   to taste
6 tablespoons olive oil
4 sprigs fresh thyme, or 2 teaspoons
   dried
2 crumbled bay leaves
4 small sprigs fresh rosemary, or
   2 teaspoons dried

¼ teaspoon jalapeño pepper, chopped
4 ripe plum tomatoes
½ cup green pepper, sliced
½ cup onions, sliced
2 teaspoons garlic, coarsely chopped
4 pitted black olives
2 teaspoons grated lemon rind
2 tablespoons red wine vinegar
4 tablespoons fresh basil or parsley,
   coarsely chopped

1.   Preheat broiler or outdoor grill to high.

2.   Sprinkle both sides of the tuna steaks with salt and pepper and brush with 2 tablespoons of the olive oil, then place the tuna in a dish. Add the thyme, bay leaf, rosemary, and jalapeño pepper. Cover with plastic wrap and let stand for 20 minutes.

3.   Meanwhile, immerse the tomatoes in boiling water for about 10 seconds. Drain, peel, and core. Chop coarsely.

4.   Place the remaining olive oil in a small saucepan over medium-high heat. When hot, add the green peppers, onions, and garlic. Cook briefly until wilted. Add the tomatoes, olives, lemon rind, vinegar, and salt and pepper to taste. Cover and simmer for 10 minutes.

5.   Transfer the mixture to a blender or food processor. Blend for 5 to 7 seconds; it should be coarse. Transfer the sauce to a saucepan, check for seasoning, and reheat briefly.

6.   If broiling, arrange the steaks on a rack and place them under the broiler about 5 inches from the heat source. Broil for 4 minutes with the door partly open.

Turn the steaks and continue broiling for about 3 minutes longer. The steaks should not be overcooked.

7. If grilling, place the steaks on a hot grill and cover with the grill's lid. Let cook for 4 minutes. Turn the steaks, cover the grill, and continue cooking for about 3 minutes.

8. Serve with the prepared sauce and sprinkle with basil. Accompany the tuna with grilled scallions (recipe follows).

YIELD: 4 SERVINGS

Oignons Verts Grillés
(GRILLED SCALLIONS)

12 scallions, cleaned and trimmed
Salt and pepper to taste

2 tablespoons olive oil

1. Preheat grill to medium high.
2. Cut the scallions into 4-inch lengths and then split them lengthwise.
3. Sprinkle with salt and pepper on both sides and brush with 1 tablespoon olive oil.
4. Place on the hot grill and cook for 2 to 3 minutes or until lightly browned, brushing from time to time with the remaining olive oil. Turn and cook the second side until tender. Keep warm until ready to serve.

YIELD: 4 SERVINGS

❧ *The chef at the Hôtel les Pyrénées is Firmin Arrambide, forty-seven years old and cooking since he was fifteen; the ease born of experience comes through. For this egg dish he used an Espelette sweet green pepper noted for its particularly thin skin, but any good green peppers can be substituted. He used Bayonne ham, but prosciutto, which is similar, would be fine, too.*

La Pipérade de Firmin Arrambide

(EGGS SCRAMBLED WITH TOMATOES, PEPPERS, AND HAM)

3 tablespoons olive oil
2 garlic cloves, cut into thin slivers
1 cup onions, coarsely chopped
1 cup green pepper, cored, seeded,
    and cut into ½-inch cubes
3 cups ripe plum tomatoes, peeled,
    seeded, and cut into ½-inch cubes

Salt and freshly ground pepper
    to taste
4 whole eggs
4 thin slices dry-cured ham, such
    as prosciutto or Bayonne

1. In a saucepan, heat the olive oil over medium heat and add the garlic, stirring until wilted. Add onions, green pepper, tomatoes, and salt and pepper to taste. Cook uncovered over low heat for 20 to 30 minutes, stirring occasionally. Most of the moisture should have evaporated.

2. Beat the eggs lightly and add them to the vegetable mixture. Stir slowly with a wooden spatula, scraping the sides and bottom of saucepan for 3 to 5 minutes. Eggs should remain slightly runny. Check for seasoning.

3. In a nonstick skillet large enough to hold the ham slices in one layer, add the ham and cook only until heated through.

4. Transfer the egg mixture to a heated serving platter. Arrange ham slices over it decoratively and serve hot.

YIELD: 4 SERVINGS

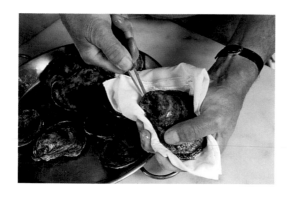

Opening an oyster for *Huîtres Panées aux Epinards,* breaded oysters with spinach

Soupe de Poisson avec Moules, fish soup with mussels, left; *Canard aux Navets et aux Epices,* duck with turnips and spices, below

*Carré d'Agneau aux Herbes
de Provence,* Provençal roast
rack of lamb

*Risotto aux Fruits de Mer
de Christian Constant,* a
seafood risotto

Filleting the fish and layering the potato slices for *Poisson à l'Ecaille de Pomme de Terre,* fish fillets with a "potato scale" crust

*Côtes de Veau aux
Champignons Sauvages,*
veal chops with wild
mushrooms, left;
*Pommes Flambées au
Calvados,* apples flamed
with Calvados, below

Poulet Vallée d'Auge,
chicken sautéed with apple
cider and cream

Shaping the dough and
letting it rise before baking
loaves of French bread, right

❧ *Traditionally, this best-known of Basque cakes was filled with cherry preserves; these days you more often find that it contains whipped cream or pastry cream, and the last-named version is the one I offer here.*

Gâteau Basque
(BASQUE CAKE)

4 cups all-purpose flour
2 whole eggs
1 cup granulated sugar
½ pound butter, softened
1 package rapid-rise yeast

4 egg yolks
2 tablespoons rum
½ teaspoon pure vanilla extract
¾ cup pastry cream (recipe
    follows)

1.   Preheat the oven to 350°.

2.   In the bowl of an electric mixer, place the flour, whole eggs, sugar, butter, and yeast and blend until smooth.

3.   Add three of the egg yolks, rum, and vanilla. Blend well and divide the dough into 2 parts. Refrigerate for 2 hours.

4.   Butter an 8-inch springform pan. Roll the first half of the dough and place it in the bottom of the mold. Spread the pastry cream over the dough, taking care that it not touch the sides of the mold. Roll out the remaining dough and lay it over the cream.

5.   Blend the remaining egg yolk with a tablespoon of water and brush lightly over the top of the cake. Bake for 45 minutes, or until lightly browned. Let cool and serve.

YIELD: 6–8 SERVINGS

Crème Pâtissière

(PASTRY CREAM)

3 egg yolks
⅓ cup granulated sugar
2 tablespoons cornstarch

1 cup warm milk (about room
    temperature)
½ teaspoon pure vanilla extract

1. Combine the egg yolks, sugar, and cornstarch in a mixing bowl. Beat well with a wire whisk until the mixture is smooth and lemon-colored.

2. Add the warm milk, stirring rapidly with the whisk.

3. Spoon and scrape the mixture into a saucepan and cook over low heat, stirring constantly with a wooden spatula until the mixture comes barely to a simmer. Take care that the sauce does not continue to cook or it may curdle. Stir in the vanilla and let cool.

YIELD: 1¼ CUPS

❧ *With the seafood of the Basque country and the sherry of Spain in mind, I put together this version of an old but wonderful standby.*

Gratin de Crabe

(CRABMEAT AU GRATIN)

3 tablespoons unsalted butter
2 tablespoons all-purpose flour
1½ cups milk
Cayenne pepper to taste
⅛ teaspoon freshly grated nutmeg

Salt and freshly ground white
    pepper to taste
¾ cup heavy cream
¼ cup dry sherry
1 egg yolk

4 tablespoons shallots, finely chopped
1 pound fresh lump crabmeat, shell
   and cartilage removed

4 tablespoons freshly grated Gruyère
   or Parmesan cheese

1.   Preheat the broiler to high.

2.   Melt 2 tablespoons of the butter in a saucepan over medium heat. Add the flour and blend well. Do not allow to brown. Add the milk and cook, stirring with a whisk, until blended and smooth. Season with cayenne pepper, nutmeg, and salt and pepper.

3.   Add the cream, bring to a boil, and simmer for 3 to 4 minutes. Stir in half of the sherry, beat in the egg yolk, and remove from heat.

4.   Melt the remaining butter in a nonstick skillet over medium heat. Add the shallots and cook until wilted. Stirring gently, add the crabmeat and cook briefly. Sprinkle with the remaining sherry.

5.   Spoon the crabmeat into a baking dish and smooth with a spatula. Pour the hot sauce over the crabmeat and sprinkle with the cheese.

6.   Place the dish under the broiler and cook until golden brown and bubbling hot.

YIELD: 4 SERVINGS

Provence

SPECIALTIES

Ratatouille, the well-cooked vegetable dish made with eggplant, tomatoes, zucchini, red peppers, garlic, onions, olive oil, and herbs

Black truffles in many dishes, from scrambled eggs to roasted pigeons

Boeuf en daube, a type of stew, braised with vegetables

Pistou, a thick vegetable soup flavored with a paste made from basil, garlic, and olive oil

Lamb, grilled or roasted, with Provençal herbs and garlic

Bourride, a thick fish stew seasoned with *aïoli,* a garlic-flavored mayonnaise

Pan bagna, a sandwich made from whole round loaves of bread dressed with olive oil and stuffed with tuna, olives, anchovies, tomatoes, and capers

Panisse, a thick porridge of polenta or chick pea flour that is molded, then fried and served sprinkled with sugar

DESSERT

Sweet melons from Cavaillon, filled with Port, sliced for a fruit platter, or made into sorbets

WINES

Côte du Rhônes, among them the illustrious red Châteauneuf-du-Pape; the sweet muscat wine Beaumes-de-Venise; other wines include the crisp whites of Cassis (not to be confused with the black-currant drink) and excellent reds and whites of Bandol

A PILGRIMAGE
TO THE SUN

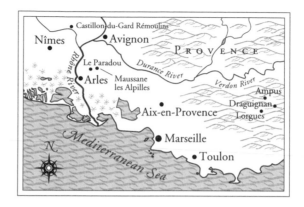

There is some concern now, voiced here and there, that Provence—sun-drenched and romantic—will soon be overrun by tourists and ruined. But I have never worried much about that possibility; first because Provence, with so many culinary and visual attractions, deserves to be seen and felt and admired by more than just some lucky few, and second because, historically, this region has not been prosperous, and much of it remains remote and poor even today. It can certainly benefit from visitors. But I have another reason, a nostalgic one, for hoping travelers will keep coming to Provence and cherish it: when I was a child, my family and I traveled this way from distant Burgundy at least once a year, a pilgrimage to the southern sun. We would always stop to picnic at one of the most startling spots in all of France, the Pont-du-Gard, a 2,000-year-old Roman aqueduct, an arched stone bridge spanning a steep, narrow gorge. The Pont-du-Gard is still exercising its ancient function today, with a pipeline carrying water to Nîmes.

Certainly, the tourists come in greater numbers now than before, but when I visited twice recently my enjoyment of the place was as great as ever. It still has a raw, unspoiled feeling. It is still possible for the boldest visitors to take their lives in their hands and climb to the very top of the aqueduct and walk across the gorge. Often there is a fierce wind—sometimes that wind is the notorious Mistral that comes roaring down the nearby Rhône, the one taint on the otherwise usually sublime Provençal weather. When one is up so high and so exposed on the uneven stones of the aqueduct's surface, a lesser breeze can feel like a Mistral, too. On the first of the two recent visits, I climbed up to the very top, strode along bravely for a while, looked way down to the river below, felt the wind buffet my body and threaten my balance, and I changed my mind, choosing a more sheltered tier of the aqueduct to continue across.

On the second visit, the main attraction for me was safely below on the bank of the Gard River where I had the opportunity to picnic on dishes prepared ahead of time by the chef of the Vieux Castillon in Castillon-du-Gard, Gilles Dauteuil. (The Vieux Castillon is a hotel-restaurant complex, ingeniously comprising the very buildings that were once individual houses in a medieval village and are now unified so unobtrusively that at first you would never imagine this village to be anything other than what it seems on the surface, certainly not a tourist establishment of such comfort.)

The Pont-du-Gard, a 2,000-year-old Roman aqueduct

Gilles promised the kind of picnic that would evoke all of Provence for us. That meant olive oil, of course, and garlic, the emblematic ingredients of the region, along with the other produce that shout its Provençal allegiance, like the tomatoes, the zucchini, and the magnificent melons. And there would be Provençal herbs aplenty, like thyme and rosemary. The sun, after all, shines in Provence most of the year, making it possible to grow many vegetables and herbs over a ten-month period. In fact thyme, rosemary, and sage grow in the wild, especially amid the rocks of the dry

The popular Provençal restaurant Le Bistro in Paradou is owned by Jean-Louis Pons and his wife Mireille; they originally bought it as a weekend home.

scrubland called the *garrigue.* Zucchini and eggplant are grown almost the entire year (no wonder *ratatouille* had to be invented—just to use up the produce). Because of this historic emphasis on vegetables and herbs, on olive oil and garlic, the Provençal diet became, according to today's understanding of nutrition, one of the most balanced and healthiest anywhere on earth.

As I visited other friends old and new in the region (actually Castillon-du-Gard is officially just outside Provence but is so enmeshed in its culture that the distinction is immaterial), the principles of Provençal cooking were driven home again and again. Just go to an olive mill, as my group and I did more than once, and witness the pride the artisans feel as they produce this magnificent oil, a food born of necessity. (In the days before refrigeration, butter, of course, could not stand the Provençal heat.)

The scraggly olive tree proffers a fruit that needs the least processing of all the vegetable oil producers to yield its oil, almost as if it were simply being juiced. One of the mills we visited was Le Moulin du Maître Cornille, an evidently profitable and somewhat modernized operation that produces spectacular extra-virgin olive oil. In the winter, the olives are picked by hand when they are rich and black, then they are ground into a paste from which comes the oil. To make a quart of extra-virgin olive oil, it takes more than ten pounds of olives. Further processing of the olives will produce more oil. One reason that all extra-virgin olive oils are not equal is that some are cold-pressed and some are processed under heat to obtain more oil. The heat is effective but it diminishes the flavor, in the view of many aficionados. Another source of variation is that the oils of various olives are blended to create the unique taste of a particular mill. I have always treasured the very best representatives of this first pressing for their fruity flavor and bouquet,

Olives and their oil are signature ingredients in Provençal cooking.

and I reserve them for salads and pastas where these characteristics are put to best use. For most cooking chores, however, I tend to turn to the less expensive olive oils and blends. But in this part of the world the oil is so plentiful I'm not sure they worry about how much of the better oil they use.

While Provence is widely and justifiably known for its gorgeous vegetables, herbs, and oils, it is relatively little known for its truffles, with the Périgord taking most of the credit for France's production of this most valuable of fungi. In fact, some people have called garlic the truffle of Provence, as if Provence didn't have bushels of the real thing just beneath its surface (so ample in supply, it is said, that Provençal truffles are often shipped off to the Périgord). Specifically, these are called *truffes du Var,* in a reference to the area of Provence that produces most of them. If one were skeptical about the truffles of Provence, both their quantity and quality, any doubt is erased at a flourishing place called Restaurant Bruno in Lorgues, where the massive chef—tall, stout, and impressive in voice, demeanor, and personality as well—Bruno himself, reaches a huge hand into a bowl of Provençal truffles and pronounces these the best of all. In fact they were representatives of the so-called summer truffles, or *truffes d'été,* which are harvested early and are milder in flavor and color.

He serves truffles in practically everything, and does so with tremendous gusto, shouting to his staff to pick up those truffle-heavy dishes and move them out, "*Enlevé Enlevé!*" And they do go marching out, sliced truffles on toast, whole truffles stuffed into pigeons, truffles in custardy scrambled eggs, and, as you will see from a recipe on page 162, truffles in peaches. Bruno is not subtle. He says that in times of worldwide recession "you have to have courage to make it" and slaps his belly for emphasis.

It was Bruno's truffle supplier, Marcel Hugou, who introduced us to a Provençal culinary experience at the other extreme—it was about as far off the beaten track as one can get—a true Provençal farmhouse serving those guests who managed to find their way to it. He guided us on a journey into the mountains and toward some of the most authentic country cooking we would find in France. The destination was Chez Marceline in the village of Argenton, a drive that took us farther and farther from civilization as we climbed the mountains of the Alpes de Haute Provence, past an occasional church or fortress, past tiny clusters of houses. The last nine miles of the road were unpaved, the fog grew thick, and the cliffs alongside the road were so steep that the ride not only seemed perilous but probably was. Occasionally we would pass a sign that said mushroom picking was forbidden—undoubtedly that meant there were some wonderful mushrooms on the hellish road to Argenton (the warnings were posted, we learned later, to fend off marauding Italians who would come across the border in search of cèpes).

We arrived in Argenton—permanent population ten but swelled in high season by tourists in residence—at the same time the sunshine did, and the town glistened. It is a little collection of stone houses, a church, and barns scattered across the hillside, with dizzying views of the valley and Coulamp River below. Logically enough perhaps, in a place so remote, Marceline Jacomet, the proprietor of Chez Marceline, cooks only what she produces on her farm—mushrooms, cheeses, duck, and the glorious Provençal herbs among them. When I asked for some eggs for an omelette she stepped out to the chicken coop and came back with eight, still warm, a few chicken feathers mingled among them. I was a happy man, in the mountains of the true and enduring Provence.

❧ *The picnic along the Gard River was prepared mostly by Gilles Dauteuil, who employs some interesting techniques. For instance, he likes to simmer garlic in milk to make it milder before using it. The total menu for the day, along with bread and wine, was roast rack of lamb with a zucchini garnish; an eggplant omelette; fillets of Mediterranean fish sautéed and served with regional vegetables; and* brandade de morue, *which is the traditional salt cod dish, along with an assortment of local olives, fresh figs, and a refreshing dessert of melon in wine. It was all laid out on a yellow Provençal cloth, and just about everything was weighted down with stones lest we lose these delicacies to the wind coursing through the gorge. Here are the recipes for three of those dishes.*

Carré d'Agneau aux Herbes de Provence

(PROVENÇAL ROAST RACK OF LAMB)

7 garlic cloves, unpeeled
½ cup milk
⅓ cup plus 1 tablespoon olive oil
¼ teaspoon dried thyme
Salt and freshly ground pepper
   to taste

1 rack of lamb, about 1½ pounds,
   most of the fat removed
¼ onion, coarsely chopped
1 shallot, coarsely chopped
¼ cup carrot, coarsely chopped
1 sprig fresh thyme

1. Preheat the oven to 425°.

2. Peel 5 of the garlic cloves and place them with the milk in a small saucepan. Bring to a boil and let simmer on a low flame for 20 minutes. Remove the garlic cloves from the milk, strain, and place them in a blender with ⅓ cup of the olive oil, ¼ teaspoon thyme, and salt and pepper to taste.

3. Meanwhile, season the rack of lamb with salt and pepper to taste and sprinkle it with 1 tablespoon of the olive oil. Place in small roasting pan with the two unpeeled garlic cloves, the onion, shallot, carrot, and the sprig of fresh thyme. Roast for 20 minutes, basting from time to time.

4. Remove the lamb from the oven and spread the garlic purée evenly over its surface. Roast the lamb for an additional 5 minutes. Serve it with tomato-zucchini garnish (recipe follows).

YIELD: 2 SERVINGS

Garni aux Tomates et Courgettes

(TOMATO-ZUCCHINI GARNISH)

1 tablespoon olive oil

2 plum tomatoes, cored and cut into
½-inch cubes

1 small zucchini, about ⅓ pound,
halved

1 clove garlic, finely chopped

Salt and freshly ground pepper
to taste

1.   In a nonstick skillet, heat the olive oil. Add the tomatoes and zucchini and cook briefly. Add the garlic and salt and pepper to taste and cook for another minute.

YIELD: 2 SERVINGS

Filets de Poisson aux Legumes

(RED SNAPPER WITH VEGETABLES)

4 red snapper fillets with skin,
weighing about ¼ pound each

Salt and freshly ground pepper
to taste

¼ cup milk

¼ cup flour

3 tablespoons olive oil

½ lemon

2 cups zucchini, thinly sliced

2 cups yellow peppers, cored, seeded,
and sliced into ¼-inch strips

¼ cup shallots, finely chopped

1 sprig fresh rosemary

½ cup cherry tomatoes

1.   Season the fish fillets with salt and pepper: dip them in the milk and then in the flour, tapping gently to remove the excess.

2.   Heat 1 tablespoon of the olive oil in a large skillet over a medium-high flame. When the oil is sufficiently hot, add the fillets, skin side up, and brown. Turn and cook the second side. Sprinkle with lemon juice and transfer to a warm platter.

3.   Heat the remaining olive oil in a skillet and add the zucchini. Season with salt

and pepper to taste and cook, stirring constantly, for 2 minutes. Add the yellow peppers and simmer, stirring constantly, for another 2 minutes. Add the shallots and rosemary and continue to cook without browning. Add the cherry tomatoes and cook until they are warmed but not wilted.

4.   To serve, place each fillet on a plate and garnish with the sautéed vegetables.

YIELD: 4 SERVINGS

❧   *At the picnic, we arranged this melon dish in an elaborate manner, with some of the cantaloupe sliced and delicately shaped to create rose petals. The same combination of flavors and pretty much the same enjoyment can be achieved more simply, as I have indicated here.*

Melon aux Figues et Menthe
(MELON WITH FIGS AND MINT)

1 medium-sized ripe cantaloupe
½ cup Beaumes-de-Venise, or other
    dessert wine
5 sprigs fresh mint

Sugar to taste
2 cups watermelon balls
2 fresh figs, quartered

1.   Halve the cantaloupe and discard seeds. To prepare the *coulis,* scoop the flesh from one half of the cantaloupe and cut it roughly into cubes.

2.   Place melon cubes, wine, 1 sprig of mint, and sugar in a blender and blend until the mixture is smooth.

3.   With a melon scooper, shape the remaining cantaloupe into balls.

4.   To assemble, place a mound of watermelon and cantaloupe balls in the center of each of 4 plates. Spoon a ring of *coulis* around each mound of melon balls. Garnish each plate with 2 fig quarters and a sprig of mint.

YIELD: 4 SERVINGS

❧ *Although Bruno is the driving force of his restaurant, the temple of truffles in Lorgues, these stuffed peaches were the creation of his young pastry chef, Gilles Herard, twenty-five, a talented man who has worked in some of the best restaurants in France and who has a great deal of freedom to employ his talents at the restaurant—as long as he remembers that this is a truffle place. And these peaches, stuffed with ice cream, are in fact—believe it or not—decorated with truffle slices. I've suggested in the recipe, however, that the truffles can be considered as optional. It's still a great peach. Keep in mind that the ice cream will have to be made well before the other ingredients.*

Pêches avec Glace à la Bruno

(PEACHES AND ICE CREAM)

FOR THE ICE CREAM:

1 cup whole milk

1 cup cream

2 vanilla beans, split lengthwise

1 tablespoon finely chopped black
    truffles (optional)

5 egg yolks

½ cup granulated sugar

2 tablespoons shelled hazelnuts,
    coarsely chopped

1. Combine the milk, cream, vanilla beans, and chopped truffles in a medium-sized saucepan. Stir the mixture and heat it to just below the boiling point (about 180°). Remove from heat.

2. In a large mixing bowl, combine the egg yolks and sugar and beat the mixture with a wire whisk until it turns a light lemony color.

3. Whisk the milk and cream mixture into the egg yolks and blend it well. Allow the mixture to cool.

4. Pour this custard into an ice-cream machine and freeze according to manufacturer's instructions.

5. As the ice cream begins to harden, but before it is completely finished, add hazelnuts and finish the ice cream in the machine. You should have 4 to 5 cups of ice cream.

TO PREPARE THE PEACHES:

4 large ripe white peaches

1. In a medium-sized saucepan, bring enough water to boil to cover the peaches.

When the water is boiling, add the peaches and simmer for about 30 seconds, or until the skin can be easily separated from the fruit. (The time will vary, depending upon the ripeness of the peaches.) Remove the peaches from the boiling water and plunge them into an ice bath to cool. Remove the skins with a sharp paring knife.

2.   Using the paring knife, cut a slice of about ¼ inch across the bottom of each peach to reveal the pit and to serve as a lid after stuffing. Set this lid aside. Cut a circle vertically around the pit, descending no deeper than the pit's length. Next, insert your knife into the peach horizontally about where the base of the pit lies. Cut across until you have released the pit, stopping before you cut entirely through the fruit. Turn the fruit upside down and slide the pit out; you may need to pry it gently loose with the knife. Replace the lid of each peach and reserve the peaches in a cool place.

FOR THE SYRUP:

2 cups water	3 lemon zests, with white part
½ cup granulated sugar	removed
Skin and pits of the 4 peeled	1 lime zest, with white part removed
peaches	2 vanilla beans, split lengthwise
3 orange zests, with white part	1 teaspoon dried mint
removed	1 teaspoon dried lemongrass

1.   In a saucepan, combine all ingredients for the sauce. Bring the mixture to a boil and simmer on a low flame for 30 minutes. Strain and chill.

YIELD: ABOUT 1 CUP

FOR THE ASSEMBLY:

16 thin slices black truffle for decoration (optional)	4 tablespoons Grand Marnier, for topping
¼ cup granulated sugar	

1.   Using a teaspoon, fill the peaches with the ice cream to the top, smooth the ice cream, and cover with the lids.

2.   Place each peach on a chilled dessert plate and spoon 2 tablespoons of the syrup over it.

3.   Make tiny slits in the lids of the peaches. Coat the truffle slices with sugar and insert truffle slices upright into the slits.

4.   Sprinkle each serving with a tablespoon of Grand Marnier.

YIELD: 4 SERVINGS

❦   *At Chez Marceline, the proprietress has strong feelings about how to go about cooking. For instance, she prefers the flavor of meats cooked in sauces the second day better than the first, and sometimes she only partially cooks a dish to impregnate the meat with the flavors and then finishes the cooking the second day. That's how she prepared duck for us, in two stages. But the recipe as I offer it to you here is less time-consuming. The duck goes well with polenta, and a recipe follows.*

Canard aux Cèpes de Chez Marceline

(CHEZ MARCELINE'S DUCK STEW WITH CÈPES)

4 cups water
3 cups dried cèpes (or other wild
    mushroom)
1 cup pitted green olives
3 small bay leaves
2 sprigs fresh tarragon, or 1 teaspoon
    dried
2 sprigs fresh thyme, or 1 teaspoon
    dried
2 tablespoons lard, or, if preferred,
    vegetable or olive oil

Salt and freshly ground pepper
    to taste
5½ pound duck, cleaned and cut into
    small serving pieces, including
    neck and gizzard
1 cup onions, thinly sliced
2 tablespoons garlic, minced
⅓ cup all-purpose flour
3 cups dry white wine
2 tablespoons parsley, finely chopped

1.   In a large soup kettle or Dutch oven, bring the water, along with the cèpes, olives, bay leaves, tarragon, and thyme, to a boil and reduce to a simmer, awaiting ingredients from following steps.

2.   Brown the duck in batches. In a large nonstick skillet, heat 2 tablespoons lard or oil over medium-high heat. Add salt and pepper to taste. Place the duck pieces in the skillet in one layer, skin side down. Cook until brown. Turn and cook the other side. Remove the duck pieces with a skimmer, leaving the fat in the skillet. Set the browned duck aside.

3.   In the same skillet, add the remaining duck and cook until both sides are browned. Then add the previously browned duck, onions, and garlic to the pan and continue to cook for 2 to 3 minutes. Add the flour, stirring until it browns. Blend in the wine and bring the mixture to a boil. Scrape to dissolve any browned particles clinging to the bottom of the skillet. Simmer until the wine is reduced by half.

4. With a skimmer, transfer the ingredients from the skillet to the kettle, leaving the fat in the skillet. Blend well, return the contents of the kettle to a boil, and then let simmer 1½ hours, or until the duck is tender.

5. Sprinkle the duck with chopped parsley and serve with polenta (recipe follows).

YIELD: 6 SERVINGS

Polenta aux Herbes

(POLENTA WITH HERBS)

4 cups water
Salt and freshly ground white pepper
   to taste
1 cup yellow cornmeal
½ cup heavy cream

½ cup grated Parmesan cheese
2 tablespoons parsley, chopped
2 tablespoons fresh basil, finely
   chopped
⅓ cup soft butter

1. Bring the water to a boil in a heavy medium-sized saucepan and add salt, pepper, and cornmeal. Blend well and return to a boil.

2. Place the saucepan in a larger pot containing 1 inch of boiling water (creating, in effect, a double boiler) and cook, covered, for 45 minutes, stirring occasionally. Add the cream, cheese, herbs, and butter. Blend well. Serve hot with the duck stew.

YIELD: 6–8 SERVINGS

❧ *Here's the reason I sent Marceline off to the chicken coop to fetch some fresh eggs. The frittata is more an Italian omelette than French—meant to be more firm and browned—but that makes sense because here in the mountains of Provence we were not so far from Italy. I cooked this frittata on Marceline's cast-iron wood-burning stove.*

Frittata Provençal

(FRITTATA WITH PROVENÇAL VEGETABLES)

2 tablespoons olive oil
1 cup eggplant, peeled and cut into
    ½-inch cubes
1 cup zucchini, thinly sliced
½ cup white onions, thinly sliced
1 teaspoon garlic, minced
8 medium-sized eggs

¼ cup fresh basil or marjoram,
    coarsely chopped
Salt and freshly ground pepper to
    taste
2 tablespoons softened butter
1 tablespoon red wine vinegar

1.   Heat the olive oil in a large nonstick skillet or omelette pan. Add the eggplant and cook over medium-high heat for 2 minutes, stirring, regularly. Add the zucchini and onions and continue cooking, stirring, until they are lightly browned. Add the garlic and cook briefly without letting it brown.

2.   Meanwhile, in a mixing bowl beat together the eggs, basil or marjoram, and salt and pepper.

3.   Add the eggs to the skillet. As they cook, stir from the bottom until the eggs start to set (about 1 minute). Cover and continue to cook on a low flame for 2 minutes.

4.   Remove the lid and dot the edges of the omelette with butter. Sprinkle the frittata with vinegar. Cover tightly and cook on low heat for 1 minute.

5.   Place a large, round serving dish over the skillet and invert the skillet to release the frittata onto the dish. It should be golden brown on top. The frittata may be served warm or cold.

YIELD: 4 SERVINGS

✤ *Throughout Provence one finds old villages perched on the hillsides or at the pinnacles of mountains; they often seem too small to be as complete as they are. Ampus, with its town hall, its grocer and bakery, its beautiful market, is like that. On the morning we arrived we visited Joel Bertaina, a forty-two-year-old baker whose growth of beard and tired eyes bore evidence of the hard work that had begun at one o'clock that morning. And on the far side of the town square, standing a bit grandly apart from the other structures, we entered the Fontaine d'Ampus, a generously proportioned restaurant (high ceilings, expansive windows) run by Marc and Alexandra Haye, who fled the noise and bustle of Paris in 1987. The dining room's beamed ceiling and terra-cotta floors lend it a rough-hewn air; the renovated kitchen, although it has a new oven, retains its old oven graced with a handsome curved chimney. The desire to hold on to tradition could be seen in the food redolent with the Provençal spirit, like the sardines in a red wine sauce and the potatoes with bacon. Small mackerel can be substituted for the sardines.*

Sardines du Pays à la Marinade au Vin Rouge

(SAUTÉED MARINATED SARDINES IN A RED WINE SAUCE)

8 large fresh sardines or small
    mackerel, cleaned
Salt and freshly ground pepper
    to taste
2 cups Côte de Provence, or
    comparable red wine
½ cup onions, chopped
⅓ cup leeks, chopped (using only
    the white part)
1 lemon
2 tablespoons olive oil

1 tablespoon garlic, minced
1 sprig fresh rosemary, or ½ teaspoon
    dried
1 sprig tarragon, or ½ teaspoon dried
½ teaspoon whole coriander seeds
½ cup tomato, peeled, seeded, and
    diced
3 tablespoons sweet butter
½ cup all-purpose flour
2 tablespoons chives, chopped

1.   Place the sardines in a flat dish with salt and freshly ground pepper. Add ⅓ cup of the red wine. Sprinkle with 2 tablespoons of the chopped onions, 1 tablespoon of the chopped leeks, and the juice of ½ lemon. Blend well and marinate for 5 minutes.

2.   Heat 1 tablespoon of the olive oil in a small saucepan. Add the remaining chopped onions and leeks and the chopped garlic. Cook over medium heat until the

vegetables are wilted. Add the rosemary, tarragon, coriander, the remaining wine, the tomatoes, and salt and pepper to taste. Boil until the mixture has been reduced by half. Blend in the butter with a wire whisk. Remove from heat and keep warm.

3.   Meanwhile, remove the sardines from the marinade and pat them dry with a paper towel. Add the remaining marinade to the cooking sauce. Place the flour in a flat dish and use it to dust each sardine lightly.

4.   In a nonstick skillet large enough to hold the sardines in one layer, heat the remaining olive oil. Add the sardines and cook over medium-high heat until lightly browned, about 2 minutes. Turn to cook the other side for an additional 2 minutes, sprinkling the fish with the juice of the remaining ½ lemon.

5.   To serve, divide the sauce onto 4 warm plates. Place 2 sardines on each plate, and sprinkle with chives. Serve with red-skinned potatoes with bacon (recipe follows).

YIELD: 4 SERVINGS

Pommes de Terre Rouge au Lardon

(RED-SKINNED POTATOES WITH BACON)

8 small red-skinned potatoes,
    about ¾ pound
Salt and freshly ground pepper
    to taste
8 thick slices of bacon

1 tablespoon olive oil
1 tablespoon fresh thyme, or
    ½ teaspoon dried
2 tablespoons water
1 tablespoon chives, chopped

1.   Preheat oven to 400°.

2.   Place the potatoes in a small saucepan with water to cover and salt to taste. Bring to a boil and simmer for 18 minutes. Add the bacon slices and simmer for 5 minutes more. Drain the contents of the saucepan. Allow the potatoes to cool, then peel them.

3.   Wrap each potato in a slice of bacon.

4.   Place the wrapped potatoes in a flat ovenproof dish. Sprinkle with the olive oil, thyme, and freshly ground pepper to taste. Add 2 tablespoons of water and bake for 20 minutes, or until the bacon is lightly browned.

5.   Sprinkle with the chopped chives and serve hot with sautéed marinated sardines in red wine sauce.

YIELD: 4 SERVINGS

❧ *My friend Michel Roux has a home in Provence and invited us there for lunch, but before that he led us to another of those startling little Provençal villages, this one called Tourtour, where the stone houses date to the tenth century and the streets are narrow even by French village standards. (We learned that the narrowness forced medieval shepherds to drive their sheep along two by two so that they could be properly counted at taxation time.) In the market there a pretty young woman was making baskets from branches that she made supple by splitting them and then repeatedly working them against her knee until they bent easily. I bought one and carried it with me to every market in France that I visited thereafter. The town holds on to its past so vigorously that it still contains a washing trough, a* lavoire, *where even now some local women come to do their laundry. A fourteenth-century olive mill is still functioning in the town, but in a gesture to the tourists who arrive in the summertime, it is converted to a gallery for local artists for the season. At Michel's house, the lunch was a rollicking affair, with many of the dishes contributed by friends in the area. Here are three of them. The first is adapted from a dish prepared by Michel's cook, Odile.*

Lapin Rôti à la Michel

(MICHEL'S ROASTED RABBIT)

1 2- to 2½-pound rabbit, cleaned
   and cut into serving-sized pieces
Salt and freshly ground pepper
   to taste
6 tablespoons olive oil
4 sprigs fresh thyme, or 2 teaspoons
   dried
2 sprigs fresh rosemary, or
   2 teaspoons dried

2 bay leaves
4 tablespoons Ricard, or other
   anise-flavored liqueur
½ cup fresh chicken broth (see
   recipe page 108), good quality
   canned, or water
4 tablespoons fresh basil, coarsely
   chopped, for garnish

1.   Place the rabbit in a shallow dish. Add the salt and pepper, 2 tablespoons of the olive oil, thyme, rosemary, bay leaves, and Ricard. Stir well and cover with plastic wrap. Place in the refrigerator to marinate for 6 hours.

2.   Preheat oven to 400°.

3.   Transfer the rabbit and herbs to a flat baking dish large enough to hold all the

pieces in a single layer. Add the remaining olive oil and bake for 30 minutes, turning and basting the rabbit as necessary.

4.   Add the chicken broth and cover with aluminum foil. Reduce oven temperature to 350° and continue to bake for 15 minutes.

5.   Remove bay leaves, sprinkle with basil, and serve.

YIELD: 4 SERVINGS

❧   *Michel's friend Paula brought a* ratatouille *to the party. Here's my version.*

Ratatouille Rapide

(QUICK RATATOUILLE)

1 eggplant, about ½ pound
3 tablespoons olive oil
3 small zucchini, about 1 pound, trimmed and cut crosswise into thin slices
1 sweet red pepper, cored, seeded, and cut into ½-inch cubes
1 green pepper, cored, seeded, and cut into ½-inch cubes
1 cup onions, thinly sliced

1 tablespoon finely chopped garlic
4 ripe plum tomatoes, cored and cut into large cubes
2 sprigs fresh thyme
1 bay leaf
Salt and freshly ground pepper to taste
4 tablespoons fresh basil, coarsely chopped

1.   Without removing the skin, cut the eggplant into ½-inch cubes.

2.   Heat the olive oil in a heavy skillet and add the eggplant, zucchini, and peppers. Stir continuously over high heat so that the pieces cook evenly (about 4 minutes). Add the onions and garlic and continue to cook.

3.   Add the tomatoes, thyme, bay leaf, and salt and pepper to taste. Stir to blend and cook over medium-high heat for about 10 minutes. Remove the bay leaf and serve sprinkled with the chopped basil.

YIELD: 4–6 SERVINGS

❧ *Here's a quiche that we also put together at Michel's.*

Quiche aux Courgettes
(ZUCCHINI QUICHE)

CRUST:

1½ cups flour
8 tablespoons cold butter, cut into
  small pieces

1 teaspoon salt
2 tablespoons ice water

FILLING:

1 tablespoon olive oil
½ cup thinly sliced green onions or
  scallions
1 pound small zucchini, cored and
  sliced thinly
Salt and freshly ground pepper
2 eggs
2 egg yolks

½ cup heavy cream
½ cup milk
⅛ teaspoon freshly grated nutmeg
¼ teaspoon red pepper flakes
1 cup Gruyère or Comté cheese, cut
  into ¼-inch cubes
¼ cup fresh basil or parsley, chopped
2 tablespoons grated Parmesan cheese

TO PREPARE THE CRUST:

1.   Preheat the oven to 400°.

2.   Using a food processor, blend the flour, butter, and salt thoroughly for 5 seconds. Add the water and blend until the pastry pulls away from the sides of the bowl and begins to form a ball.

3.   Gather the dough into a ball and, using a floured rolling pin, roll the dough into a round 13 inches in diameter and ¼ inch thick.

4.   Pick up the dough by rolling it onto the pin and transfer it to a 10½-inch

black tart pan with a removable bottom. Press the dough gently into the pan, gathering it in toward the wall of the pan to thicken the sides of the shell. Trim off the excess dough. Press a kitchen fork around the rim to create a crimped design.

5.   Line the shell with wax paper or kitchen parchment and weigh down with aluminum weights or dried beans. Bake for 10 minutes, remove the weights and paper, and bake for 5 minutes more. Remove from the oven and let cool.

TO PREPARE THE FILLING:

1.   Heat the olive oil in a shallow skillet over medium-high heat, add the onions and zucchini and sauté for about 5 minutes. Do not let the vegetables brown. Sprinkle with salt and pepper to taste. Drain in a colander.

2.   In a mixing bowl, use a wire whisk to beat the eggs and the yolks. Then add the cream, milk, nutmeg, pepper flakes, and salt and pepper, if necessary, and continue beating until well blended.

TO ASSEMBLE THE QUICHE:

1.   Use a slotted spoon to place the zucchini and onions evenly in the shell. Cover with the Gruyère and ladle the egg mixture over the cheese and zucchini. Sprinkle with basil and Parmesan cheese.

2.   Place the quiche on a cookie sheet on the bottom shelf of the oven and bake for 45 minutes.

3.   Let cool on a rack, unmold, and serve warm.

YIELD: 6–8 SERVINGS

❧ *Before leaving Provence, I devised several other typical recipes, which follow.*

Daube Provençal

(PROVENÇAL BRAISED BEEF)

4 pounds brisket of beef or any
shoulder cut, well trimmed and
cut into 1½-inch cubes
Salt and freshly ground pepper to
taste
2 tablespoons olive oil
16 small pearl onions, peeled
6 garlic cloves, unpeeled
24 small green olives, pitted and
blanched in boiling water, then
drained

3 tablespoons flour
1 bottle red Provençal wine, or other
red wine
1 cup water
4 sprigs fresh thyme, or 1 teaspoon
dried
1 bay leaf
2 whole cloves
2 allspice
1 tablespoon tomato paste

1.   Sprinkle the beef with salt and pepper.

2.   Heat the oil over high heat in a large nonstick skillet large enough to hold the meat in one layer. Cook, stirring, until well browned.

3.   Transfer the meat to a heavy casserole and add the onions, garlic, and olives. Cook for 5 minutes, then add the flour and blend well, stirring, for 1 minute more. Add the wine, water, thyme, bay leaf, whole cloves, allspice, and tomato paste. Blend well and bring to a simmer.

4.   Cook, covered, over low heat for 3 hours, or until tender. Remove the thyme sprigs and bay leaves and skim off any fat that may have floated to the top of the casserole before serving.

YIELD: 4 SERVINGS

Gigot d'Agneau aux Herbes de Provence

(ROAST LEG OF LAMB WITH PROVENÇAL HERBS)

1 leg of lamb, 6 to 7 pounds
1 tablespoon olive oil
2 sprigs fresh thyme, or 1 teaspoon
    dried
2 sprigs fresh rosemary, or 1 teaspoon
    dried

Salt and pepper to taste
2 small white onions, peeled
6 garlic cloves, unpeeled
1 bay leaf
½ cup Rose de Provence wine

1. Preheat oven to 425°.

2. Prepare the lamb by removing the outer fat and skin and the hip bone, which runs at a 45-degree angle from the leg bone. Run a knife along it on all sides to free it. You will see the ball joint of the socket that connects the leg to the hip. Cut through the tendons that connect the joint to the socket. The bone should now come free. Set aside.

3. Rub the lamb with the olive oil and herbs and sprinkle it with salt and pepper. Place it in a roasting pan. Add the onions, garlic, bay leaf, and the hip bone.

4. Roast the lamb on the bottom rack of the oven, basting every 15 minutes. After 1 hour, reduce the heat to 400°. Remove the fat from the pan and add the wine.

5. Continue roasting for 15 minutes, or until the internal temperature reaches 140° for medium rare.

6. Remove the lamb from the oven, placing the bone underneath it to serve as a rack. Let it stand in a warm place for 15 minutes, so that the juices continue to drip into the pan gravy, enriching it. Carve and serve with the gravy.

YIELD: 4 SERVINGS

Daube Niçoise

(PROVENÇAL BEEF STEW)

4 pounds of beef, round steak or
    chuck, well trimmed and cut into
    1½-inch cubes
3 tablespoons olive oil
Salt and freshly ground pepper
    to taste

12 small white onions, peeled
¾ pound small mushrooms, washed
    and dried
2 tablespoons garlic, minced
¼ cup flour
½ cup canned crushed tomatoes

1 cup fresh beef broth, or good
    quality canned
1 cup dry red wine
1 bay leaf
½ teaspoon saffron threads
4 sprigs fresh thyme, or 1 teaspoon
    dried

¾ pound carrots, cut into 2-inch
    pieces
18 black Niçoise olives, pitted,
    blanched for 30 seconds, and
    drained
¼ cup parsley, finely chopped

1.   In a large black cast-iron pot, heat the oil over high heat and brown the beef thoroughly on all sides. Season with salt and pepper.

2.   Add the onions, mushrooms, and garlic and blend well. Pour off the fat. Add the flour, stirring to coat the meat and vegetables. Cook, stirring, for about 3 minutes.

3.   Add the tomatoes, beef broth, wine, bay leaf, saffron, thyme, and salt and pepper to taste and bring to a boil. Scrape the bottom of the pot as you stir, so that nothing sticks and burns. Cover and simmer for 1 hour, stirring occasionally.

4.   Add the carrots and continue cooking for ½ hour, or until the meat is done. Remove the bay leaf and thyme sprigs. Add the olives, simmer briefly, check for seasoning, and serve with chopped parsley as a garnish.

YIELD: 8 SERVINGS

Soupe à l'Ail Provençale
(GARLIC SOUP PROVENCE-STYLE)

24 garlic cloves, peeled
4 cups water
Salt and freshly ground pepper to
    taste
1 bay leaf
1 tablespoon olive oil

6 fresh sage leaves, or 1 teaspoon
    dry rubbed sage
1 French baguette (see recipe
    page 42)
2 egg yolks
½ cup grated Parmesan cheese

1.   Crush the cloves of garlic lightly. Place them in a saucepan with the water, salt and pepper, bay leaf, olive oil, and sage. Simmer uncovered for 15 minutes.

2.   While the soup cooks, slice the French bread into slices ⅛ inch thick. Toast lightly on both sides.

3.   When the soup is ready, place the egg yolks in the bottom of a soup tureen and beat with a wire whisk. Continue to beat vigorously while straining the piping hot garlic broth over them.

4.   Add the toasted bread and sprinkle with the Parmesan cheese. Strain in the remaining broth. Stir and serve immediately in hot soup plates.

YIELD: 4 SERVINGS

Poulet Sauté Provençal
(CHICKEN SAUTÉED PROVENÇAL-STYLE)

1 3½-pound chicken, cut into
   serving pieces
Salt and freshly ground pepper
   to taste
2 tablespoons olive oil
2 tablespoons butter
2 teaspoons fresh rosemary,
finely chopped, or 1 tablespoon
   dried
2 garlic cloves, peeled
2 tablespoons shallots, minced
½ cup dry white wine from Provence
¾ cup fresh chicken broth (see recipe
   page 108), or good quality canned

1.   Sprinkle the chicken with salt and pepper.

2.   Heat the olive oil and 1 tablespoon of the butter in a heavy skillet large enough to hold all the chicken pieces in one layer. When hot, add the chicken pieces skin side down. Cook over medium heat for 10 minutes, or until golden brown on one side.

3.   Turn the chicken pieces and add the rosemary and garlic cloves. Cook for 10 minutes longer.

4.   Pour half the fat out of the skillet, add the shallots, and cook briefly. Add the wine and chicken broth, stirring to dissolve the brown particles that cling to the bottom and sides of the skillet. Cover and cook for 10 minutes more.

5.   Remove the chicken pieces to a serving dish and keep warm. Continue to cook the sauce until it is reduced to about ¾ cup, then add the remaining tablespoon of butter. Return the chicken to the skillet, along with any juices that may have accumulated on the dish. Bring to a boil and serve immediately.

YIELD: 4 SERVINGS

Côte d'Azur

SPECIALTIES

Stuffed or fried zucchini flowers

Tiny stuffed vegetables, like mushroom caps or onions

Pissaladière, an onion tart laced with anchovies

Tapenade, the black olive and anchovy paste used as
a sauce or dip

Bass (called bar) grilled in fennel-scented smoke, as well as
a myriad of other Mediterranean fish, including
rascasse, lotte, rouget

Ravioli à la Niçoise, pasta stuffed with stewed beef

Fougasse, a rich, flat, olive oil bread

Pistou, a thick vegetable soup flavored with a paste made from
basil, garlic, and olive oil

Bouillabaisse, saffron-flavored seafood stew

Bourride, a fish soup of white fish, garlic, and olive oil, served
with garlicky mayonnaise called *aïoli*

Socca, a Provençal crêpe made of chick pea flour, served hot

Salade Niçoise, usually with olives, anchovies, capers,
tomatoes, and other vegetables

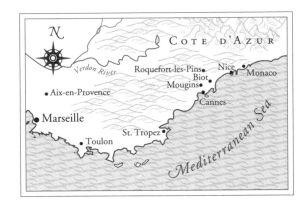

HAIL THE NEW PRINCE

Of all the great cooks I know in France, it may be Alain Ducasse of the Hôtel de Paris in Monte Carlo for whom I have the greatest admiration—because of the absolute perfection of his cooking, his eagerness to serve as a mentor to gifted young chefs, and because of the terrible adversity he suffered just a few years ago. He was flying to Lake Annecy in the Savoy with a few other men intent on starting a new business. In the deep fog their plane went down, and all perished, except for Alain (although he believed, trapped in the wreckage, that he was finished, too). He remembers seeing a pair of legs work their way into the remnants of the plane; he thought he was imagining it. The rescue took an hour. Although Alain survived, he had been badly injured—the glasses he wears today attest to the damage done to his eyes in the crash.

If you get the chance to visit Ducasse and sample his work, you just might agree with me that his is the dedication of someone—no matter how accomplished he may have been before the accident—who knows he is fortunate to be alive and is determined to make the most of it. His diligence and intensity are obvious in every dish. He believes in the purest and freshest of ingredients—but any good French chef will tell you that. The difference here is that the freshness is more evident in the final product than I have seen anywhere else. One gets the sense that each morsel is truly the very best he could find. He arranges for butter to be made especially for him by a farmer in the southwest of France; there is a single supplier—in Spain—that he turns to for the best fish he can get; he brings white truffles in from Italy. (All across America, home and restaurant cooks cannot always obtain the same ingredients he has found, of course, but his approach is instructive: when the cooking matters, don't stint—go out of your way to find the very best there is.) Having arranged for such fine produce, he sees it as his duty to prepare it in ways that show

it off and do not in any way mute the magnificence of it. So he cooks lightly and simply but with supreme skill, illustrated by the sumptuous but unpretentious dish of vegetables, pears, and chestnuts that appears later in this chapter.

Alain Ducasse of the opulent Hôtel de Paris in Monte Carlo

He runs his establishment with military precision. The whole staff listens with absolute attention as he calls out the assignments for the day, and then, in unison, the young cooks respond, *"Oui, chef!"* They know that, should one of them fail, there's a whole line of others waiting for the chance to work with Ducasse. Most of the twenty-five on his staff will be gone in a year in any event, because he believes it is his job to train them and send them out into the world, as the emissaries of his cooking.

The irony is that the simplicity and directness of Ducasse take place in one of the

The markets in and around Nice are much as they always were, but it is rare to find an old-style fishing port, like the one below, that has escaped domination by yachts and tourism.

most chic spots on the Côte d'Azur. The restaurant itself glitters with gilt moldings, and hand-painted murals (portraits of the mistresses of Louis XV) grace the walls; one's feet sink into the Aubusson carpet. The wine list is fabulous, and a waiter gracefully rolls a silver cart to the table to offer Champagne by the glass. This is, after all, Monte Carlo, where the notion of the glitzy Côte d'Azur was born at the turn of the century when European nobility began to frequent it as a winter resort. In a way, of course, Ducasse's understated approach, so elegant in its purity, is not at all out of place here, any more than a perfect diamond would be.

For me and my companions, on this journey through France, Monte Carlo was an exception. During most of the time we spent along the Côte d'Azur (when we weren't enticed by some brilliant, varied market like the one at Nice), we tried to stay on the margins, away from the overwhelming self-absorption and pretension that one too often encounters in the most touristic spots. They are fine in their way, and I do enjoy all the commotion in short takes, but I must say sometimes it saddens me: I was disappointed by how thoroughly the little fishing villages and ports are being squeezed out by monied tourism and by yachts as big as the Ritz. Although all is not completely lost, a few fishermen do remain tending their nets, dragging deeply on their cigarettes. If you find yourself yearning to see a fishing village in a condition that recalls its past—and want to dine on its superb seafood while you're at it—make your way to Villefranche near Nice. Or, if you just need a break from all the commotion, travel (as many visitors and locals who are looking for simpler areas near the coastline often do) to what is called the *arrière pays,* the back country, for some extraordinary Provençale food. We did just that.

When we visited Mougins, overlooking Cannes, it was to drop in on Jean-Pierre Giordano of the Bistro de Mougins, certainly one of the least self-important dining spots, and most delightful, in this quaint village with its several fine restaurants. There one finds straightforward southern French cooking—zucchini flowers coated in batter and fried, basil soup, stuffed sardines, and the like. And later we visited Jean-Pierre's house for an old-fashioned picnic in his backyard. When we stayed overnight in the area it was far from the crowds at the Auberge du Colombier in Roquefort-les-Pins. The word *colombier* refers to a dove's aviary, and as you sit outside having a drink with Jackie Wolff, the owner, you can watch his doves as they leave an aviary on the property to fly low across the horizon, one at a time, and then return home.

↬ *During our picnic in Jean-Pierre's backyard, we enjoyed these lovely fish brochettes, and I contributed a rack of lamb and a side dish of sautéed shredded vegetables. Although salmon and cod are not Mediterranean fish, Jean-Pierre was able to purchase them and was pleased to employ them anyway. He used vegetables from his sister's garden and herbs from his own backyard. His barbecue was particularly Provençal in that he kindled the fire with branches of dried fennel. It was wild fennel that grows on the hillsides of the region. Jean-Pierre used a grilling basket that stands on its own legs about four inches from the coals. He placed some dried fennel branches in the basket along with the skewers.*

For the salmon and cod brochettes, I prefer metal skewers; they're simply easier to handle than the wooden ones. A possible side dish is the rice with pine nuts I offer just after the marinade recipe.

Brochettes de Poisson à la Jean Pierre

(JEAN PIERRE'S SALMON AND COD BROCHETTES)

1 or 2 sweet red peppers, cored, seeded, and cut into 16 1-inch cubes

6 ounces skinless salmon fillet, cut into 12 1½-inch cubes

6 ounces skinless fresh cod fillet, cut into 12 1½-inch cubes

1 large white onion, peeled, halved lengthwise, cut into 16 1-inch cubes

1 fennel bulb, halved lengthwise, cut into 16 1-inch cubes

Marinade for salmon and cod *brochettes* (recipe follows)

2 tablespoons fresh basil, finely chopped

2 sprigs fresh thyme, or 1 teaspoon dried

Salt and freshly ground pepper to taste

1 lemon, cut into 4 wedges as a garnish

1. Prepare the outdoor charcoal barbecue.

2. Begin each skewer with a piece of red pepper. Continue by alternating the salmon and the cod with pieces of vegetable between each cube of fish. Finish each skewer with a piece of red pepper. To assure even cooking, do not press the ingredients too tightly together.

3. Place skewers in a deep dish. Brush generously with the marinade (recipe follows) and sprinkle with the basil and thyme. Let sit at least ½ hour. (Ideally, the skewers should marinate overnight.) Cover with plastic wrap and refrigerate.

4.   Sprinkle the skewers with salt and pepper to taste and place them on hot grill about 4 inches from the coals. Cook on first side for about 4 to 5 minutes. Brush again with the marinade and turn and cook on second side for an additional 4 to 5 minutes. Do not overcook.

5.   Garnish each serving with a lemon wedge. Serve with rice dish (recipe follows).

YIELD: 4 SERVINGS

Marinade

4 tablespoons olive oil
1 tablespoon garlic, peeled and finely
   chopped
Juice of ½ lemon
1 tablespoon crushed coriander seeds

1 sprig fresh thyme, or ½
   teaspoon dried
Salt and freshly ground pepper
   to taste

1.   In a small bowl, combine the olive oil, garlic, lemon juice, coriander, thyme, and salt and pepper.

YIELD: ½ CUP

Riz aux Pignons
(RICE WITH PINE NUTS)

2 tablespoons butter
4 tablespoons chopped onions
¼ cup pine nuts
1 cup parboiled (converted) rice
1½ cups water

2 sprigs fresh thyme, or ½ teaspoon
   dried
1 bay leaf
Salt and freshly ground pepper to
   taste

1.   Preheat the oven to 400°.

2.   Melt 1 tablespoon of the butter in a heavy ovenproof saucepan and add the onions and pine nuts. Cook and stir until wilted. Add the rice, water, thyme, bay leaf, and salt and pepper.

3.   Bring to a boil, stirring to make sure there are no lumps in the rice. Cover with a close fitting lid and place in the oven.

4.   Bake for 17 minutes. Then remove the cover and discard the thyme sprigs and bay leaf. Using a fork, stir in the remaining butter and serve.

YIELD: 4 SERVINGS

❧   *When I cooked this lamb at Jean-Pierre's place, I first seared the meat on the grill and then transferred it to the oven. But all the cooking can be done in the oven, if you like. If you do it that way, it is necessary to start by cooking under the broiler for 2 to minutes to sear the meat before adding the bread crumb topping and then finish the meat by roasting it.*

Carré d'Agneau Côte d'Azur

(RACK OF LAMB CÔTE D'AZUR-STYLE)

3 tablespoons olive oil
4 tablespoons dried bread crumbs,
    pressed through a fine sieve
1 tablespoon shallots, finely chopped
1 teaspoon garlic, finely chopped
1 teaspoon parsley, finely chopped
Salt and freshly ground pepper
    to taste
2 racks of lamb, well trimmed of
    the fat and skin

2 sprigs fresh rosemary, or ¼
    teaspoon dried
2 sprigs fresh thyme, or ¼ teaspoon
    dried
4 sprigs fresh thyme or rosemary,
    for garnish
Vegetable garnish (recipe follows)

1.   Prepare outdoor charcoal grill (with a lid) to high heat.

2.   In a small mixing bowl, combine 1 tablespoon of the olive oil, the dried bread crumbs, shallots, garlic, parsley, and salt and pepper to taste. Mix well.

3.   Sprinkle the racks of lamb with salt and pepper and brush them with 1 tablespoon olive oil. Be sure to brush especially well on the meat side.

4.   Place the lamb on the hot grill, meat side down, about 4 inches from the coals. Sprinkle with rosemary and thyme. Cook until lightly browned, then turn and cook on second side (about 5 minutes total).

5.   Transfer the lamb to an ovenproof dish and sprinkle both sides of each rack with equal amounts of the bread crumb mixture and the remaining olive oil. With the barbecue lid shut, roast the lamb for about 12 to 15 minutes more, basting from time to time with the cooking juices.

6.   Remove the lamb from the grill and let sit in its dish in a warm place for about 5 minutes before slicing. Leaving the racks in the dish, slice them into two-chop sections. The juices will blend with the bread crumbs. Place 2 pieces on each

of 4 warmed serving plates and spoon the cooking juices over the meat after removing the herb sprigs. Spoon vegetable garnish (recipe follows) beside the lamb and garnish each plate with a sprig of fresh thyme or rosemary.

YIELD: 4 SERVINGS

Sauté de Julienne de Légumes
(SAUTÉED JULIENNE VEGETABLES)

1 cup carrots, peeled and trimmed
1 cup white turnips, trimmed
1½ cups zucchini, trimmed
1 tablespoon olive oil

½ tablespoon garlic, finely chopped
1 tablespoon parsley, finely chopped
Salt and freshly ground pepper to taste

1.   Using a mandoline or a vegetable slicer, shred the carrots, turnips, and zucchini.

2.   In a large nonstick skillet, heat the olive oil over medium heat and add the carrots. Cook, stirring, for about 2 minutes.

3.   Add the turnips and continue to cook for 1–2 minutes. Add the zucchini and garlic and toss the vegetables together. Continue to cook until tender but still slightly crisp. The total cooking time should be about 5 minutes.

4.   Sprinkle with parsley and salt and pepper to taste.

YIELD: 4 SERVINGS

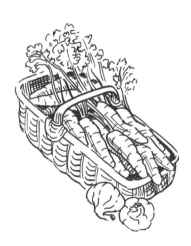

❧ *Another restaurant we visited on the Côte d'Azur was L'Auberge du Jarrier at Biot, near Antibes. Christian Metral runs the kitchen while his wife, Brigitte, takes care of the gracious dining room. The restaurant is at the end of a little passage in the middle of a Provençal village known for pottery making. (Jarrier refers to the ceramic pots.) Christian promised that the dish he would prepare would be deceptively easy, even though the recipe might seem involved. I think he's right. Here's his* dorade *with potatoes meant to resemble scales (I have substituted other fish for the unavailable* dorade*). The only delicate operation in the recipe is flipping the fish into the skillet while keeping the scales of potato intact. Tilting the skillet to meet the fish will help.*

Poisson à l'Ecaille de Pomme de Terre

(FISH FILLETS WITH A "POTATO SCALE" CRUST)

2 medium Idaho potatoes, peeled and
    cut into 1½-inch cylindrical shapes
2 skinless fish fillets, such as sea bass,
    sea trout, or red snapper, about
    6 ounces each
Salt and freshly ground white pepper
    to taste

1 garlic clove, peeled and cut in half
⅓ cup plus 1 tablespoon olive oil
½ cup tomatoes, peeled, seeded, and
    cut into small dice
1 lemon, peeled, seeded, and diced
20 black Niçoise olives, pitted (about
    ¼ cup)

1.   Using a mandoline or vegetable slicer, cut the potato cylinders into very thin slices. They should be almost transparent. Do not wash the slices once they have been cut. You will need about 30 slices per portion.

2.   Season the fillets on both sides with salt and pepper to taste. Place the fish fillets side by side and slightly overlapping on a plate. They should look like one large flatfish fillet.

3.   Layer the potato slices over the fillets in overlapping rows so that they cover the entire surface, with the "tail" remaining uncovered. Rub the potato slices gently with garlic and sprinkle with salt and pepper. Place the fish in the freezer for 5 minutes to help the potato adhere.

4.   In a large nonstick skillet, heat 1 tablespoon olive oil over medium heat. Insert a large, thin spatula underneath the fish fillets. Carefully lift and flip the fish into the skillet, potato side down, tilting the skillet up toward the fish slightly to help catch it as you flip it. The natural starch of the potatoes holds the slices together. Do

not move the fish around in the skillet until after about 2 minutes, when the potatoes have begun to brown lightly.

5.   To turn the fish, cover the skillet with a plate and invert it. Slide the fish back into the pan. Cover and continue to cook for 3 to 4 minutes or until the fish is done. Cooking time will depend on the thickness of the fillets. Remove and keep warm.

6.   Meanwhile, in a medium-sized saucepan, combine ⅓ cup olive oil, tomatoes, lemon pieces (be sure all lemon pits are removed), and olives. Season with salt and pepper to taste (because the sauce contains so much lemon, it should not require much salt). Bring to a boil over medium heat and remove. Cooking for too long will cause the lemon pieces to fall apart. Check for seasoning.

7.   Place the fish in the center of warmed serving plates and spoon the sauce around.

YIELD: 2 SERVINGS

✢   *And then there is Ducasse's vegetable masterpiece. The recipe illustrates his values perfectly. What could be simpler than these braised vegetables? But every vegetable, as he prepared it, was a perfect representative of its kind, not to mention the deep flavor of the broth he used—his kitchen is famous for its stocks. Finally there is the Mediterranean touch of a few drops of olive oil at the very end. Here, once again, only the very finest virgin olive oil was used. To keep the spirit, I suggest you, too, go to the best shop or open market you know for these ingredients.*

Légumes d'Automne à l'Etouffé d'Alain Ducasse
(ALAIN DUCASSE'S SIMMERED AUTUMN VEGETABLES)

3 tablespoons extra-virgin olive oil

1 2-inch cube of salt pork cut into
    4 chunks, blanched for
    2 minutes

1 new potato, with skin on, cut into
    ¼-inch slices

Coarse salt and freshly ground
    pepper to taste

1 large carrot, peeled and cut on bias
    into ¼-inch slices

1 white turnip, peeled and cut on bias
    into ¼-inch slices

1 large salsify, peeled and cut on bias
    into 1-inch lengths

2 garlic cloves, chopped

½ cup cèpes or other wild
    mushrooms, trimmed
1 large branch of Swiss chard, leafy
    part torn into bite-sized pieces
    and rib cut into 1-inch lengths

1 small pear, peeled and cut in half
½ cup strong fresh chicken broth
    (see recipe page 108), or good
    quality canned
5 chestnuts, peeled

1.   In a heavy, medium-sized saucepan, heat 2 tablespoons of the olive oil over medium heat. Add the salt pork and cook, stirring, until lightly browned on all sides. Add the potato and salt and pepper to taste. Stir, cover, and cook for about 2 minutes.

2.   Add the carrots, turnips, salsify, and garlic and cook, stirring, for about 2 minutes. Cover and cook for an additional 5 minutes.

3.   Add the mushrooms, the rib of the Swiss chard, the pear, and salt and pepper to taste and cook, stirring, for about 2 minutes. Cover and cook for an additional 5 minutes. The mixture should begin to caramelize.

4.   Add the chicken broth and continue to cook until most of the liquid has evaporated and the cooking juices are a light caramel color. Add the chestnuts and the leafy part of the Swiss chard. Stir occasionally until these last two ingredients are heated through. Check for seasoning. The total cooking time for the dish should be about 30 minutes.

5.   Sprinkle with remaining olive oil. Serve immediately in warmed deep dishes.

YIELD: 2 MAIN COURSE SERVINGS OR 4 APPETIZER PORTIONS

✤ *In honor of the Côte d'Azur, I put together my own seafood and vegetable recipe.*

Filets de Rouget aux Crevettes, Tomates, et Courgettes

(RED SNAPPER FILLETS WITH SHRIMP, TOMATOES, AND ZUCCHINI)

4 small red snapper fillets, about
⠀⠀¼ pound each, skin on
8 jumbo shrimp (6 to the pound),
⠀⠀peeled and deveined
Salt and freshly ground pepper
⠀⠀to taste
½ cup flour
4 tablespoons olive oil
1 tablespoon finely chopped shallots

1 cup ripe tomato, peeled, seeded,
⠀⠀and cut into 1-inch cubes
1 cup zucchini, cut into fine strips
⠀⠀about 1½ inches long
1 tablespoon red wine vinegar
1 tablespoon black or green olives,
⠀⠀pitted and chopped
3 tablespoons flat green parsley,
⠀⠀finely chopped

1.⠀Sprinkle the fish and shrimp with salt and pepper to taste and then dip them in flour, shaking off the excess.

2.⠀Heat 2 tablespoons of the oil over high heat in a nonstick skillet large enough to hold the fish in one layer. Add the fish skin side down and cook for 3 minutes or until lightly brown. Turn and cook for about 3 minutes more, or until done. Remove and keep warm.

3.⠀In the same skillet, add the shrimp and cook briefly on both sides until done. Remove and keep warm.

4.⠀In the same skillet, heat the remaining olive oil. Add the shallots and cook briefly until wilted. Add the tomato, zucchini, and salt and pepper to taste, and cook over high heat, stirring and tossing, for about 3 minutes. Add the vinegar and the olives and cook, stirring, for another minute. Blend in the 3 tablespoons of parsley.

5.⠀To serve, divide this mixture onto 4 plates and place the fish fillets and shrimp on top. Sprinkle with remaining parsley.

YIELD: 4 SERVINGS

In Marseilles—a rough-and-tumble coastal city that is not part of the Côte d'Azur but was in fact our first stop as we neared it—we chose a spot just outside the center of the city and near the old port called the Petit Nice (a Côte d'Azur name, to be sure). Here you are hardly aware of the cosmopolitan city as you look out the expansive windows at the Bay of Marseilles, its waves crashing against the rocks. Just a short distance out in the bay are a group of islands adorned with crumbling fortresses. This was, of course, the place to dine on the quintessential Mediterranean dish, bouillabaisse.

At the Petit Nice, the chef, Gerald Passedat, explained that a genuine bouillabaisse is made with typical Mediterranean fish and that the soup base he uses is made of crabs and six different types of tiny rockfish. Larger fish are marinated overnight in dry spices such as powdered saffron, garlic, fennel, and bay leaf. But since you are not going to make that particular dish at home because the ingredients will be unavailable, here's an accessible version.

Note: Among the European fish Gerald used were John Dory, rascasse, and rouget, for which I have made substitutions, and you can feel free to substitute, as well, with other reasonably firm, non-oily fish.

Courragou Phocéen

(MEDITERRANEAN SEAFOOD STEW)

⅓ cup virgin olive oil

2 cups potatoes, peeled and shaped into 2-inch cylinders, then cut into ⅛-inch slices

½ cup shallots

2 cups tomatoes, skinned, seeded, and cut into small cubes

Salt and freshly ground pepper to taste

1 teaspoon dried thyme

1 tablespoon coriander seeds

1 tablespoon crushed white peppercorns

2 garlic cloves, unpeeled

1 whole bay leaf

4 stems dried fennel

1 teaspoon tomato paste

1 orange wedge

1 lemon wedge

3 cups fish broth (see recipe page 199)

1 tablespoon saffron strands

¼ pound bay scallops

¼ pound tilefish fillet, skin on

¼ pound eel, cleaned and cut into 2-inch lengths

¼ pound sea bass fillet, skin on

¼ pound red snapper fillet, skin on

¼ pound monkfish fillet, skinned

1.   In a large nonstick skillet (about 12 inches in diameter) heat the olive oil over high heat and add potatoes (well drained), cooking until they are lightly browned on both sides. Add shallots, stirring constantly until wilted; do not brown. Add tomatoes, stirring carefully so that the potatoes do not break. Sprinkle with salt to taste. Add thyme, coriander, crushed peppercorns, garlic, bay leaf, fennel, tomato paste, orange, and lemon. Combine well.

2.   Add fish broth, bring to a boil, and simmer for 10 minutes, skimming off any impurities and excess oil that rise to the surface. Add saffron. Cover and simmer for about 5 more minutes, or until potatoes are three-fourths of the way cooked.

3.   Season the seafood with salt and freshly ground pepper to taste. Set the seafood over the cooking liquid, cover, and shake the skillet so that the cooking liquid covers the seafood. Cook over low heat for 3 to 4 minutes. Do not overcook. Check for seasoning. Remove garlic cloves, bay leaf, fennel stems, and orange and lemon pieces.

4.   Serve in warmed bowls with Parmesan *croûtons* on the side (see recipe page 133).

YIELD: 4 SERVINGS

✣   *Another of the dishes redolent of Marseilles is a fish soup with mussels.*

Soupe de Poisson avec Moules

(FISH SOUP WITH MUSSELS)

2 pounds boneless cod, red snapper,
   or any other white-fleshed fish
2 pounds unshelled mussels,
   well scrubbed
6 cups water

1 cup dry white wine
3 tablespoons olive oil
1 cup leeks, minced
1 cup onions, finely chopped
1 cup celery, finely chopped

1 tablespoon garlic, minced

3 sprigs fresh thyme, or 1 teaspoon dried

1 bay leaf

1 teaspoon saffron threads

2 teaspoons turmeric

4 cups crushed tomatoes

¼ teaspoon red pepper flakes

Salt and freshly ground pepper to taste

1 pound medium shrimp, shelled

2 tablespoons Ricard, Pernod, or other anise-flavored liqueur

2 tablespoons parsley, chopped

1. Cut the fish into 1-inch cubes and set aside.

2. Place the mussels in a kettle. Add the water and wine and bring to a boil. Simmer just until the mussels open. Drain, reserving the broth.

3. Remove the mussels from their shells and set them aside.

4. Heat the oil in a soup kettle and add the leeks, onions, celery, garlic, thyme, bay leaf, saffron, and turmeric. Cook, stirring, for about 5 minutes, then add the tomatoes, red pepper flakes, salt and pepper, and the mussel broth. Simmer for 20 minutes, stirring occasionally.

5. Add the fish and stir to blend. Bring to a boil and cook for 3 minutes. Add the shrimp, mussels, and Ricard. Cook for 5 minutes. Check for seasoning and remove thyme sprigs and bay leaf. Sprinkle with parsley and serve piping hot with *croûtons* on the side (see recipe page 133).

YIELD: 10 SERVINGS

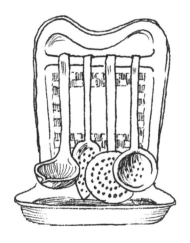

❧ *Anywhere along the sunny coast of France you are likely to be overtaken by the desire for a really good* sorbet. *This fits the bill.*

Sorbet au Citron avec Pamplemousse
(LEMON SHERBET WITH GRAPEFRUIT)

2 cups plus 2 tablespoons sugar
4 cups water
Grated rind of 2 lemons
2½ cups fresh lemon juice

2 large, juicy grapefruits, peeled and
   cut into sections
¼ cup vodka
Fresh mint leaves for garnish

1.   Combine 2 cups of sugar with the water in a saucepan and boil for 5 minutes, stirring to dissolve. Add the lemon rinds and juice and allow to cool. Chill thoroughly.

2.   Pour the mixture into the container of an electric or hand-cranked ice-cream maker. Then freeze and pack according to the manufacturer's instructions.

3.   Meanwhile, place the grapefruit sections in a mixing bowl and add the remaining 2 tablespoons of sugar and the vodka. Chill until ready to serve.

4.   Using an ice-cream scoop, place a scoop of *sorbet* in the center of a refrigerated dessert plate. Arrange the sections of grapefruit around it and pour the juice around. Decorate with fresh mint leaves.

YIELD: 6–8 SERVINGS

Rhône Valley

SPECIALTIES

Fresh fruits are everywhere, especially peaches, apricots, pears, cherries, melons, apples, and strawberries

Fresh vegetables and herbs are widely used, notably green beans, Swiss chard, asparagus, eggplant, wild thyme, rosemary, and bay leaf

Lamb of Remuzat, often roasted with garlic, rosemary, and thyme

Guinea fowl of the Drôme area, stewed with wine or herb-roasted

Ravioli, filled with goat cheese and herbs (one type of ravioli, *caillettes* of Chabeiul, boasts eight different aromatic herbs)

CHEESES

Tommes de chèvre (fresh goat cheese, cured for just three or four days)

Saint Marcellin (another mild cheese, from goat's or cow's milk)

Picodon, a tangy cheese from cow's or goat's milk steeped with *marc,* the dried grape skins left after pressing

DESSERTS

Pogne of Romans, a sweet brioche with flower blossoms

Praline tarts

WINES

Fine pungent Rhône reds (primarily from the Syrah grape), such as the apellations Crozes-Hermitage, Hermitage, and St. Joseph. Production of whites is less significant but includes those of Condrieu, St. Joseph, Saint Peray, and Hermitage.

THE ROAD TO LYON

On the way up from the sea and into the interior toward Lyon, there is a point where the south and north start to blur in terrain and cooking; you leave the maritime mountains of Provence and enter the plains of the Rhône River at the margin of the high region known as the Rhône-Alpes. There you pass through villages and cities where some relatively isolated culinary genius may well be plying his trade and, of course, drawing a clientele from as far away as Paris—or New York or Tokyo. Two such establishments, as you near Lyon, are especially startling to visit, disparate in every way except in the excitement offered by the food. One is the Restaurant Michel Chabran, in pretty Pont-de-l'Isère, a few miles outside of Valence. There the fine chef told us once, as we spent an entire rainy afternoon savoring lunch, that he always reminds himself he is running a restaurant and that people show up hungry: "I am not a sculptor or a painter," he says, "I am a chef."

The other restaurant I have in mind is in St. Etienne, a homely industrial city that would attract few tourists were it not for the work of Pierre Gagnaire, one of the most talked-about young chefs in all of France, who assembles his dishes as if each were a brand-new creation every time it is made (and will disassemble it in the kitchen, if something doesn't please him, to begin again).

Gagnaire has been called France's craziest chef, and also one of its most innovative. "Cooking," he says, "is like playing," and as you watch this big blond man work, decorating a dish as he splashes beet juice and pea purée in a swirl across the plate, he does look a little like a giant kindergartner, an extraordinarily focused one. When we visited Pierre it was not long after he had won a third Michelin star, an award so rarefied that only nineteen chefs possess it. (Gagnaire would have made it

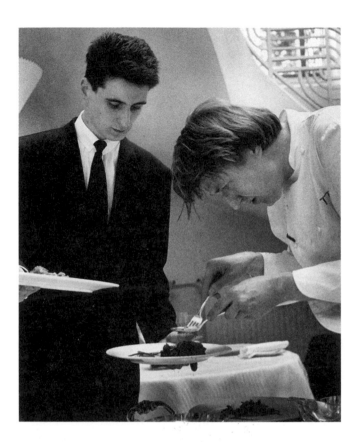

Pierre Gagnaire finishes a dish in the dining room of his restaurant in St. Etienne.

a round twenty were it not for the fact that my good friend Roger Verge at Moulin de Mougins near Cannes was demoted to two stars on the very same day Gagnaire was elevated.) His typical creations—typical for him if for no one else—might include a lettuce stuffed with crab and surrounded by pearl onions along with red currant *coulis* and sour cherry juice. Or his fancy might turn to a *fricassée* of rabbit with cinnamon and fresh juniper, or to cockscombs flavored with honey. He says he refuses to limit himself to the commoner ingredients: "Today," he says, "our garden is the world." When I dine with Pierre I am never sure this is actually French cooking in the sense that I have always known it. It is not simply a matter of taking traditional dishes and dealing with them in an inspired way. No, it is idiosyncratic; it is purely Pierre Gagnaire.

The fact that what he does is so risky and entertaining, while still managing to succeed as food, is what draws well-heeled crowds (the price, like many three-star restaurants, is easily more than $100 a person) to this remarkable, airy establishment.

It is a restaurant in which the columns are hand-painted in vivid blue and green, blasts of color imposed on a basic Art Deco theme that make this an almost unsettlingly modern place. What keeps the flamboyant Gagnaire here in this city of no renown is a bit of a mystery to some. When a reporter for the *New York Times* asked him he said, "It's not Cannes; it's not Miami. Nothing disturbs me here." And I think I understand that perfectly. This self-taught man is completely immersed in his cooking, his artistry, and bland St. Etienne serves as his garret.

Michel Chabran, also off on his own, is, as I have suggested, something else entirely. His interests go beyond food. He talks about his passion for tennis and race-car driving. He intensely enjoys his surroundings, a countryside that produces so much fruit that he describes it as something like the American Midwest in its ability to supply much of France. The commercial fruit and vegetable market in Pont-de-l'Isère is one of the most rambunctious I have seen. It is enclosed behind a wire fence and, every Monday as 5:00 p.m. approaches, the buyers gather outside the gate, jostling for position. At exactly five o'clock, a whistle blows, the mayor unlocks the gate, and buyers go charging through; it looks more like a running of the bulls than anything else. But the chaos is harmless, and it is fun. Because of the agricultural productivity of the area, the cooking leans heavily on herbs, particularly rosemary and thyme, and vegetables: the guinea fowl of the area will be amply herbed before it is roasted, for instance, and when the cooks prepare cheese-filled ravioli here, there is one called a *caillettes* of Chabeiul that contains no less than eight different herbs.

Chabran's restaurant is both rustic and modern, with bare stone columns, but also elegant, ballooning white-on-white tablecloths in subtle geometric patterns. And just because he describes himself as something other than an artist is no reason to assume his food is anything but stunning.

I can well remember, for instance, a fillet of *sandre* (a widely used freshwater fish in France) with caramelized onions and a citrus sauce. The fish's coating was grated zest of orange and lemon and the onions were hidden beneath the fish so that you dipped into them as a sweet surprise, a present. Naturally, he uses fruit in much of his cooking, particularly the apricots and peaches of the region. Since his is an area between Provence and Lyon, Michel finds himself cooking with the butter and cream of Lyon and the olive oil of Provence, often mixing them together. It is, in fact, a combination that I like very much myself—for reasons of both taste and health.

❧ Lotte *is the French name for the monkfish Americans have become so fond of, and here's a wonderful roasted monkfish, served with mashed potatoes, that was prepared by Michel Chabran's sous-chef; it is a recipe that employs both olive oil and cream. Most of the monkfish we see in American shops is sold as fillets; Chabran much prefers to cook it on the bone, which he feels adds flavor. If you would like to do it this way, it may require a special request at the shop.*

Note: The fish broth below must be prepared before the monkfish is cooked.

Lotte Rôtie à la Michel Chabran

(MICHEL CHABRAN'S ROASTED MONKFISH)

2-pound monkfish still on the
    bone, but head and skin removed
Salt and freshly ground pepper
    to taste
½ cup olive oil

1 carrot, coarsely diced
1 onion, coarsely chopped
5 garlic cloves, unpeeled
1 cup dry white wine
½ cup fish broth (recipe follows)

1.   Preheat oven to 425°.

2.   Season fish with salt and pepper to taste.

3.   Heat 3 tablespoons of the olive oil in a large nonstick skillet. Over high heat, cook the first side of the fish until golden brown, about 1 minute. Turn and brown second side. Add carrot, onion, garlic, wine, and fish broth and simmer 2 to 3 minutes.

4.   Transfer the contents of the skillet into an ovenproof baking dish and cover tightly with aluminum foil. Roast fish in oven for 5 minutes. Remove the fish to a serving platter and keep warm.

5.   Meanwhile, in a saucepan boil the cooking liquid and vegetables over high heat until reduced by half. Stir in the remaining olive oil to bind the sauce.

6.   Spoon sauce and vegetables over fish and serve with mashed potatoes (see recipe page 199).

YIELD: 4 SERVINGS

Fumet de Poisson

(FISH BROTH)

3 pounds fresh fish bones, including
   the head but with gills removed
6 cups water
1 cup dry white wine
1 cup sliced onions
1½ cups sliced celery

1 cup sliced leeks, green portion only
4 sprigs fresh parsley
1 bay leaf
1 teaspoon dried thyme
6 whole peppercorns

1.   Chop the fish bones.

2.   Combine all the ingredients in a kettle or saucepan. Bring the mixture to a boil and simmer for 20 minutes. Strain and discard the solids. Leftover stock can be frozen.

YIELD: 6 CUPS

✻   *Chabran's inclination to mix olive oil and cream is reflected in this version of mashed potatoes.*

Purée de Pommes de Terre à l'Huile d'Olive

(MASHED POTATOES WITH OLIVE OIL)

1½ pounds Idaho or Washington
   State potatoes, peeled and cut
   into 2-inch cubes
2 cups milk, or enough to cover
Salt to taste

½ cup heavy cream
⅓ cup olive oil
Freshly grated nutmeg to taste
Freshly ground white pepper
   to taste

1.   Place the potatoes and milk, salted to taste, in a large saucepan. Bring to a boil. Reduce to a simmer, cover, and cook 25 minutes.

2.   Strain the potatoes and reserve the milk. Put the potatoes through a food mill or ricer and transfer to a large saucepan.

3.   Heat the cream and olive oil in a small saucepan and then add them to the potatoes, stirring well with a wooden spatula. To obtain a looser consistency, stir in some of the reserved hot milk.

4.   Season with grated nutmeg, salt, and freshly ground pepper. Serve hot.

YIELD: 4 SERVINGS

❧ *In Chabran's fruit-rich region, we of course had to do something interesting with peaches and here they are,* flambéed *and garnished with fresh mint.*

Pêches Flambées au Grand Marnier
(PEACHES FLAMBÉED WITH GRAND MARNIER)

5 large ripe peaches, peeled, pitted, and halved
3 teaspoons fresh lemon juice
4 tablespoons Grand Marnier

½ cup sugar
2 tablespoons butter
¼ cup water
4 sprigs fresh mint, for garnish

1.   Sprinkle the peach halves with 1 teaspoon of the lemon juice to prevent them from discoloring.

2.   To prepare a *coulis,* place 2 peach halves, 1 teaspoon lemon juice, 2 tablespoons Grand Marnier, and ¼ cup sugar in a food processor and blend until smooth.

3.   Place the butter and remaining sugar and lemon juice in a nonstick skillet large enough to hold the 8 remaining peach halves in a single layer. Cook, stirring, over medium heat until the sugar is completely dissolved. Add the peaches, rounded side down, and cook over low heat for 10 minutes. When the sugar begins to caramelize, swirl in the water and continue to cook for 2 to 3 minutes, until the liquid reaches a thick, syrupy consistency.

4.   Add the remaining Grand Marnier and *flambé* the peaches.

5.   Place 2 peach halves on each plate, spoon the *coulis* around them, and garnish with sprigs of fresh mint. Serve warm.

YIELD: 4 SERVINGS

✤ *Pierre Gagnaire composed the following striped bass dish with its array of vegetables, fruit, and juices. It looks more complicated than it is because it really is an assemblage, a spontaneous work of art that is in fact marvelous to behold—as well as to eat. The recipe is for two servings, which makes a certain sense if you intend to try it for an intimate dinner.*

The pea purée and beet juice garnishes should be prepared in advance.

Bar Façon Gagnaire

(SEA BASS WITH A PURÉE OF SWEET PEAS AND BEET JUICE)

PURÉE OF SWEET PEAS FOR GARNISH:

1½ cups sweet peas
Salt to taste
1 cup fresh chicken broth (see recipe
    page 108), or good quality canned

¼ cup milk
Freshly ground white pepper to taste
4 tablespoons butter

1.   Place the peas, along with salt to taste and chicken broth to cover, in a small saucepan. Bring to a boil. Simmer for 2 minutes. Strain, reserving the cooking liquid.

2.   Set aside ¾ cup of the blanched peas to be used in the assembly (recipe follows).

3.   In a food processor, place the remaining ¾ cup peas, the milk, enough of the reserved cooking liquid to cover, and salt and freshly ground white pepper to taste, and process to a fine purée.

4.   In a small saucepan, cook the purée over medium-high heat for about 2 minutes. Add butter, stirring with a wire whisk. Cover and keep warm.

YIELD: ABOUT ¾ CUP

BEET JUICE FOR GARNISH:

2 tablespoons butter
3 small beets (about 1½ inches in
    diameter), peeled and thinly
    sliced

¾ cup fresh chicken broth (see recipe
    page 108), or good quality canned
Salt and freshly ground white
    pepper to taste

1.   Melt 1 tablespoon of the butter in a small saucepan. Add beets and cook, stir-

ring, until wilted. Add chicken broth and continue to cook for about 3 minutes. Season with salt and freshly ground white pepper to taste.

2. Strain through a fine sieve or cheesecloth, pressing the beets to extract as much liquid as possible. Return the beet juice to the saucepan. (The cooked beets can be reserved for another use.)

3. Bring the beet juice to a boil and simmer for 2 minutes. Remove from heat and swirl in the remaining butter. Cover and keep warm.

YIELD: ½ CUP

BASE FOR POACHING BROTH:

1 cup red muscat grapes, cut in half
½ cup freshly squeezed grapefruit
    juice, with pulp

¼ cup water

1. Purée grapes, grapefruit juice, and water in a food processor.
2. Strain and transfer the liquid to small saucepan.

YIELD: ABOUT 1¼ CUPS

MAIN INGREDIENTS FOR ASSEMBLY:

1 small white cabbage, cored,
    and outer leaves removed
1 teaspoon mild curry powder
1 teaspoon pink peppercorns
2 whole cloves
12 whole almonds, shelled and
    blanched
½ cup butter
Salt and freshly ground white
    pepper to taste

2 boneless sea bass fillets with skin
    on, 1 pound total (red snapper,
    striped bass, or any non-oily fish
    may be substituted)
½ cup white seedless grapes
2 sprigs whole chives plus 2 table-
    spoons finely chopped for garnish

1. Separate 4 good-looking, intact leaves from the cabbage and place them in a saucepan with water to cover and salt and pepper to taste. The leaves should be a little larger than the fish fillets. Bring to a boil and simmer until wilted. Remove and reserve (save the remainder of the cabbage for another use).

2. In a small saucepan combine poaching broth, curry powder, pink peppercorns, cloves, and almonds. Bring to a boil and whisk in the butter. Season with salt and freshly ground white pepper to taste.

3. In a small roasting pan large enough to hold the fillets in a single layer, place

fillets skin side up and season on both sides with salt and freshly ground white pepper to taste. Cover the fillets with the blanched cabbage leaves and the poaching broth mixture.

4. Set the roasting pan into a larger roasting pan big enough to hold it along with 1 inch of hot water. Cover both pans tightly with foil. Bring to a boil and cook for 3 minutes. Turn the fillets and cook 3 minutes more or until done. Do not overcook. Check for seasoning.

5. Meanwhile, in a small saucepan combine the reserved blanched peas and the grapes. Heat briefly and add whole sprigs of chives.

6. Place a cabbage leaf on each warmed plate. Lay a fillet over each, and top with remaining cabbage leaves. Divide almonds equally over each fillet and spoon 4 tablespoons of poaching liquid over them. Sprinkle pea and grape mixture on top, carefully arranging the chive sprigs.

7. With a soup spoon drizzle pea purée and beet juices separately around fish to form a decorative pattern. Sprinkle with chopped chives.

YIELD: 2 SERVINGS

⚜ *After we left Gagnaire's unusual world of cooking, we headed back to a charming little place called the Hostellerie du Bois Prieur in Cottance, not far from Lyon. It's run by a young couple, Jean-Louis Bonnard and his wife, Hélène. The hotel is situated in a romantically beautiful, lonely spot in the middle of hills and endless vistas. A good way to get there is by private plane, if you happen to be a pilot, which Jean-Louis is. (He created his own landing strip on a steep hillside; so he lands by going uphill to slow up and takes off whooshing downhill.) We drove. That night I was craving a good old-fashioned chicken in the pot, which I cooked in the fireplace that opens onto the dining room, and here it is, along with the assumption that you'll be using a stove.*

Poule au Pot
(CHICKEN IN THE POT)

2 3- to 4-pound chickens
3 quarts water

Salt to taste
2 veal bones, cracked

2 cups white wine
Bouquet garni tied together with
    string and consisting of:
    4 sprigs fresh parsley, or
      1 teaspoon dried
    4 sprigs fresh thyme, or
      1 teaspoon dried
    2 bay leaves
2 medium onions, cut in half and

each half stuck with a clove at
    the ends
2 garlic cloves, peeled
6 whole peppercorns
2 large leeks, cleaned and cut into
    1-inch lengths
10 large carrots, peeled and left whole
8 white turnips, peeled and left whole
¾ cup parboiled (converted) rice

1.   Cut each chicken into 10 serving pieces (including the backs, which should be cut into 3 pieces each). Remove and reserve the wing tips.

2.   In a large pot combine the water, salt to taste, veal bones, wing tips, wine, and *bouquet garni*. Bring to a boil.

3.   Add the chicken pieces, onions stuck with cloves, garlic, and peppercorns. Return the soup to a boil, and add the vegetables. Simmer for 20 minutes.

4.   Add the rice and continue simmering for an additional 15 minutes, being careful not to overcook.

5.   Remove and discard the *bouquet garni* and the cloves from the onions. Chop the onions coarsely and return them to the pot. Check for seasoning.

6.   Serve in large, warmed soup plates with plenty of broth spooned over the chicken and vegetables.

YIELD: 8 SERVINGS

Lyon

SPECIALTIES

Tripe, served as the dish called *gras double,* cooked twice, flavored with wine, onions, and tomatoes
Chicken, from nearby Bresse, often poached
Fromage Blanc aux fines herbes, a soft fresh cheese, mixed with herbs
Salade Lyonnaise, comprising eggs, bacon, and greens
Dandelion salads
Quenelles Sauce Nantua, fish dumplings in a crayfish sauce
Onions, with calf's liver and many other dishes
Meat *pâtés* of many varieties, often in rustic versions
Veau sous la mère, tender veal fed only on its mother's milk
Pêches de vignes, red-skinned and red-fleshed peaches

DESSERTS

Chocolate truffles, and countless other chocolate concoctions

WINES

Beaujolais is not far away and is favored, but so are other wines
from Burgundy and from Bordeaux

THE BIG APPETITE

Although I have often been to Lyon, perhaps the most admired restaurant city in France—a place that has sent off so many of its chefs as missionaries to the rest of the world—I had never seen anyone there quite like Jean-Paul Lacombe. A soft-spoken, intense man who has done as much for Lyon as it has done for him, Jean-Paul is, I believe, the single most important restaurateur in the city. He is the proprietor of the famed Léon de Lyon as well as four flourishing bistros. He was instrumental in converting a dreary red-light district along the rue Mercière into a vibrant showcase for small restaurants and cafés, warmly lit and friendly, suggesting something like the Left Bank of Paris. One of Jean-Paul's establishments, Le Bistrot de Lyon, is in a building that was once, naturally enough, a brothel. Then, I suppose, the clientele carried on its business as privately as possible; today, it's the spot where people go to see and be seen.

During one of the brilliant days we spent in Lyon, Jean-Paul and I strolled through the outdoor market of the Quai St. Antoine, overlooking the banks of the Saône River (both it and the Rhône wind through Lyon) and the indoor market, Les Halles. Jean-Paul conveys a kind of controlled casualness. On this day, wearing a white sweater and pleated blue slacks, his thinning brown hair falling across his forehead, he moved from stall to stall in the market in his low-key, generous-spirited way, greeting the vendors like the old friends they are. At one outdoor stall, I got to meet Lucien, a merchant who specializes in *pêches de vigne,* flavorful peaches that make a particular impression because their light-colored fuzz is so stark against their reddish skin, and the skin in turn echoes their red insides. The reason for the *vigne* in their name is that historically they were grown in vineyards (but Lucien says they no longer are). At another stall, this one at Les Halles, I met a man named Jacques,

*A young American cook
who found a job in the
prestigious kitchen of Léon
de Lyon*

the butcher known for his *veau sous la mère,* veal from calves fed only with their own
mother's milk.

Touring Lyon this way you quickly get the central idea about its consummate
culinary success. The food that is available here draws from the variety and ampli-
tude of the produce all around the city: chickens from Bresse, vegetables from the
Rhône Valley, the wine of Beaujolais and Burgundy. It is as if Lyon were actually at
the mouth of the horn of plenty and all the fruits of the fertile neighboring regions
just came cascading out right here. Certainly, it helped that Fernand Point, one of
the seminal French cooks of all time, once practiced his trade just outside Lyon in
Vienne at La Pyramide (since his death the establishment has lost much of its lus-
ter). His influence, bringing subtlety to naturally heavy foods, refined all of Lyonnaise cooking for miles around.

Another important factor is that Lyon has always been an international cross-

roads. Merchants and warriors have been passing through for more than 2,000 years, sometimes stopping for a while, bearing with them their ideas, their wares, their foods. One of the most important develop-

The bistros of Lyon have given new life to the city.

ments—because it contributed greatly to the prosperity of this city—was the introduction of the silk industry by Italian refugees fleeing the civil wars of the fifteenth century.

A tradition of the silkworkers that has been pretty much lost in the bustle of modern life is the *mâchon,* a mid-morning meal made up primarily of inexpensive cuts of meat, *les bas morceaux.* It was meant to keep the workers, who had been on the job since 5:00 a.m., going strong until lunchtime. Jean-Paul organized a *mâchon* for us, to give us a sense of the past. One typical Lyonnaise dish was the *gras double,* made from four different parts of the cow's stomach and simmered for hours with onions, tomatoes, and white wine. It requires extraordinarily lengthy cooking to be tender. It cooks for two different periods of six hours each. In the first stage, it in effect creates its own sauce, and in the second stage it cooks in it, a type of cooking the French call *les viandes en sauce.* "Like any good dish," Jean-Paul said, "you have to wait for it." (I don't know how true that is, but it sounded appropriate just then.)

In that dish, we experienced two of the signature elements of Lyonnaise cooking, organ meats and onions. I can't say that the onions here are better than elsewhere in France (and maybe they aren't even used in any greater quantity) but long ago the people of Lyon came to realize that the common onion had the versatility of a piano—in the music of cooking, it can blend with almost any score or take the dominant role—so virtually any dish called Lyonnaise will contain these cherished onions.

They eat big in Lyon. We also had a variety of spectacular sausages and something amusing called *la cervelle de canut,* literally, "silkworkers' brains." Actually, it isn't brains of any kind, much less a silkworker's. It is a dish common to the area comprised of the soft, young cheese called *fromage blanc,* seasoned with shallots, *fines herbes,* oil, vinegar, and salt and pepper—a simple combination that in one variant or another has always been a favorite of mine. (Regrettably, *fromage blanc* is hard to find in the United States, but a fair substitute can be made by combining equal parts cottage cheese and plain yogurt or sour cream and blending well with a whisk; see recipe page 214.)

The food writer Waverley Root once complained that Lyon struck him as too bourgeois: "while providing superlative food on the luxurious level to those able to pay for it, it offers somewhat contemptuous treatment of the lower classes." If that were ever as true as Root contended, it does not seem to be now. The newer bistros have taken hold with their reasonably priced and straightforward food. And some of the older, still simpler blue-collar establishments—called *bouchons*—today attract people from all strata of life (often welcoming foreigners as if they were regulars), and the workers of the past who may have been treated poorly then are, if anything, idealized now.

Although the silkmakers are long gone, at Léon de Lyon the waiters pay daily tribute to the silk trade, wearing leather aprons like the workers once wore. It is more than simply a matter of show. When we had dinner there, a blend of the sensibilities associated with prosperity and those linked to the tastes of the working class could be seen clearly in the cooking: the delicate elegance of a terrine of leeks and cheese with truffles, for example, alongside the organ meats—beautifully prepared tripe and liver.

⚜ This is a version of the leek and cheese terrine Jean-Paul Lacombe served us at his restaurant. A significant difference is that he serves it with a truffle vinaigrette, and I want to make it more accessible than that, so I offer instead a straightforward, less extravagant vinaigrette.

Note: Jean-Paul unmolds the terrine and then wraps it in cellophane to hold it together as he slices it.

Terrine de Poireaux au Fromage de Chèvre à la Jean-Paul Lacombe
(JEAN-PAUL LACOMBE'S TERRINE OF LEEKS AND GOAT CHEESE)

4 cups fresh chicken broth (see recipe page 108), or good quality canned

Bouquet garni, tied together with string and consisting of:
   6 sprigs parsley
   3 sprigs thyme
   2 bay leaves

2 carrots, coarsely chopped

1 large onion, cut in half

10 cloves, 5 each stuck into the onion halves

2 whole shallots, peeled

2 garlic cloves, peeled

Salt and freshly ground pepper to taste

12 large leeks

1 tablespoon powdered gelatin

2 tablespoons parsley, chopped

2 tablespoons chives, finely chopped

2 tablespoons chervil, finely chopped

½ cup tomatoes, peeled, seeded, and diced

¾ pound goat cheese, softened to room temperature

1.   In a large pot, bring to a boil the chicken broth, *bouquet garni,* carrots, onion halves stuck with cloves, shallots, garlic, and salt and pepper to taste. Simmer.

2.   To prepare the leeks, cut away the roots, outer leaves, and the top, dark green portion so that the trimmed leeks match the length of your terrine. Slit the leeks lengthwise (leaving the base intact to hold each leek together) and rinse them under running water to wash away any grit. Add the leeks to the simmering liquid, reduce heat, and cook for about 20 minutes, until tender.

3.   Remove the leeks from the broth. Strain and reserve 3 cups of the broth.

4.   To extract as much liquid as possible from the leeks, place them on a tray lined with paper towels. Cover with an additional layer of paper towels and a weighted object and chill for 3 hours.

5.   Meanwhile, in a saucepan, bring the reserved broth to a boil and reduce it to 1½ cups. Add gelatin and stir until dissolved. Return to a boil briefly, check for seasoning, and set aside.

6.   Cover the bottom of the terrine with a layer of leeks, alternating the direction of the stems and the tips, and brush with the gelatin-thick broth to moisten. Sprinkle with 1 tablespoon each of parsley, chives, and chervil, ¼ cup of the tomatoes, and salt and pepper to taste.

7.   Place goat cheese in the center and spread out evenly. Line the walls of the terrine with leeks. Brush the leeks again with gelatin. Sprinkle with the remaining herbs and tomatoes, and cover with the remaining leeks, reserving 2 leeks for decoration. Press lightly to pack the ingredients into the terrine. Brush with the remaining gelatin, cover, and chill overnight.

8.   Dip the terrine in a basin of hot water briefly to loosen it. Cover it with a cutting board or serving platter and invert. The contents should slide out; give a few firm taps if necessary.

9.   Wrap the unmolded terrine in plastic. Using a very sharp knife, saw the terrine into ½-inch slices and serve with vinaigrette (recipe follows).

10.   Garnish with the 2 remaining cooked leeks.

YIELD: 4–6 SERVINGS

Vinaigrette

1 tablespoon shallots, finely chopped
½ teaspoon garlic, minced
2 tablespoons parsley, finely chopped
1 tablespoon red wine vinegar

¼ cup olive oil
Salt and freshly ground pepper
   to taste

1.   Place all the ingredients in a mixing bowl and blend vigorously with a wire whisk.

YIELD: ½ CUP

Lyon   ❧   *211*

❧ *Sautéed calf's liver with onions is, of course, the familiar and classic Lyonnaise dish. Here's one from Jean-Paul, garnished with sliced carrots and snow peas (recipe follows).*

Foie de Veau aux Oignons et Câpres

(SAUTÉED CALF'S LIVER WITH ONIONS AND CAPERS)

4 tablespoons all-purpose flour
Salt and freshly ground pepper
   to taste
4 slices calf's liver, about 1 pound
4 tablespoons butter
1½ cups white onions, thinly sliced

4 tablespoons green capers
1 teaspoon garlic, minced
1 teaspoon rosemary, finely chopped,
   or ½ teaspoon dried
2 tablespoons red wine vinegar
4 tablespoons parsley, finely chopped

1. Blend the flour and salt and pepper to taste. Dredge the liver slices on both sides with the flour mixture, tapping to remove excess.

2. Heat 1 tablespoon of the butter in a nonstick skillet. Add the onions and salt and pepper to taste. Cook, stirring, until wilted. Add the capers, garlic, and rosemary. Continue cooking over medium-high heat for 5 minutes longer.

3. Meanwhile, heat 2 tablespoons of the butter in a second nonstick skillet large enough to hold the liver slices in one layer. Cook the liver over high heat. It will take about 2 minutes on each side for medium rare. Transfer the liver to a heated serving plate to keep warm.

4. In the same skillet used for the liver, add the onion mixture and the vinegar. Bring to a boil over high heat. Add the remaining butter, swirling it around. Pour the onion mixture over the liver, sprinkle with parsley, and serve with sliced carrots and snow peas.

YIELD: 4 SERVINGS

Carottes et Pois Mange-Tout

(SLICED CARROTS AND SNOW PEAS)

½ pound carrots
Salt to taste
½ pound snow peas, trimmed
1 tablespoon butter
1 tablespoon olive oil

2 tablespoons sesame seeds
¼ teaspoon ground cumin
3 tablespoons scallions, chopped
2 tablespoons parsley, chopped

1.   Peel and trim the carrots and slice them thinly.

2.   Place the carrots in a saucepan and cover with water salted to taste. Bring to a boil and simmer for 1 minute. Add the snow peas, return to a boil, and cook for 1 minute. Drain.

3.   Heat the butter and olive oil in a nonstick skillet. Add the sesame seeds and cook, stirring, until lightly browned. Add the carrots, snow peas, cumin, and scallions. Sauté, stirring, for 1 minute. Check for seasoning. Sprinkle with parsley and serve.

YIELD: 4 SERVINGS

❧   *You don't have to be a silkworker in Lyon to have an affection for this robust, classic dish.*

Tripes à la Lyonnaise

(TRIPE LYONNAISE STYLE)

2 pounds honeycomb tripe, with
   fat removed
Salt to taste
1 bay leaf
6 whole peppercorns
Bouquet garni, tied together with
   string and consisting of:
   4 sprigs parsley
   2 celery stalks
   2 sprigs fresh thyme (if dried

   thyme is used, add 1 teaspoon to
   the water)
1 medium onion, stuck with 2 cloves
1 large carrot, cut into 2-inch lengths
⅛ teaspoon red pepper flakes
2 tablespoons butter
2 cups onions, thinly sliced
2 teaspoons garlic, finely chopped
1 tablespoon red wine vinegar
2 tablespoons parsley, finely chopped

1. Place the tripe in a kettle with salted water to cover. Add the bay leaf, peppercorns, *bouquet garni,* the onion stuck with cloves, carrot, and pepper flakes. Cover, bring to a boil, and simmer for about 4 hours, or until tender. Let cool.

2. Drain the tripe and cut it into bite-sized strips. There should be about 2½ cups.

3. Heat the butter in a large nonstick skillet. Add the tripe and cook, stirring, over high heat for about 8 minutes. Add the sliced onions and cook over medium heat, stirring, until the onions start to brown. Add the garlic and cook for 10 minutes more over low heat, stirring frequently.

4. Add the vinegar and cook, stirring, over high heat for 1 minute. Sprinkle the chopped parsley over all. Check for seasoning. Blend well and serve.

YIELD: 6 SERVINGS

⅄ *This cheese and herb dish is one of the soul-satisfying staples of Lyon. Since* fromage blanc *is rarely available in the United States, I offer an adaptation.*

Fromage Blanc aux Fines Herbes

(COTTAGE CHEESE AND SOUR CREAM WITH HERBS)

1 pound small-curd cottage cheese
1 cup sour cream
1 teaspoon garlic, minced
2 tablespoons chives, finely chopped

3 tablespoons parsley, finely
   chopped
2 tablespoons chervil
Salt and pepper to taste

1. In a bowl blend all the ingredients thoroughly. Chill and serve with French bread (see recipe page 42).

YIELD: ABOUT 3 CUPS

❧ *Good, rustic meat loaf abounds in Lyon. Virtually all the recipes involve combinations of meats, rather than just one or another. Here we have pork, veal, and beef.*

Gâteau de Viande

(FRENCH MEAT LOAF)

1 tablespoon butter
2 tablespoons shallots, finely chopped
1 teaspoon garlic, minced
¼ pound mushrooms, finely diced
2 teaspoons ground coriander
½ cup fresh tomatoes, finely chopped
2 pounds mixed ground meat consisting of pork, veal, and beef, in any combination

4 tablespoons onions, chopped
½ pound fresh chicken livers, finely chopped
1 cup fine fresh bread crumbs
¼ teaspoon freshly grated nutmeg
1 egg
4 tablespoons parsley, finely chopped
Salt and freshly ground pepper to taste

1.   Preheat the oven to 400°.

2.   Melt the butter in a saucepan and when hot add the shallots and garlic. Cook, stirring, until wilted. Add the mushrooms and salt and pepper. Cook over high heat, stirring, until all the moisture disappears. Add the coriander and tomatoes and cook for about 5 minutes. Let cool.

3.   Place the meat in a mixing bowl. Add the tomato mixture and onions. Add the livers, bread crumbs, nutmeg, egg, parsley, and salt and pepper to taste. Blend well by hand.

4.   Spoon the mixture into a loaf pan measuring 9 × 5 × 3 inches. Pack it well and smooth over the top. Set the pan in a larger pan and pour boiling water around it. Then place both pans together on top of the stove and bring the water to a second boil. Cover the meat with foil and bake the loaf in its water bath in the oven for one hour. Remove the foil and bake for 15 minutes longer. Serve hot or cold as an appetizer with cornichons and Dijon mustard.

YIELD: 8 SERVINGS

❧ *I didn't have this dish in one of the many bistros in the city, but I might well have; it is appropriate for Lyon in its hearty simplicity.*

Poitrine de Volaille au Vinaigre

(CHICKEN BREASTS WITH VINEGAR)

4 5-ounce boneless chicken breasts, with skin on
Salt and freshly ground pepper to taste
3 tablespoons sweet butter
2 teaspoons garlic, finely chopped
¼ cup red wine vinegar

½ cup fresh chicken broth (see recipe page 108), or good quality canned
1 bay leaf
1 teaspoon tomato paste
2 tablespoons parsley or chervil, finely chopped

1.   Sprinkle the chicken with salt and pepper. Heat 1 tablespoon of the butter in a nonstick skillet. Add the chicken skin side down. Brown over medium-high heat on one side and turn and brown lightly on the other side. This should take about 8 minutes.

2.   Add the garlic and cook briefly, taking care not to let it burn. Add the vinegar, chicken broth, bay leaf, and tomato paste. Bring to a boil, cover, and simmer for 5 or 6 minutes or until done. Remove the chicken to a warm platter, cover with foil, and keep warm.

3.   Reduce the cooking liquid by half. Check for seasoning. Add to the sauce any juices that have accumulated around the chicken breasts. Bring to a boil. Remove the sauce from the heat, swirl in the butter, sprinkle with the parsley or chervil, and serve.

YIELD: 4 SERVINGS

❋ *Onions in profusion show up in this pork dish; you want to keep in mind that they should be slightly browned to draw out the flavor, but not overcooked or they become harsh.*

Medaillons de Porc aux Oignons et Fromage
(MEDALLIONS OF PORK WITH ONIONS AND CHEESE)

8 3-ounce pieces thin boneless pork loin, trimmed of excess fat
Salt and pepper to taste
2 tablespoons olive or vegetable oil

2 cups onions, finely sliced
1 tablespoon garlic, minced
1 cup grated Gruyère or Comté cheese

1. Preheat the oven to 425°.

2. Sprinkle the pork with salt and pepper to taste. Heat 1 tablespoon of the oil in a heavy skillet large enough to hold the pork slices in one layer. When the oil is quite hot, add the pork and cook until brown on one side, about 5 minutes. Turn the slices and cook for another 5 minutes. Remove from the pan and keep warm.

3. Meanwhile, in another skillet, heat the remaining oil and cook the onions and garlic, stirring, over medium heat, until the onions are slightly browned, about 10 minutes.

4. In a large, flat ovenproof dish, place the pork slices side by side and spread an equal amount of onion mixture over each. Sprinkle the grated cheese on top.

5. Place the dish in the oven and bake for about 8 minutes, or until the cheese melts and browns slightly. Serve immediately.

YIELD: 4 SERVINGS

✤ *One destination not to be missed in Lyon is the chocolate shop called Bernachon, the most famous in the city and run by one of the truly delightful people in France, the eighty-year-old Maurice Bernachon, who began in this very place as a fourteen-year-old apprentice and eventually took it over. The shop is dominated by brown tiles on the walls and ceiling so that, on entering it, you feel a little like you just stepped into chocolate itself. The candies are displayed with great care and beauty—glistening rows of perfect, tiny gems. Bernachon prepares its own chocolate, starting with cocoa beans from South America and Madagascar that are roasted right in the shop. Here is a recipe for one of those chocolate gems, a simple, fail-safe candy if you make certain to use high-quality chocolate.*

Truffes au Chocolat Bernachon
(BERNACHON'S CHOCOLATE TRUFFLES)

10 ounces bittersweet chocolate	2 ounces butter
1 cup heavy cream	½ cup cocoa

1.   Chop the chocolate into small bits.
2.   Bring the cream to a boil and stir in the chocolate.
3.   Add the butter, blend until the mixture is smooth, and chill overnight.
4.   Using your hands, shape the chocolate into truffle-sized drops. Chill until each one is set and roll the truffles in the cocoa.

YIELD: 18 TO 24 TRUFFLES

❧   Here's my own chocolate contribution, inspired by Bernachon.

Gâteau au Chocolat

(CHOCOLATE CAKE)

8 ounces unsweetened chocolate	1 cup walnuts or pecans, chopped
1 cup sweet butter at room temperature	1 cup heavy cream
	1 tablespoon granulated sugar
3 cups confectioners' sugar	Powdered cocoa, for decoration
8 eggs, separated	(optional)

1.   Preheat the oven to 350°.

2.   Butter the bottoms of two 9-inch cake pans and cut out 2 rounds of wax paper to fit the bottoms. Line the cake pans with the paper rounds and set aside.

3.   Place the chocolate in a saucepan and set the pan in a larger pan of gently simmering water. Let stand until melted, stirring occasionally. Remove and let it cool partially.

4.   Place the butter in the bowl of an electric mixer and gradually beat in the confectioners' sugar. When light and fluffy, add the egg yolks, beating constantly. Beat in the melted chocolate.

5.   Beat the whites until stiff and fold them into the chocolate mixture.

6.   Remove ⅓ of the mixture and set aside as a filling.

7.   Stir the chopped nuts into the remaining batter.

8.   Spoon equal amounts of the batter containing the nuts into the prepared cake pans and smooth the tops. Place in the oven and bake for 17 minutes.

9.   Remove from the oven and run a knife around the sides of the pans to loosen the cakes. Cover the pans one at a time with racks and, protecting your hands with pot holders, quickly invert the cakes onto the racks. They should come out easily. Peel off the wax papers and let the cakes cool.

10.   Spoon the reserved filling onto one of the cakes. Place the other on top. When ready to serve, whip the cream and add granulated sugar to taste. Frost the outside of the cake with whipped cream. Sprinkle the top with cocoa, if desired.

YIELD: 12 SERVINGS

Iles Flottantes

(FLOATING ISLANDS)

4 cups milk
1 vanilla bean, or 1 teaspoon
    vanilla extract
1¼ cups granulated sugar
6 eggs, separated

1 teaspoon cornstarch
Salt to taste
4 tablespoons Grand Marnier
¼ cup water

1.   Bring the milk to a boil in a large skillet. Add the vanilla and 6 tablespoons of the sugar. Stir to dissolve. Reduce to a simmer.

2.   Beat the egg whites until stiff, gradually adding 6 tablespoons of sugar, the cornstarch, and salt as you beat.

3.   When the meringue is stiff, outfit a pastry bag with a star tube (No. 4). Fill it with the meringue and pipe it out onto a baking sheet in 3-inch circles to form rosette designs. Using a metal spatula, transfer as many rosettes into the milk as the skillet will hold.

4.   Simmer for about 30 seconds and then use a slotted spoon to turn the rosettes over. Poach the other side for 30 seconds.

5.   As the rosettes finish cooking, transfer them onto paper towels to drain and cool while you poach the next batch.

6.   Strain the milk and remove the vanilla bean (if used). Beat the egg yolks until light and lemon-colored and pour them slowly into the strained milk. Stir over low heat until the custard coats the spoon. Remove from the heat. Continue stirring for 30 seconds.

7.   Add the Grand Marnier. Strain the custard into a wide, shallow serving dish. Place the meringues over the top. Chill.

8.   Combine the remaining sugar with ¼ cup water in a saucepan. Cook until the caramel is dark amber in color but do not let it burn. Before the caramel has a chance to set, pour it in a thin thread all over the tops of the meringues.

YIELD: 10 SERVINGS

Burgundy

SPECIALTIES

Beef Bourguignon, beef stewed in red wine
Dijon mustard in cooking and salads and as a table condiment
Jambon persillé, ham with parsley set in gelatin
Andouillettes, chitterling sausages
Gougère, a buttery puffed pastry made with Gruyère cheese
Daube, beef braised in red wine
Pike cooked in wine or with cream
Crayfish in many different preparations
Snails in garlic butter
Ham steaks cooked with cream

DESSERTS

Pain d'épice, a dark brown gingerbread from Dijon
Crêpes Parmentiers, little potato pancakes
Cherry *clafouti,* a custardy tart

WINES

Great whites such as Chablis and Pouilly-Fuisse
The revered reds and whites from the area known as Côte d'Or, or
golden slope (from near Dijon to south of Beaune), which are produced
by small vineyards and are extremely rare, given their fame
Beaujolais
Crème de Cassis, thick black currant liqueur

HOME AGAIN

Any return to Burgundy is, for me, an almost gleeful reentry into my childhood. I grew up in a village, St. Vinnemer, on the Burgundy canal, so small that you will not find it on some otherwise adequate maps, but it is near the reasonably well-known Tonnerre. And my Burgundian neighborhood, in the grander sense, included places like Chablis (close enough for routine visits) and Dijon, a bit of a trek to the northeast, although my father went there often, always returning home with mustard, of course. We lived the sort of lives in which food and wine occupied a position at the core of our experience. We grew and raised much of what we needed, hunted and fished for most of the rest. It was very rare for anyone, male or female, growing up in a Burgundian village during my time to be anything but a good cook.

On my most recent return to St. Vinnemer, I was accompanied by my daughter Claudia and my six-year-old grandson, Nicolas. Like any grandfather, I wanted to be sure that Nicolas had a visceral feeling for the family roots, that he saw the canal where I fished as a boy and where, in the early part of the century, my grandfather and grandmother worked maintaining the lock. I wanted him to visit the little school I attended in the 1920s and to touch the stone walls of the houses that have always been here. Naturally, I also hoped he would meet some of my friends from childhood, especially Guy Mignard, a wonderful fellow who never moved away. We did drop in on Guy; he is a man close to the earth, and, if I needed any reminding of it, I no longer did after he insisted that I taste a concoction of snake alcohol (an actual snake is preserved in it) that he had prepared himself with the intention of warding off heart disease and who knows what else. Evidence of his outdoor life is all over the wall of his barn, where he has mounted hunting and fishing trophies,

Guy Mignard, a child-hood friend, who has never left the little village of St. Vinnemer

including the jaws of pike, the huge, voracious river fish notorious for its brutal teeth.

The memory of the Burgundy canal has coursed through my mind all my life and wherever I am. But to outsiders, landlocked Burgundy presents a deceptively dry picture, I think, because they just don't realize how dominated it is by water. It is a region held together and given its character by its waterways—746 miles of rivers and canals, once full of commerce and now almost entirely devoted to recreation. To get to the canal, Nicolas and I had to walk no more than a few steps from the house my family used to own.

The latest lockkeeper is a young woman who spends her quiet days watching the passage of tourist barges that regularly ply the canal (Nicolas got a chance to open one of the gates so he could see the water come rushing through). As in any similar canal with locks, the water, as it floods each lock or drains from it, acts as a hydraulic

elevator, transporting vessels from one level to the next.

I spent some time on the tourist barges in Burgundy this time around, vessels operated by Guy Bardet and his company, Compagnie Continental des Croisières, in Dijon. Despite a superficial resemblance, these are definitely not the barges of my boyhood: aboard one of those I visited there is an ample bar, a dining room for twenty-two, fine sleeping quarters below decks, and a kitchen that is much more professional and workable than many on yachts. On the deck are six bikes, so that the travelers can take turns visiting the countryside when the barge pulls into a dock somewhere along the canal. And the barge is so wide that it barely fits through some of the locks, with just about 1½ inches on either side to allow for error. Commenting on the tight fit, Guy, an immensely confident and personable man, noted, "The captain must be very sober." Because of limited refrigeration on board, the cooks make daily sojourns onto the land, dropping in on local markets and shops, to fashion the day's meals, although it needn't be anything terribly special (sausages, salads); it's the freshness and variety that count.

There are no hotels in St. Vinnemer so we stayed in Tonnerre at L'Abbaye Saint-Michel, a regal hotel and restaurant where I also cooked with the chef, Christophe Cussac. The hotel—an impressive combination of the old and new with its crum-

A Burgundian butcher shop extends its own sort of welcome.

bling abbey walls adjacent to a modern steel-and-glass main building—is as fine a place as any to use as a home base for journeying north to Chablis or east to Dijon.

Drive over to Dijon and you will find yourself in the world's mustard center, a culinary distinction that derives from the fact that the town was situated on the Gallo-Roman spice route, and its inhabitants developed a craving for food with a bit of heat. Six hundred years ago, the mustard seeds—which, fortunately, grew wild in the Dijon area then—were ground and mixed with wine to create a mustard. Today, they are more often blended with vinegar and spices, but the seeds no longer are native (other crops proved more profitable). The people of the area neither hide the fact nor, of course, shout it out, but the mustard seeds are now imported from Canada. Nevertheless, the craftsmanship and the care still reside here in abundance, as evidenced by a visit to the ETS Fallot company in Beaune, near Dijon. There we saw the seeds as they were ground by old-fashioned millstones; their pungency filled the air, so strong it made my eyes tear.

The mustard manufactured in and around Dijon has a sharper, stronger taste than the product we know as "Dijon mustard" in the States and it is also generally smooth and lemony yellow in color. (Cold-processed mustard remains yellow; it turns gray if it is cooked during processing.) The assertive quality of good mustard matters a great deal because it is used with such frequency in French cooking, creating under-tones for everything from salad dressings to sauces for roasts. Mustard was so impor-tant in my childhood that my family, like many Burgundians, served it as a ubiquitous condiment, and even ate it as if it were a food all by itself—a mustard sandwich was a familiar after-school snack.

Take a ride over to Chablis and the aroma of the primary product is somewhat mel-lower. It is, of course, the white Burgundy wine they produce there that has made Chablis a magnet for wine lovers everywhere. Just on the outskirts of town are the most important vineyards, those designated Grand Cru, sprawling on a slope that puts the wine at peril year in and year out because, here in northern Burgundy (not so far from Paris), the vineyards are less exposed to sun and suffer lower tempera-tures than the wine regions to the south. Thus frost has always been the enemy; the great freeze of 1956 will be long remembered for the devastation it brought to the Chardonnay harvest. Yet the people of Chablis argue that it is precisely this marginal weather that gives the crisp, dry white wine here its lively character, distinguishing

it from Chardonnay elsewhere in France and the world.

A man with a character lively enough to match his wine is Christian Moreau, an impressive force in Chablis, whose company produces wines at a variety of official quality levels and designations (all of them, even the humblest, are remarkably good, and some, as you might imagine, are superb). The Moreau label shows up in stores throughout much of the United States. Christian's company owns vineyards that produce a Grand Cru (25 acres), another 25 acres devoted to the next level, Premier Cru, and 160 acres for the third level, simply Chablis.

Christine and Christian Moreau behind their home in Chablis

Christian, round-faced and dimple-cheeked, is a big, vigorous man who regularly dresses in jeans and a workshirt and isn't afraid to soil his hands or take personal charge in the fields: in the wintertime, for instance, he has a thermometer in the vineyard rigged to sound an alarm in his bedroom when the temperature drops too low, and then he leaps out of the house, shouting to his crew, "Come on, let's go!" so that they can light the diesel heaters among the vines. As he walked us through one of the vineyards, Christian pointed to some of the older vines, fifty and sixty years old, with great satisfaction because he believes they produce the best grapes as their roots reach ever deeper for nutrients; he showed us how the vines were wrapped in wire in such a way as to present the grapes to the mechanical picker as it came by, with minimum damage to the vines themselves. He said it takes the production of two or three vines to make one bottle of wine.

He strikes me as so expert and so comfortable in his work that it comes as a shock to learn that it is only through the most circuitous of routes that Christian finds himself here at all. His father expelled Christian from home when he was just seventeen and sent him off to live with relatives in Canada because the boy seemed just too unmotivated to carry his weight in so prestigious a family. "You don't want to go to school and you don't want to work in the vineyard," his father said in exasperation, as he came to his harsh decision. He bought Christian a ticket to Canada, one way.

As it happens, I knew Christian's father because he was part of the same 1939 World's Fair contingent that brought me to America for the first time, but I knew him as a great wine man and never really saw the stern side that Christian experienced.

Christian says he arrived in Canada ready to be his own man, to put Chablis and parents behind him, maybe never to go back. He intended to work hard and build a life doing whatever it took. As we sat over lunch at the Hostellerie des Clos he recalled that he said to himself, "Come on, wake up." So he worked as a lumberjack, bought a truck, and built one vehicle into a profitable business. He met a beautiful college student named Christine and married her (she would give birth to two sons), and he settled further into his new Canadian life. Until the summons came.

In 1972, his sister urged him to return to France; she said the family needed him. But Christian wasn't thrilled about going; he agreed to visit but didn't stay, at first. Eventually, he did return, a hardworking businessman who happened to have a vintner's skills, even if he had rejected them earlier. Now, as we sat outside his gracious home in Chablis, alongside the pool, sipping one of his marvelous wines, it seemed indisputably true that both he and his wife were Chablisienne to the core.

When we dined on several occasions in Chablis it was at the restaurant Christian favors, and for manifestly good reason, the Hostellerie des Clos, presided over by the chef Michel Vignaud. Slender, with a huge mustache that is still not large enough to conceal a broad smile, Michel knows how to cook with white wine, particularly this astonishing Chablis, as well as anyone I've met. He also is eager to show off some of the typical Burgundian treats, like a ham with cream, the sausages called *andouillettes,* the custardy cherry tart known as a *clafouti.*

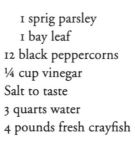

✻ *When I was growing up, not far from Chablis, I often went off with friends to catch crayfish in the streams. Here is Michel Vignaud's recipe for a sort of crayfish stew. There are three stages in the procedure: preparing the crayfish, making the sauce, and then assembling the last of the ingredients.*

Fricassée d'Ecrevisses au Chablis

(BRAISED CRAYFISH IN WHITE WINE SAUCE)

1 cup onions, coarsely chopped	1 sprig parsley
1 cup carrots, coarsely chopped	1 bay leaf
½ cup celery, coarsely chopped	12 black peppercorns
¼ cup shallots, coarsely chopped	¼ cup vinegar
Bouquet garni, tied together with	Salt to taste
string and consisting of:	3 quarts water
1 sprig thyme	4 pounds fresh crayfish

1. In a large pot, add the onions, carrots, celery, shallots, *bouquet garni,* peppercorns, vinegar, salt, and 3 quarts of water, bring to a boil, and simmer for about 5 minutes.

2. Meanwhile, to prepare crayfish, place them belly up, one by one, in the palm of your hand. With the thumb and forefinger of your other hand, remove the midsection of the tail flap. Pull gently so that the intestinal tube comes out along with the piece of tail flap.

3. Add the crayfish to the simmering *court bouillon.* Cover and return the liquid to a boil. Remove the crayfish from the *bouillon* immediately. Allow them to cool briefly so they can be handled for shelling.

4. Reserve 4 whole crayfish with shells on for decoration. For the rest, gently separate the head section from the tail section, reserving the heads for the sauce (recipe follows). Remove the tail meat in one piece from its casing by squeezing the shell gently to loosen it and then pulling away each ring of the tail shell, one by one.

FOR THE SAUCE:

Crayfish heads (see above)
2 tablespoons butter
⅓ cup carrots, coarsely chopped
⅓ cup leeks, coarsely chopped
⅓ cup celery, coarsely chopped

½ cup tomatoes, peeled, seeded, and
 coarsely chopped
1 cup Chablis, or other dry white
 wine
2 cups water

1.   Crush the reserved crayfish heads, using a kitchen mallet.

2.   In a large saucepan, melt the butter and add the carrots, leeks, celery, and tomatoes. Cook, stirring, over medium heat. Add the crayfish heads and continue to cook about 5 minutes. Add the wine and 2 cups water. Simmer for 15 minutes. Strain through a fine sieve and reserve.

TO ASSEMBLE THE DISH:

4 tablespoons butter
1 tablespoon sweet red pepper, finely
 chopped
¼ cup carrots, finely diced
¼ cup celery, finely diced
½ cup Chablis, or other dry white
 wine
1 cup crayfish sauce (see above)
2 tablespoons fresh peas, blanched

2 tablespoons fava beans, blanched
 and skinned
Salt and freshly ground pepper to
 taste
Crayfish, cooked and shelled (see
 above), and 4 whole crayfish for
 garnish
4 sprigs fresh tarragon for garnish

1.   In a medium-sized saucepan, heat 1 tablespoon of the butter and add sweet red pepper, carrots, and celery. Cook, stirring, over medium heat for about 3 minutes. Add the wine and continue to cook until the liquid is reduced by half. Add the crayfish sauce (see above) and cook until the liquid is reduced, once again, by half. Whisk in remaining butter over medium heat, being careful not to let the sauce return to a boil.

2.   Add peas and fava beans and continue to cook only until ingredients are heated through. Check for seasoning and sprinkle with salt and pepper.

3.   Divide the shelled crayfish evenly among 4 warmed soup plates. Pour sauce over them. Top each serving with a whole crayfish in the shell and decorate with a sprig of tarragon.

YIELD: 4 SERVINGS

Burgundy   ⚜   *229*

❧ *Ham with cream is one of those cherished Burgundian dishes. This is a version of it, to be served with sautéed spinach and tomatoes.*

Jambon Rôti à la Chablisienne

(BAKED HAM STEAKS WITH CREAM)

3 tablespoons butter
4 lean country ham steaks, about
   6 ounces each
2 tablespoons shallots, finely chopped
½ cup ripe tomatoes, cut into small
   cubes

1 cup Chablis, or other dry white
   wine
1 cup heavy cream
Salt and freshly ground pepper
   to taste

1. Over medium heat, melt 2 tablespoons of the butter in a nonstick skillet large enough to hold all the ham in one layer. Add the ham steaks and cook for about 2 minutes. Turn and cook on the other side for about 1 minute. Transfer to a platter and keep warm.

2. In the same skillet add the shallots and tomatoes and cook, stirring, until wilted. Add the wine, bring to a boil, and simmer until most of the wine has evaporated. Add the cream and salt and pepper to taste and return to a simmer. Cook, stirring, for about 3 minutes.

3. Place a fine mesh strainer over a small bowl and pour the tomato and cream mixture through it, using a rubber spatula to push the solids through. Return the sauce to the skillet and allow it to simmer briefly. Swirl in the remaining butter and check for seasoning.

4. To serve, divide sautéed spinach and tomatoes (recipe follows) among 4 warmed serving plates. Place a steak over each serving of vegetables and spoon the sauce over all.

YIELD: 4 SERVINGS

Sauté d'Epinards et Tomates

(SAUTÉED SPINACH AND TOMATOES)

1½ pounds fresh spinach
2 large ripe tomatoes
2 tablespoons butter

1 garlic clove, peeled
1 pinch freshly grated nutmeg
Salt and pepper to taste

1.   Remove the stems of the spinach and wash the leaves thoroughly in cool water. Drain well and let stand.

2.   Core the tomatoes, halve them, squeeze out the seeds, and cut the tomatoes into small cubes.

3.   In a large skillet, add butter, tomato, and garlic and cook briefly over high heat while stirring. Add the spinach, nutmeg, and salt and pepper to taste. Cook quickly, stirring with a wooden spatula, until the spinach is wilted. Do not overcook. Serve immediately.

YIELD: 4 SERVINGS

❧   *A terrific dessert to go with any of these Burgundian dishes is a fruit compote like the one Michel prepared for us.*

Compote de Figues et Oranges au Grand Marnier
(FIG AND ORANGE COMPOTE WITH GRAND MARNIER)

4 seedless oranges
2 cups sugar
1 cup water
2 tablespoons Grenadine syrup

8 ripe figs
6 tablespoons Grand Marnier
4 sprigs fresh mint

1.   Using a zester, remove the zest of one of the oranges in long strips. You will need about 3 tablespoons.

2.   Using a sharp knife, carefully remove the skin from all the oranges so that the flesh is completely exposed. Cut the oranges crosswise into slices a little less than ¼-inch thick (remove any pits) and place the slices in a large bowl.

3.   Meanwhile, blend the sugar and water in a small saucepan. Stir well to completely dissolve the sugar. Bring the mixture to a boil and simmer for 10 minutes to produce a syrup. Remove from the heat and add the Grenadine. Blend well. Allow to cool.

4.   Place 4 figs in a saucepan small enough so they fit snugly. Pour enough syrup over them so that the figs are barely covered. Add the strips of orange peel. Bring to a boil, cover, and simmer for 10 minutes. Remove and let cool.

5.   Place the 4 poached figs on top of the orange slices. Add the cooking liquid, 4 tablespoons Grand Marnier, and the remaining syrup. Cover with plastic wrap and refrigerate.

6.   Just before serving, slice the remaining uncooked 4 figs into 5 slices each.

7.   Divide the cooled orange slices and their juice onto 4 chilled plates. Place the 5 fig slices over the orange and top each with a poached fig. Sprinkle the remaining 2 tablespoons of Grand Marnier over the plates and garnish each with a sprig of fresh mint.

YIELD: 4 SERVINGS

✢ *When we visited the L' Abbaye Saint-Michel in Tonnerre to join Christophe Cussac and his father Daniel in the kitchen, we turned out a splendid stuffed tomato dish, with clams and salmon roe giving the whole composition true elegance.*

Tomates Farcies aux Fruits de Mer

(TOMATOES STUFFED WITH SEAFOOD)

8 ripe plum tomatoes, peeled, about
    1¼ pounds
Salt and freshly ground pepper
    to taste
24 fresh mussels, cleaned
2 tablespoons Chablis, or other dry
    white wine
1 tablespoon finely chopped onions
16 littleneck clams, cleaned, or any

variety of fresh clams or mussels
    available
1 3-ounce salmon fillet, skinned and
    boned
Vinaigrette (recipe follows)
4 teaspoons salmon roe
Tomato *coulis* (see recipe page 233)
4 sprigs fresh basil or parsley for
    garnish

1.   Core the tomatoes and cut them in half lengthwise. Scrape out the flesh and seeds with a teaspoon, being careful to leave the tomatoes intact for stuffing. Sprinkle them with salt and pepper to taste.

2.   In a saucepan large enough to hold the mussels in one layer, bring the wine and onions to a boil. Add the mussels, cover, and cook until the mussels open, about one minute. Remove from the pot immediately and reserve. Do not overcook.

3.   Place the clams in a saucepan large enough to hold them in one layer. Cover and cook over high heat just until they open. Remove from the pot immediately and reserve.

4. Shell the cooked clams and mussels.

5. Cut the salmon into ¼-inch cubes.

6. Toss the shellfish and raw salmon in the vinaigrette (recipe follows) and combine well. Stuff the tomatoes with the seafood mixture. Reserve the excess.

7. Divide the excess stuffing into the center of 4 serving plates. Place 4 tomatoes around the center. Garnish the center stuffing with a teaspoon of salmon roe. Divide the *coulis* (recipe follows) evenly around the tomatoes. Decorate with sprigs of fresh basil or parsley.

YIELD: 4 SERVINGS

Vinaigrette Piquante

(SPICY VINAIGRETTE FOR TOMATOES STUFFED WITH SEAFOOD)

Salt and freshly ground pepper
   to taste
1 teaspoon sherry vinegar
1 tablespoon extra-virgin olive oil

4 drops Worcestershire sauce
2 drops Tabasco sauce
2 tablespoons chopped basil

1. Combine salt and pepper and vinegar in a small mixing bowl and stir until salt is dissolved. Stir in the olive oil. Add the Worcestershire, Tabasco, and basil and combine well.

YIELD: ⅓ CUP

Coulis des Tomates

(COLD TOMATO COULIS FOR TOMATOES STUFFED WITH SEAFOOD)

2 large tomatoes, peeled, cored,
   seeded, and quartered
Salt and freshly ground pepper
   to taste

¼ teaspoon sherry vinegar
1 tablespoon ketchup
1 tablespoon extra-virgin olive oil

1. To peel tomatoes, immerse them in boiling water for about 10 to 20 seconds, or just long enough to loosen the skin. Remove immediately and pull away the skin. Small tomatoes will require less time in the boiling water than larger ones.

2. Quarter the tomatoes and scrape away the seeds.

3. In the container of a food processor combine the tomato quarters, salt and pepper to taste, vinegar, ketchup, and olive oil. Blend to a smooth purée.

YIELD: 1 CUP

꙳ *Yet another great pleasure for me in this most recent visit to Burgundy was to pay a call on the restaurant La Côte d'Or in Saulieu; this was the establishment made famous by one of the two greatest chefs of the early twentieth century, Alexandre Dumaine (the other was Fernand Point at Pyramide in Vienne, near Lyon), but it is now the stage of one of the nation's most innovative cooks, the balding, ebullient Bernard Loiseau. He is a chef who believes in lighter fare than is common in much of France. His purées are moistened with milk or water, for instance, and there will be a minimum of butter or cream, if any is used at all.*

Loiseau produces the Burgundian snail dish below with its traditional garlic-parsley accompaniments, but he chooses to purée them to join the snails in a final assemblage. The garlic purée is particularly noteworthy because of his approach. To tame the garlic, he repeatedly blanches it in water before it is puréed with milk. It may strike you as fussy, but the technique seems to work. He uses fresh snails, but canned French escargots *will do the trick in the American kitchen.*

Escargots à la Purée d'Ail

(SNAILS IN GARLIC SAUCE)

24 canned *escargots,* drained
    (imported from France)
1 cup Chablis, or other dry white
    wine
1 small onion, cut in half and stuck
    with 4 cloves
1 carrot, peeled and sliced
Bouquet garni, tied together with
    string and consisting of:
    Outer leaves of the green
      of a leek
    1 sprig thyme

1 sprig parsley
1 bay leaf
½ teaspoon black peppercorns
Salt and freshly ground pepper
    to taste
2 large heads of garlic (10 to 12
    large cloves)
⅓ cup milk
3 cups flat leaf parsley, trimmed
    and stemmed
⅓ cup flour
2 tablespoons clarified butter

1.   In a small saucepan, place the snails, wine, onion with cloves, carrot, *bouquet garni,* peppercorns, and salt. Bring to a boil, cover, and simmer over low heat for 15 minutes. Drain and reserve.

2.   Meanwhile, prepare the garlic purée. Pound each head of garlic firmly with

the palm of your hand to loosen the cloves. Place the cloves, with skin on, in a small saucepan with water to cover. Bring to a boil and cook for 5 minutes, then drain and peel the cloves. Trim the root from each one, pulling gently to remove the string that forms the core.

3.　Return the garlic cloves to the saucepan, cover again with water, bring to a boil, cook for 5 minutes, and drain. Repeat the procedure 4 more times. (As the garlic oil is removed in this fashion, the garlic is finally ready to yield a rich, smooth flavor.)

4.　In a small food processor, purée the garlic, milk, and salt and pepper to taste. Scrape the sides of the container from time to time to obtain a smooth consistency.

5.　In a small saucepan, boil the parsley briefly in salted water, cooking only until leaves are wilted but still bright green. Remove the parsley from the hot water with a slotted spoon and plunge it into a bath of ice water to prevent it from cooking further. This will also help the parsley maintain its color. Drain.

6.　In a small food processor, blend the parsley and salt and pepper to taste. Add enough water to make a runny purée.

7.　Heat each of the purées separately over low heat in small saucepans and check them for seasoning. Add water if either purée becomes too thick.

8.　Pat the snails dry and dredge them in the flour. Toss them in a sieve to remove any excess flour.

9.　In a nonstick skillet, heat the clarified butter until it is lightly browned. Add the snails and toss them in the butter until they are well browned. Place the cooked snails on a paper towel to absorb any excess butter. Keep warm.

10.　To assemble the dish, divide the garlic purée onto 4 warmed serving plates, spooning it carefully into the center of each one. Next, spoon the parsley purée around it. Place 6 snails, flat side up, on each plate over the garlic purée. Serve with crusty French bread.

YIELD: 4 SERVINGS

❦   *After I observed Loiseau at work for a while, I devised this mashed-potato dish, very garlicky, and stunningly green (thanks to the parsley juice).*

Purée de Pommes de Terre Verte

(GREEN MASHED POTATOES)

1½ pounds potatoes (Washington
  State or Idaho)
6 large garlic cloves, peeled
Salt and freshly ground white pepper
  to taste

2 cups loosely packed parsley,
  with stems
1¼ cups warm milk
2 tablespoons butter

1.   Peel the potatoes and cut them into ½-inch cubes.

2.   Place the potatoes and garlic in a large saucepan with water to cover and salt and white pepper to taste. Bring to a boil and simmer for 15 minutes, or until tender. Drain.

3.   Push the potatoes and garlic through a food mill or ricer. Return the ingredients to saucepan.

4.   Meanwhile, blend the parsley and ¼ cup of the milk in a food processor or blender until the parsley is coarsely chopped.

5.   Place a strainer lined with cheesecloth over a small bowl. Pour the parsley and milk mixture through the cheesecloth. To extract all the juice, wrap the cloth around the parsley and wring tightly.

6.   Add the remaining milk, the butter, and the parsley juice to the potatoes. Beat with a wooden spoon until well blended. Add white pepper and check for seasoning.

YIELD: 4 SERVINGS

❧ *Both veal and a crisp Chablis are so light they make a beautiful combination.*

Médaillons de Veau à la Chablisienne
(MEDALLIONS OF VEAL IN CHABLIS)

8 3-ounce medallions of lean veal
  cut from the fillet or the rack
  (each about ½ inch thick)
Salt and freshly ground pepper
  to taste
½ cup flour
6 plum tomatoes, cored
4 tablespoons butter
2 cloves garlic, minced

1 sprig fresh thyme, or ¼ teaspoon
  dried
1 bay leaf
½ cup Chablis, or other dry white
  wine
1 cup fresh chicken broth (see
  recipe page 108), or good quality
  canned
2 teaspoons shallots, finely chopped

1. Season veal medallions on both sides with salt and pepper to taste. Dredge lightly in flour, tapping to remove any excess.

2. Bring enough salted water to a boil to cover the tomatoes. Add tomatoes and let stand 10 seconds, or long enough to loosen skin. Drain and peel. Cut them into quarters and scrape away the seeds.

3. In a skillet large enough to hold the meat in a single layer, heat 1½ tablespoons butter and add the veal, garlic, thyme, and bay leaf. Cook over medium heat for 3 to 4 minutes, or until lightly browned. Turn and lightly brown second side. Remove only the meat and keep warm.

4. In the same skillet, add the wine and stir, scraping to dissolve the brown particles clinging to the bottom and sides of the pan. Add the chicken broth and any juices that may have accumulated around the veal. Continue to cook until the sauce is reduced by half. Swirl in 1 tablespoon butter.

5. In a small skillet, heat the remaining butter and add the tomatoes, shallots, and salt and pepper to taste. Cook briefly over medium heat, stirring only until warmed through. Do not overcook.

6. To serve, spoon green mashed potatoes (see recipe page 236) into the center of each of 4 warmed plates. Place 2 medallions on each plate on opposite sides of the potatoes, separating them with 6 tomato quarters.

YIELD: 4 SERVINGS

⁂ Just outside of Beaune is the Hostellerie de Levernois, an eighteenth-century white country manor with gabled roofs, a formal French garden, and a kitchen that relies heavily on the region's wine and its produce. (While we were there, an escargot *vendor showed up and hauled from his car a sack containing 2,000 snails.) It is a charming, light-drenched establishment where two generations of Jean Crotet's family are constantly developing dishes to make Burgundians proud.*

Note: In preparing this dish be sure to slice the potatoes at the last minute so they do not discolor.

Blanc de Volaille en Croustade de Pomme de Terre

(CHICKEN BREAST IN POTATO CRUST LEVERNOIS-STYLE)

2 large Idaho or Washington State
    potatoes
2 5-to-6-ounce boneless, skinless
    chicken breasts

Salt and freshly ground pepper
    to taste
3 tablespoons vegetable oil

1.   Peel the potatoes and cut them into fine julienne strips with a food processor or by hand. Do not wash them; it is important to retain the starch so that it helps the potatoes adhere. Salt well, let them sit 3 to 4 minutes, and wring them dry in a clean cloth.

2.   Season the chicken breasts with salt and freshly ground pepper to taste.

3.   Wrap each chicken breast completely with a generous amount of potato strips, packing the potato around it by cradling it between both hands. Do not execute this step too far in advance of cooking time or the potatoes will darken.

4.   Heat the oil in a nonstick skillet and cook the chicken breasts until well browned on the first side. Turn and brown second side.

5.   Slice breasts diagonally with a serrated knife and serve hot with sautéed spinach on the side (recipe follows).

YIELD: 2 SERVINGS

Epinards en Branches Sautés

(SAUTÉED SPINACH)

½ pound fresh spinach
2 tablespoons olive oil
⅛ teaspoon freshly grated nutmeg

Salt and freshly ground pepper
 to taste

1. Pick over the spinach leaves and remove the large stems. Wash, drain, and remove all the moisture by placing the spinach between paper towels and patting dry.

2. Heat the olive oil in a large nonstick skillet over high heat, then add the spinach and nutmeg. Add salt and pepper to taste. Cook very quickly, tossing constantly, until the spinach is just wilted. Drain and serve hot.

YIELD: 2 SERVINGS

✧ *An interesting use of Dijon mustard is to blend it with fennel; the result has a distinct but not overpowering character that marries well with salmon.*

Saumon Grillé à la Sauce Moutarde et Fenouil

(GRILLED SALMON FILLETS WITH FENNEL MUSTARD SAUCE)

4 boneless salmon fillets, about
 6 ounces each, with skin on
1 tablespoon olive oil
4 sprigs fresh thyme, or 2 teaspoons
 dried
Salt and freshly ground pepper
 to taste
1 head of fennel, about ¾ pound

3 tablespoons butter
2 tablespoons shallots, finely chopped
½ cup Chablis, or other dry white
 wine
¼ cup water
2 tablespoons Dijon mustard
2 tablespoons chives, chopped
12 chive sprigs for decoration

1. Brush the salmon on both sides with olive oil. Sprinkle with thyme and add salt and pepper to taste. Cover with plastic wrap and marinate at least 10 minutes.

2.   Trim the fennel, removing all but the white bulb at the center, and cut it into thin slices.

3.   In a small saucepan, melt 1 tablespoon of the butter and add the shallots and fennel. Cook over medium heat briefly, stirring until wilted. Add the wine, water, and salt and pepper to taste. Bring to a boil and simmer about 5 minutes, or until reduced by half.

4.   Pour the contents of the saucepan into a blender or food processor. Add the mustard and blend to a fine, smooth sauce. Transfer this sauce to a small saucepan and simmer for about 3 minutes. Stir in the remaining butter and chopped chives, and keep warm until ready to serve.

5.   Preheat the grill and place the salmon on it skin side down for about 3 minutes. Turn the fish and cook it for another 2 minutes. It will still be pink inside. If you prefer it cooked more thoroughly, increase the cooking time.

6.   Lay the salmon fillets on warmed plates. Spoon sauce around the fish and garnish with chive sprigs. Serve with vegetable mélange (recipe follows).

YIELD: 4 SERVINGS

Matignon

(VEGETABLE MÉLANGE GARNISH)

¾ cup white turnips, peeled and cut
    into ¼-inch cubes
¾ cup carrots, peeled and cut into
    ¼-inch diagonal slices
¾ cup string beans, trimmed
2 tablespoons olive oil

2 tablespoons finely chopped shallots
¾ cup snow peas, trimmed and sliced
    in half on the diagonal
½ cup small yellow cherry tomatoes
Salt and freshly ground pepper
    to taste

1.   Blanch turnips, carrots, and string beans in boiling salted water for about 2 minutes. Strain and reserve.

2.   Heat the olive oil in a large nonstick skillet and add the blanched vegetables and the shallots, stirring briefly over medium heat. Add the snow peas and cook until just wilted. Add the cherry tomatoes and continue to cook until they are warmed through but not softened. Season with salt and pepper to taste.

YIELD: 4 SERVINGS

❧ *Onion soup is a specialty in any number of French regions and cities, but we are particularly proud of the Burgundian version, which relies heavily on white wine.*

Soupe à l'Oignon Bourguignonne
(ONION SOUP BURGUNDY-STYLE)

3 pounds onions

4 tablespoons butter

1 tablespoon garlic, minced

Salt and freshly ground pepper
   to taste

2 tablespoons flour

4 cups water

4 cups fresh chicken broth (see recipe
   page 108), or good quality canned

2 cups Chablis, or other dry white
   wine

1 bay leaf

3 sprigs fresh thyme, or 1 teaspoon
   dried

12 slices French bread (see recipe
   page 42), ¼ inch thick

2 cups grated Gruyère or Comté
   cheese

1. Preheat the oven to 400°.

2. Peel the onions, cut them in half, and slice them very thin.

3. Heat the butter in an ovenproof deep skillet and add the onions, garlic, and salt and pepper. Cook, stirring, over medium heat until the onions are wilted and beginning to brown, about 10 minutes. Place the skillet in the oven and bake for 10 minutes.

4. Remove the skillet from the oven and sprinkle the onion mixture with the flour, stirring to coat the onion pieces evenly. Add the water, chicken broth, and wine. Cook over high heat, scraping around the bottom and sides of the skillet to dissolve the brown particles. Add the bay leaf and thyme and simmer for 20 minutes, stirring frequently. Check for seasoning.

5. Meanwhile, place the bread slices on a baking sheet and bake until brown and crisp.

6. Increase the oven heat to 450°.

7. Pour the soup into 6 individual onion soup terrines or 1 large ovenproof terrine. If individual terrines are used, place 2 slices of toast on top of the soup. If a large terrine is used, cover it with the toast pieces overlapping. Sprinkle the toast with cheese, place the terrine on a baking dish to catch the drippings, and bake for about 10 minutes, or until the soup is bubbling and brown on top.

YIELD: 6 SERVINGS

❧ *In Burgundy, when you marinate with red wine, you don't hold back. This pork dish requires a full bottle.*

Rôti de Porc à la Bourguignonne

(MARINATED LOIN OF PORK BURGUNDY-STYLE)

1 5-pound center-cut loin of pork with bone, most of the fat removed
1 garlic clove, peeled
1 teaspoon paprika
2 cups onions, coarsely chopped
1 cup leeks, coarsely chopped
1 cup carrots, cut in rounds
1 bay leaf
1 sprig fresh rosemary, or 2 teaspoons dried
2 teaspoons coriander seed

Salt and freshly ground pepper to taste
2 sprigs fresh thyme, or 1 teaspoon dried
1 bottle dry red Burgundy wine
4 sprigs fresh parsley
3 tablespoons flour
½ cup fresh chicken broth (see recipe page 108), or good quality canned
¼ teaspoon grated nutmeg
2 tablespoons butter

1. Rub the pork loin all over with the garlic clove and paprika. Place in a deep casserole, and add the onions, leeks, carrots, bay leaf, rosemary, coriander, salt, pepper, thyme, wine, and parsley. Cover and let stand in the refrigerator for 24 hours, turning the meat occasionally.

2. Preheat the oven to 400°.

3. Remove the meat from the marinade, strain the liquid, and reserve both the liquid and the vegetables.

4. Place the pork loin, fat side down, in a preheated Dutch oven over medium-high heat. Cook for about 5 minutes, turning, until sizzling. Place the uncovered pot in the oven and bake for 30 minutes. Remove the pork and pour off the fat.

5. Return the pork, fat side up, to the casserole and scatter the vegetables around it. Return to the oven and bake for 10 minutes uncovered. Sprinkle the vegetables with the flour. Bake for 5 minutes longer. Stir in the marinade and add the chicken broth. Cover and bake for 1 hour.

6. Remove the meat and keep warm. Strain the sauce and skim off the fat. Reduce the sauce by half, by simmering it for about 10 minutes. Add the nutmeg and swirl in the butter. Slice the meat and serve with the sauce and puréed potatoes (see recipe page 199).

YIELD: 8 SERVINGS

⚜ *The little potato pancakes called* crêpes Parmentiers *are served in Burgundy restaurants as a savory side dish to accompany the main course or at the end of the meal sprinkled with sugar. At home, the pancakes are especially handy when you're entertaining.*

Note: The variations are endless. To each cup of batter you may add 2 tablespoons chopped chives, chopped ham, or Parmesan cheese.

Crêpes Parmentiers
(FRENCH POTATO PANCAKES)

3 large Idaho or Yellow Gold
   potatoes, about 1¼ pounds
Salt and freshly ground pepper
   to taste
1 cup milk

⅛ teaspoon grated nutmeg
2 tablespoons flour
6 whole eggs
3 tablespoons heavy cream
4 tablespoons melted butter

1. Peel the potatoes and cut them into 1½-inch cubes. Place them in a saucepan and cover with salted water. Bring to a boil and simmer uncovered for 20 minutes.

2. Drain the potatoes and put them through a food mill or potato ricer, then return them to the saucepan.

3. Heat the milk and add it to the potatoes, stirring with a wire whisk. Add salt and pepper to taste, nutmeg, and flour. Blend well and scrape the mixture into a mixing bowl.

4. Add the eggs one at a time, stirring gently but thoroughly after each addition with a wooden spatula. Do not beat. Stir in the cream. This will make about 4 cups of batter.

5. Lightly butter a large nonstick skillet over medium heat. Add about one tablespoon of batter for each pancake. Cook until golden brown on one side, then turn and cook on the other side. One cup of batter makes about 18 pancakes. Leftover batter may be stored in a tightly closed jar for a day or longer.

YIELD: ABOUT 75 SMALL PANCAKES

Charolles and the Auvergne

SPECIALTIES

Grilled meats, especially beef, and beef and calf's liver

Pot-au-feu, boiled beef and vegetables (using all the cow)

Oeufs en Meurette, eggs poached in red wine

Omelette Brayaude, made with potatoes and cubed ham, and cooked with cream

Lentilles de Puy, green lentils in stews and many soups

Cabbage soup (*potée*)

Rissoles, a pastry filled with *pâté* or ground meats, and either fried or baked

Fricandeau, veal coated with a layer of salt pork lard and simmered in a broth with vegetables

Gigot Brayaude, leg of lamb that is larded and cooked with white wine and herbs, and served with beans

CHEESES (MOSTLY COW'S MILK) FROM AUVERGNE

Cantal, Bleu d'Auvergne, Fourme d'Ambert (another blue cheese), and Saint-Nectaire (creamy, thick)

DESSERTS

Clafouti, a type of custard tart with fruit

Chestnut cakes and tarts

Crêpes filled with apples, cherries, or candied fruit

THE STEAK SOURCE

In the United States, the distances are great and the highway system dominant, so the art of the side trip—the out-of-the-way destination along the way—is pretty much a thing of the past. In France nowhere seems so very far from anywhere else, and yet it is possible for two places just a few miles apart to be so different in terrain, cuisine, economy, and even culture that a short hop from one to the other is a momentous journey. No, the side trip is not dead in France; it is almost unavoidable. Thus, on our way to meet my friend Marc Sarazin in Charolles, the area in Burgundy that lent its name to the best-known French beef cattle, the *charollais,* we took a left turn and headed west, back toward central France to the Auvergne region, known for its cold winters, its hot baths, and its rustic cuisine.

Auvergne, more specifically the town of Thiers, is also a center of knife-making—and as much as I love my winter skiing and country food, the passion and dedication I feel for a good knife matches it all. It was the knives that drew me to Auvergne. I have used some knives for decades, honed them, protected them, traveled with them. There was no question, close as we were, that we had to visit Thiers. There, knife shops can be found all over town and the manufacture of Sabatier knives still flourishes despite clear evidence—some deserted forges and factories—that the knife-making business as a whole isn't what it used to be.

I had never seen knives made before, and my appreciation for a good knife would be—if you can imagine it—even greater after I did. The manufacturing process to this day, at least in this place where they have been forging blades for 500 years, remains a true craft. There are 120 different procedures involved in making a good-quality knife, and we saw three of the principal ones, each in a different factory, although the word "factory" connotes perhaps too large an operation. Each was more like a small workshop. The first was a fiery place of forges and furnaces black-

In the tempering workshop of a Thiers knife-maker, blades are heated and then cooled to strengthen the steel.

ened by soot, where green-tinted orange flames could be seen erupting from their confinement. There smoldering blades were transferred by workers from the forge to stamping machines. The work might seem monotonous or dangerous but the intensity on the workers' faces as they perfectly positioned each blade in the stamper before it came crashing downward told you that this work demanded alertness. As each man held a blade in place to be stamped, it looked like nothing so much as a thrust in a deadly battle of warriors. The pounding noise of the place made my ears ring.

After that came the tempering workshop where the blades are heated to tremendous temperatures and then cooled to strengthen the steel. And then they are ground on a stone—just as they always have been. Finally, they are polished, in this case, by a middle-aged couple working alone in a shop on the side of their home, husband

The charollais *cattle, France's most important source of beef, require more personal attention than other breeds.*

and wife on benches, side by side and deeply concentrating, as they sit in front of the whirling polishing stones.

Witnessing this work put me in mind of the clues that allow a buyer to spot a high-quality knife in the store back home, whether Sabatier's or any of the other well-known brands: the steel should be the kind known as high-carbon stainless (simple stainless steel will not sharpen as well and is usually cheap in every respect); the blade should be a single piece that reaches all the way through the handle and isn't just attached to it in some flimsy fashion; the knife should feel well balanced and it should be comfortable in the hand. All of this, reflecting the work of artisans I have just described, is so important. A bad knife will leave you feeling clumsy and is even dangerous, since it may cause you to use too much force or to slip and, in either case, risk a nasty cut.

Jean-Marie Feneon, a prosperous middleman who fattens charollais *cattle for the market*

After the knife-making experience among people working just as their predecessors had in the deep past, we managed to spend the night in exactly the sort of place that made sense, the Château de Codignat. This hotel with a turreted stone exterior and elaborate gilt interior was, I imagine, the sort of refuge feudal lords would have chosen as a stopover on the way to battle, although to hold on to that feeling it was necessary to ignore the view of the swimming pool out on the lawn.

Anyway, we didn't do any swimming because we were hurrying off to our main destination, Charolles, home of the beef cattle the French praise to the skies. I admire it, too, although this animal yields beef that Americans, at least in the past, would find less appealing than the richer meat they can obtain from breeds raised in the States. The *charollais* are big, lean, grass-fed cattle. The meat is not marbled (I realize, of course, that in the United States we are looking for less fat these days, too) and it can be quite tough, especially if grilled. Pan-frying is often a safer approach.

Although the *charollais* have been raised in America, my friend Marc Sarazin (who lives both in Charolles, a handsome village of rivers and churches, and New York, a somewhat larger place blessed with rivers and churches) explains that the breed is not well suited for the mass production of beef required in the United States. For one thing, its head is too large, so calving is never an easy matter and a vet always needs to be present; this is, however, exactly the sort of personal care that the French indulge with such pride, even if productivity suffers.

The cattle themselves—like wine or cheese—infinitely vary depending on *le terroir,* the nature of the land they have available for grazing; even neighboring fields, the French contend, may produce cattle of differing quality. Here, as in Auvergne, there remain echoes of feudalism. The farmers often rent their land, for example, although they work it as if it were their own, and the rent—thanks to a benign governance—is adjusted according to the price the cattle are fetching in a given period. To underline that sense of a feudal past, the farm that Phillippe Pacaud supervises with his family is in the shadow of a fourteenth-century château. The château is mostly in ruins and the only nobility strolling about it these days tend to have four legs.

One of the most beautiful fields we saw, rolling and green and made brilliant by yellow flowers, was off a narrow road. The land was owned by Jean Marie Feneon, whose crumpled hat and weathered cane are belied by his importance as a major middleman in *charollais.* It is his job to take the cattle from places like the Pacaud farm and fatten them (as much as *charollais* are fattened, in any case) for market. The reason his field can be seen so easily from the road, by the way, is that the hedges that were once high to protect the cows are now trimmed to enhance the view for travelers, of which there are not so very many: when you are here, among the fields, cattle, and stone houses, you are in deepest France, away from the urbane world and conventional tourism.

Nothing could be more timeless than the old cattle market in St. Christophe where, every Thursday morning, the farmers leave behind their isolated lives and bring their cattle—thousands of them—to the stone-wall-enclosed yard, as farmers have been doing for 500 years. It is the fifth largest cattle market in the country, and every year 100,000 cattle pass through this village of a mere 600 inhabitants.

Although in open fields one is rarely aware of cows actually mooing, here, with so many of them standing cheek by jowl, the mooing fills the air in a din that can be heard for great distances.

❧ *After the rough-and-tumble of the cattle world we turned toward some gentility—at the Château de La Chaize, and its Beaujolais vineyard, overseen by the genteel and generous Marquise Roussy de Salle, who described the virtues of her Grand Cru Brouilly wine to us in impeccable English. Beaujolais, derived from the Gamay grape (and much fruitier than the Pinot Noir that produces the richer Burgundies), is grown in the southern section of Burgundy in one of the largest wine-producing areas of France (fifty miles long and nine miles wide). Nine other Grand Cru wines emanate from these hills, but the Brouilly is a great favorite abroad, particularly in the United States. It is grown just beyond the stunningly formal Château de La Chaize, with its classic gardens and calm reflecting pond. After the Marquise showed us around, she escorted us to the nearby Château de Pizay, a hotel and restaurant, where we drank her wine in copious amounts. In honor of that fine Brouilly, I later put together this recipe for a wine-rich chicken.*

Coq au Vin Brouilly

(CHICKEN WITH BROUILLY WINE)

1 3-pound chicken, cut into 8 serving
   pieces, reserving the back for
   another use
Salt and freshly ground pepper
   to taste
3 tablespoons butter
4 tablespoons shallots, finely chopped
1 teaspoon garlic, finely chopped
4 sprigs fresh thyme, or 1 teaspoon
   dried

1 bay leaf
1 tablespoon flour
2 tablespoons Cognac
3 cups Château La Chaize Brouilly,
   or other good red wine
1 whole clove
4 sprigs parsley
1 chicken liver

1.   Remove and discard excess fat from the chicken pieces. Sprinkle the chicken with salt and pepper to taste.

2.   In a deep, heavy skillet, melt 1 tablespoon of the butter over high heat. Add the chicken pieces skin side down. Cook until brown, about 5 minutes on each side, over medium heat. Pour off the fat.

3.   Return the skillet with the chicken pieces in it to the heat and add the shallots, garlic, thyme, and bay leaf. Sprinkle the contents of the pan with flour and stir well. Add the Cognac, tilt the pan slightly, and ignite. When the flame dies down,

stir in the Brouilly wine and bring to a boil. Add the clove, parsley, and liver. Return to a boil for 1 minute, then reduce to a simmer. Cover and continue to cook over low heat for 45 minutes, or until tender.

4. Remove the parsley, the thyme sprigs, the clove, and the bay leaf. Swirl in the remaining butter. Check for seasoning and serve.

YIELD: 4 SERVINGS

❧ *Another of our side trips, not far from Charolles, in Roanne, was a visit to the world-esteemed Restaurant Troisgros, where Pierre Troisgros was a gracious host and the picture of the perfect chef, with his small mustache and his toque jauntily tilted. More than three decades ago, in an attempt to use up an overabundant supply of sorrel in his garden, he developed a salmon dish that is simple pan-cooked fish embellished with a sumptuous sauce of mushrooms, vermouth, and cream among ingredients that also include a full two cups of fresh sorrel. It is redolent of the garden and so smooth that it is no wonder it became a signature dish among his many other dishes vying for the honor. As a measure of the regard for this dish around here, the train station is painted pink and green to evoke the salmon and the sorrel.*

Saumon à l'Oseille Façon Troisgros
(TROISGROS'S SALMON WITH SORREL SAUCE)

¾ cup white mushrooms, cleaned
  and sliced
½ cup shallots, finely chopped
¼ cup dry white vermouth
1 cup dry white wine
¾ cup fish broth (see recipe page 199)
1 teaspoon fresh lemon juice

¾ cup heavy cream
Salt and freshly ground white pepper
  to taste
2 cups fresh sorrel, washed and
  stemmed
1 10- to 12-ounce center-cut salmon
  fillet, boneless and skinless

1. In a small saucepan, combine the mushrooms, shallots, vermouth, white wine, fish broth, and lemon juice. Cook over high heat until the mixture is reduced to a quarter of its volume. It should have a syrupy consistency. Add the cream, stir-

ring with a wire whisk, and bring the mixture to a boil for a few seconds (do not overcook). Then remove it from the heat and season with salt and freshly ground pepper. Strain the sauce through a fine sieve into another small saucepan.

2. Tear the sorrel into pieces with your hands and drop it into the sauce. Do not cut the sorrel with a knife; cutting the leaves will give it a bitter taste. Stir the sauce with a wooden spoon so as not to cut into the sorrel leaves. Check for seasoning and keep warm.

3. Cut the salmon into 12 ¼-inch-thick pieces. Season on one side with salt and white pepper. Without using butter or oil, cook the fillets in a heated nonstick skillet for about 20 seconds on each side. Do not brown.

4. Divide the sauce evenly onto 2 warmed plates, arranging strands of sorrel around the outer edges. Place 6 salmon fillets in the center of each plate and serve hot.

YIELD: 2 SERVINGS

✿ *Here's my suggestion for a handsome side dish to go with the salmon and sorrel.*

Riz aux Tomates à la Créole
(CREOLE RICE WITH TOMATOES)

4 cups water	1 sprig fresh thyme, or ¼ teaspoon
Salt to taste	dried
1 cup parboiled (converted) rice	1 bay leaf
1 tablespoon olive oil	1 tablespoon fresh lemon juice
1 tablespoon butter	2 tablespoons parsley, finely chopped
½ cup onions, finely chopped	2 tablespoons fresh basil, finely
1 teaspoon garlic, minced	chopped
½ cup tomatoes, cored and diced	Freshly ground pepper to taste

1. Salt the water and bring it to a boil in a large saucepan. Add the rice and cook at a full rolling boil, stirring often, for 17 minutes. Drain immediately. Return the rice to the saucepan and keep warm.

2. Meanwhile, heat the olive oil and butter in a skillet. Add the onion and gar-

lic and cook, stirring, until wilted. Add the tomatoes, thyme, and bay leaf, and continue to cook, stirring, for an additional 3 minutes. Discard thyme sprig and bay leaf.

3. Transfer the contents of the skillet to the rice and add the lemon juice, parsley, basil, and pepper. Mix well and serve.

YIELD: 4 SERVINGS

✢ *The Troisgros restaurant boasts one of the most attractive kitchens I have seen, with spacious work areas and bay windows looking out over a garden studded with pink geraniums. It's a wonderful place to work, reflecting the kind of aesthetic amenities one doesn't find in the best kitchens in many other places in the world, like New York, for instance. The kitchen is open and flooded with natural light from a garden that was actually created to give the cooks a view. This work area rivals the dining room in its beauty. Naturally, I lingered to prepare a broiled peppered beef—after all, Charolles was in hailing distance—to be served with mashed potatoes and carrots.*

Filet de Boeuf Grillé au Poivre à la Sauce Vodka
(BROILED PEPPERED FILLET OF BEEF WITH VODKA)

1¼ pounds center-cut fillet of beef,
    well trimmed
2 tablespoons cracked black peppercorns
2 garlic cloves, crushed
2 bay leaves
2 sprigs fresh rosemary, or 1 teaspoon
    dried
1 cup dry red wine, such as Pinot
    Noir

2 tablespoons Absolut Peppar,
    or other pepper vodka
1 tablespoon olive oil
1 tablespoon red wine vinegar
Salt to taste
½ cup fresh chicken broth (see
    recipe page 108), or good quality
    canned
1 teaspoon tomato paste
2 tablespoons butter

1. Rub the beef with the cracked black pepper and place it in a nonaluminum deep dish. Add the garlic cloves, bay leaves, rosemary, red wine, vodka, olive oil, vinegar, and salt. Cover and let stand for 30 minutes. Drain and pat dry, reserving the marinade.

2.   Preheat the charcoal or the oven broiler to high.

3.   If the fillet is to be cooked on a hot, clean grill, place it over the coals and sear it all around evenly for about 12 to 15 minutes for rare. If it is to be cooked in an oven broiler, place the fillet on a rack about 3 inches from the source of heat. Broil, turning to sear it evenly, for about 12 to 15 minutes for rare. Cook longer if greater doneness is desired. Transfer to a warm platter and keep warm.

4.   Meanwhile, heat the reserved marinade in a small saucepan over high heat and reduce it by half. Add the chicken broth and tomato paste and any juices that may have accumulated around the fillet.

5.   Reduce the sauce by more than half, stir in the butter, and check for seasoning. Remove and discard the bay leaves and rosemary sprigs.

6.   Cut the meat into thin slices and serve with the sauce and mashed potatoes and carrots (recipe follows).

YIELD: 4 SERVINGS

Purée de Pommes de Terre et Carottes

(MASHED POTATOES AND CARROTS)

1 pound russet or Idaho potatoes	1 cup milk
¾ pound carrots, peeled and sliced about ¼ inch thick	2 tablespoons butter
	1 pinch freshly grated nutmeg
½ cup white onions, sliced	1 pinch ground cumin
Salt and freshly ground pepper to taste	2 tablespoons parsley, finely chopped

1.   Peel the potatoes and rinse well. Cut them lengthwise into large cubes.

2.   Place the potatoes, carrots, and onions in a saucepan with water to cover and salt to taste. Bring to a boil and simmer for 12 to 15 minutes or until the potatoes are tender. Drain.

3.   Meanwhile, heat the milk in a saucepan.

4.   Put the vegetable mixture through a food mill or potato ricer. Return it to a saucepan, and mix in the butter, using a wooden spoon to stir. Add the nutmeg, cumin, parsley, and pepper to taste. Add the warm milk gradually, while stirring. Check for seasoning and keep warm.

YIELD: 4 SERVINGS

✂ *Anytime you are in beef country, there will, of course, be veal and calf's liver, too. The following two recipes are an homage to the calf.*

Fricadelles de Veau Panées

(BREADED VEAL PATTIES)

1 pound lean veal, all gristle removed
⅛ teaspoon freshly grated nutmeg
Salt and freshly ground white pepper
   to taste
1 cup heavy cream, or ½ cup heavy
   cream and ½ cup plain yogurt

1½ cups fresh bread crumbs, rubbed
   through a fine sieve
4 tablespoons butter
1 tablespoon corn oil
1 tablespoon fresh lemon juice

1. Have the veal ground twice by the butcher, or use a food processor to give the texture of twice-ground veal.

2. Place the veal in a mixing bowl and refrigerate until very cold.

3. Remove the veal from the refrigerator and add the nutmeg, salt, pepper, cream, and 1 cup of the bread crumbs. Beat briskly with a wooden spoon until well blended and smooth.

4. Divide the mixture into 4 equal portions and shape into patties about ¾ inch thick. Coat thoroughly with the remaining bread crumbs, shaking off the excess.

5. Heat 1 tablespoon of the butter and the corn oil in a nonstick skillet large enough to hold the patties in one layer without crowding. Brown the patties lightly over medium heat for about 5 minutes. Turn and continue cooking and browning on the second side until the meat is cooked through but not dry. Do not overcook.

6. Transfer to a warm plate. Wipe out the skillet. Add the remaining butter and cook until foamy. Continue cooking until the butter is a hazelnut color. Stir in the lemon juice and pour the butter sauce over each patty.

YIELD: 4 SERVINGS

Foie de Veau Meunière

(CALF'S LIVER MEUNIÈRE)

4 slices calf's liver, about 1¼ pounds
Salt and freshly ground pepper
   to taste
⅓ cup flour

2 tablespoons olive oil
4 tablespoons butter
1 tablespoon fresh lemon juice
2 tablespoons parsley, finely chopped

1.   Season the liver with salt and pepper. Dredge the liver slices in the flour on all sides, shaking to remove the excess.

2.   Heat the olive oil in a large nonstick skillet over high heat. Add the liver and cook on one side for about 2 minutes. Turn the liver and cook 2 minutes, or until the liver is cooked according to taste. Transfer to hot serving plates or platter.

3.   Add the butter to the skillet, let it brown briefly, then add the lemon juice. Pour the sauce over the liver. Sprinkle with parsley and serve.

YIELD: 4 SERVINGS

❧   *In Charolles, two very satisfying classics—you will find them at almost any local restaurant—are eggs poached in Beaujolais wine and apple crêpes (Normandy isn't the only region proud of its apples), and here they are in the next two recipes.*

Oeufs en Meurette

(POACHED EGGS IN BEAUJOLAIS WINE)

5 tablespoons butter
2 tablespoons flour
8 slices of French baguette (see recipe
   page 42), about ¼ inch thick
16 small pearl onions, peeled
2 teaspoons garlic, minced
2 cups Beaujolais wine
1 cup fresh chicken broth (see
   recipe page 108), or good quality
   canned
2 cloves

Bouquet garni, tied together with
string and consisting of:
   4 parsley sprigs
   2 sprigs fresh thyme, or 1 teaspoon
   dried, added to the broth
   1 bay leaf
   1 branch celery
Salt and freshly ground pepper
   to taste
8 fresh whole eggs
2 tablespoons parsley, finely chopped

1. Make a *beurre manié* by combining 2 tablespoons butter and 2 tablespoons flour with your fingers until smooth. Break the mixture into small pieces and reserve.

2. To make *croûtons,* toast the bread slices and brush them with 2 tablespoons of butter. Set them aside and keep warm.

3. Melt 1 tablespoon of butter in a saucepan or skillet over medium heat. Add the onions and cook to color lightly. Add the garlic, wine, broth, cloves, *bouquet garni,* and salt and pepper. Bring to a boil and simmer for 20 minutes. Remove the onions with a slotted spoon and set aside. Strain the liquid into a bowl and return it to the saucepan. Heat to simmering.

4. Break one egg at a time without damaging the yolk into a teacup and slide it gently into the simmering wine. You can poach up to 4 eggs at a time, and the cooking time should be about 3½ minutes. Do not overcook; the yolks should be runny. Transfer the finished eggs to a plate and keep warm. Repeat the procedure for the remaining eggs.

5. Add the *beurre manié* to the simmering liquid and stir constantly with a wire whisk until smooth. Add the onions and return to a simmer. Remove from heat and check for seasoning.

6. Serve by placing 2 *croûtons* on each of 4 warm plates. Place an egg over each bread slice. Use a slotted spoon to remove the onions from the sauce and place 4 on each serving. Divide the sauce over each. Sprinkle with chopped parsley.

YIELD: 4 SERVINGS

Matefins aux Pommes

(THICK APPLE CRÊPES)

3 eggs
¼ cup flour
Pinch of salt
1 cup milk
⅓ cup melted butter
2 large Golden Delicious apples

½ cup sugar
2 tablespoons water
¼ cup heavy cream
¼ cup fresh orange juice
2 tablespoons Grand Marnier

1. Put the eggs in a mixing bowl and beat them lightly. Add the flour and salt and mix well with a wire whisk. Add the milk slowly, blending until smooth. Add 3 tablespoons of the melted butter and mix well.

2. Peel, core, and quarter the apples, then cut them into thin slices. Blend the apple slices into the batter.

3. Meanwhile cook the sugar and water in a small saucepan over medium heat until the sugar is thoroughly dissolved. Do not caramelize. Add the cream and orange juice. Bring to a simmer, stirring constantly, then remove from heat and add the Grand Marnier.

4. Use 1 teaspoon of the melted butter to coat a nonstick skillet about 6 to 7 inches in diameter, and add about ¾ cup of the apple batter. Cook over medium heat for about 2 minutes, or until the crêpe is lightly browned. Turn and cook for about 2 minutes more. Transfer the crêpe to a plate and keep warm. Repeat with another teaspoon of butter and ¾ cup batter until all the batter is used.

5. Serve on warm plates with Grand Marnier sauce around the crêpes.

YIELD: 4 SERVINGS

Franche-Comté (Jura)

SPECIALTIES

Trout and other freshwater fish, which are sautéed and grilled, or served as *truite au bleu* (boiled with vinegar and salt), or made into fish stews with white or red wine; pike is made into *quenelles*

Frog's leg soup
Panada, a bread-and-butter soup

Charcuterie includes smoked ham, caraway-flavored Morteau sausages (called *Jesus*), and stuffed tongue

Bresse chicken cooked with cream

CHEESES

Comté, a nutty, semi-firm cheese used in salads, soups, fondues, and other dishes

Morbier, a spicy cheese with a layer of ash in the center

Vacherin, a creamy, pungent cheese

WINES

Red, white, and rosé from Côtes du Jura

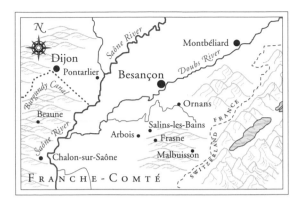

THE CO-OP SPIRIT

As we hugged the Swiss border and headed into the Franche-Comté region, we were on a journey toward a cheese of great character: Comté, a semi-firm cheese like Gruyère, with a marvelous nutty flavor. As we approached, the terrain became wild: there are deep gorges walled by stone cliffs, dense pine forests, and the magnificent river called La Loue, which travels great distances underground before it emerges to carve this stunning landscape out of the stone and through the woods. Here there is marvelous trout fishing, as you might expect, and the fisherman's center is the town of Ornans. The fishing brings tourists, and so do the skiing, hunting, and hiking. Those who seek out this place are the outdoors-oriented, back-to-nature sort of visitors, part of what the French call *le tourisme vert,* the green tourism. But mostly this is a still-secret part of France, with little industry or agriculture. The perfect, tight pine cones, sold around the world for their decorative value and for seeding forests, are among the few sources of income (the trees also contribute to the logging and furniture-making industries).

In the region—its best-known area is the Jura—the people know that because it's such a hard place to make a living they must band together to survive, and they do that through co-ops that produce their wonderful Comté cheese (although it is similar to Gruyère, you will recognize it in the store by its virtual absence of holes). Here, the locals eat cheese daily and don't hesitate to melt it into virtually any dish, from potatoes to salads to soups.

I have a great fondness for this region that goes beyond the trout and the cheese and the pine trees because one of my dearest relatives, my nephew Roland Saillard— young, bearded, and good-natured—lives here with his family. He tends his own herd of Montbéliard cows, which are white with reddish-brown patches, and they

are one of the mainstays of Comté cheese. They are known for their productivity and have been exported to, among other places, Africa for that reason. These cows each give five gallons of milk a day, but as ample *Roland Saillard and one of his favorite bulls*

as that sounds it is meager when you consider that a single wheel of dense Comté cheese will require 100 gallons. I have mentioned the cows of France elsewhere, and I admire them all for one reason or another, but here, besides producing great volumes of wonderful milk, they are remarkable for their almost pet-like intelligence and friendliness.

Back in the States the cows one sees are always so lethargic, as they move sluggishly through their routines of eating and milking, but here on the green pastures that stretch out as calm interludes in the rough-hewn landscape, the cows seem energetically happy and alert and—dare I say it—they appear capable of smiling. As Roland took us out to the field, he first pointed out one of his favorites, chewing while standing under a tree. But he walked on to another cow and paid it more

attention, putting his arms around its massive neck, stroking it, and talking to it. (I do think it smiled.) At that moment, the first cow, the putative favorite, simply reached a point of agitation where it couldn't stand this anymore. I don't want to belabor the point, but I believe you could see jealousy in its eyes. Ignoring the crowd of

An important source of income in the Jura is Comté, a nutty semi-firm cheese.

observers standing around, it came jogging over at what for a cow must be full speed, its bell clanging loudly over the whistling of a stiff breeze, and presented itself for some affection, too.

After this scene, we went off to see where the milk from these cows is transported, a plant that produces the cheese for Roland's co-op in the town of Frasne. There the milk is partly skimmed, cultured, heated, and stirred in big vats. This procedure, far from being routine, requires years of experience, as each cheesemaker gradually raises the temperature in the vats and, reaching into the curdling milk, attempts to determine, by feel, when the curds have reached the desired stage. The small plant is utterly clean; the floor is continuously hosed down so that, at times, you feel you are standing in a shallow river. And nothing is discarded: the curds are separated from the whey and then pressed into molds before they leave the plant as new cheese in need of aging; the whey is trucked off to pig farms as feed.

Next in the cheesemaking process comes the aging—and because this is France that step turns out to be as picturesque as everything else. The cheese isn't simply placed in some practical building with artificial environmental controls. No, the rounds are held in an imposing stone fortress deep in the woods. It was built in 1882, a decade after the Franco-Prussian War, in the hope that it would stave off further invasion. But it was never needed and, in 1964, when overproduction of milk and cheese made the need for storage desperate, the fortress proved, finally, to have a use. Its temperature is naturally cool and constant, like a cave's; its humidity is constant, too. Most of the cheese will remain here—at any one time there may be as many as 90,000 wheels—to be aged twelve months on average. The older the cheese, the more intense the flavor. Some rare few are twenty months old, reserved for the best customers. Although the flavor of the fully aged cheese is strong, it is still sweet and smooth. In Franche-Comté, despite the co-op spirit, the cheese of each producer is kept separate so that buyers can choose based on what they believe to be discernible and distinct, if highly nuanced, characteristics of taste.

❧ *While we were in the area we stayed at the Hôtel de France in Ornans, owned by Serge Vincent, a trout fisherman without parallel. He took us fishing on the Loue; Serge, a stocky man, decked out in his brown fisherman's vest and brown cap, strode into the middle of the fast-coursing river and cast with the fluidity that only the best ever master. Of course, the expedition was successful. Afterwards, Serge and I and the young chef Jean-Michel Tannières, from the restaurant that bears his name in nearby Malbuisson, worked together to prepare the fish. A traditional approach is called* truite au bleu, *which often involves striking the trout on the head to kill it, gutting it with great speed, and dropping it into boiling water along with vinegar and salt; the trout's body curls and turns blue as it interacts with the vinegar. Since it is unlikely, unless you are a trout fisherman, that you will be able to duplicate that process, here is a perfectly wonderful recipe for brook trout sautéed with chanterelles.*

Truite de Ruisseau aux Chanterelles

(BROOK TROUT SAUTÉED WITH CHANTERELLES)

¼ cup milk

2 brook trout, about ½ pound each, cleaned

Salt and freshly ground pepper to taste

⅓ cup flour

2 tablespoons vegetable oil

4 tablespoons butter

1½ cups chanterelle mushrooms, cleaned and cut into bite-sized pieces

2 tablespoons shallots

4 tablespoons capers

Juice of ½ lemon

1 tablespoon parsley, chopped

6 whole chive sprigs

1. Pour the milk into a flat dish and add the fish, turning them several times to coat well. Season the trout, both inside and out, with salt and pepper.

2. Pour the flour into a second flat dish and dredge the fish, tapping them to remove any excess.

3. Heat the oil over medium heat in a nonstick skillet large enough to hold the trout in a single layer and add the trout. Cook the first side for about 4 minutes; turn and cook the second side for 6 to 8 minutes, basting frequently with the oil, so that they brown evenly. Be careful not to burn the skin; that would give the fish a bitter flavor. Transfer the fish to a heated serving platter and keep warm. Discard any oil remaining in the skillet.

4.   In the same skillet, heat 2 tablespoons of the butter over high heat. Add the mushrooms and sprinkle with salt and pepper to taste. Cook tossing until lightly browned. Add the shallots and capers and cook briefly. Add the lemon juice and swirl in the remaining butter. Check for seasoning.

5.   Spoon mushrooms over the trout, sprinkle with the parsley, and garnish with chives.

YIELD: 2 SERVINGS

❧   *Although I mention the fish called* omble chevalier, *which is so closely related to trout that it virtually is one, in the next chapter in connection with Lake Annecy in Savoy, where it is better known, it also resides in the clear lakes of the Jura in Franche-Comté. It is a clean-tasting fish, resonating with the freshness of its pure waters. Unless you find yourself cooking in the Jura or Savoy you will have to turn to commoner trout. So here is a recipe—I'll keep the* omble chevalier *in the name for the romance of it—for rainbow trout cooked in the way we prepared its rarer relative.*

Omble Chevalier Pöelé aux Amandes

(PAN-FRIED LAKE TROUT WITH ALMONDS)

¼ cup milk

4 rainbow trout, about ¾ pound each

Salt and freshly ground pepper to taste

⅓ cup all purpose flour

3 tablespoons corn or vegetable oil

6 tablespoons butter

⅓ cup sliced almonds

2 tablespoons shallots, finely chopped

2 tablespoons Absolut Citron or other lemon vodka

16 sprigs chervil or flat leaf parsley

1.   Pour the milk into a flat dish and add the fish, turning them several times to coat well. Season the fish, both inside and out, with salt and pepper.

2.   Pour the flour into a second flat dish and dredge the fish, tapping them to remove any excess.

3.   Heat the oil over medium heat in a nonstick skillet large enough to hold the fish in a single layer and add the fish. Cook the first side for about 4 minutes; turn and cook the second side for 6 to 8 minutes, basting frequently with the oil, so that

the fish brown evenly. Be careful not to burn the skin; that would give the fish a bitter flavor. Transfer the fish to a heated serving platter and keep warm. Discard any oil remaining in the skillet.

4.   In the same skillet, heat 2 tablespoons of the butter over high heat. Add the almonds and cook, tossing, until they are lightly browned. Add the shallots and cook briefly. Add the vodka and cook until the liquid reduces slightly, about 1 minute. Swirl in the remaining butter. Check for seasoning.

5.   Spoon the almond mixture over the fish and garnish with the chervil or parsley.

YIELD: 4 SERVINGS

⅌   *Another fish of the region is the* féra, *although recipes for it can also employ trout or salmon, as I have in this instance. This is a dish prepared for us by Jean-Michel Tannières.*

Gratin Minute de Féra aux Herbes du Potager

(GRATIN OF LAKE FISH WITH FRESH HERBS)

2 1-pound rainbow trout, filleted
1 tablespoon vegetable oil
Salt and freshly ground pepper
   to taste
½ cup mayonnaise

¼ cup whipped cream
1 tablespoon fresh herbs, finely
   chopped (use any combination
   of parsley, thyme, chervil,
   chives, etc.)

1.   Preheat broiler until it is very hot.

2.   Cut each fillet into very thin slices.

3.   Brush 4 ovenproof plates with vegetable oil. Divide the fish slices onto the plates, arranging them so they overlap slightly. Season with salt and pepper.

4.   In a small mixing bowl, combine the mayonnaise, whipped cream, and herbs. Spread a thin layer of this mixture over each plate of fish.

5.   Place the dishes under the broiler for about 1 minute rotating them so that the fish browns evenly. Serve immediately.

YIELD: 4 SERVINGS

❧ *I could not leave the Franche-Comté region without trying my hand at a couple of noodle dishes using its cheese. They sound similar but as you will see from the ingredients lists they are quite distinct, one with cucumbers and the other with tomatoes and an ample infusion of herbs. The servings are deliberately small because I intend these as side dishes.*

Note: If Comté cheese is unavailable, substitute Gruyère.

Pâte au Fromage de Comté et Concombres

(PASTA WITH COMTÉ CHEESE AND CUCUMBERS)

½ pound dried rotelli or other
    noodles
Salt to taste
2 cucumbers

1 tablespoon butter
1 tablespoon olive oil
¾ cup grated Comté cheese
Freshly ground pepper to taste

1. Bring enough salted water to a boil to cook the pasta. Add the pasta.
2. Meanwhile, wash the cucumbers, leaving the skin on. Split them into quarters lengthwise and cut each quarter into 2-inch-long pieces. Round the edges of the strips to create olive-shaped pieces.
3. Two minutes before the pasta is finished, according to manufacturer's instructions, add the cucumbers to the pot. When the pasta is done, strain it and reserve ½ cup of the cooking liquid.
4. In a large nonstick skillet heat the butter and olive oil. Add the pasta and cucumbers and cook briefly, incorporating the reserved hot water. Sprinkle with ½ cup of the grated cheese and combine thoroughly. Season with salt and freshly ground pepper to taste.
5. Transfer to a warm serving bowl and sprinkle with remaining cheese.

YIELD: 4 SIDE-DISH SERVINGS

Nouilles au Fromage de Comté et Herbes

(NOODLES WITH COMTÉ CHEESE AND HERBS)

½ pound thin noodles
Salt to taste
3 small ripe plum tomatoes
1 tablespoon olive oil
Freshly ground pepper to taste
2 tablespoons butter

1 pinch freshly grated nutmeg
2 tablespoons basil or parsley,
   coarsely chopped
4 tablespoons Comté cheese, freshly
   grated

1. In a large saucepan, bring enough salted water to a boil to cook the noodles. Add the noodles and cook, stirring from time to time, until done. Do not overcook. Drain the noodles, reserving ¼ cup of the cooking liquid, and set the noodles aside.

2. Core and peel the tomatoes and cut them into ¼-inch cubes.

3. Heat the olive oil in a saucepan and add the tomatoes and salt and pepper to taste. Cook over high heat, stirring occasionally until the tomatoes are warmed through.

4. In the same saucepan in which the noodles were cooked, melt the butter and add the noodles, the reserved cooking liquid, tomatoes, nutmeg, and basil. Blend well over low heat and add the cheese. Toss and serve.

YIELD: 4 SIDE-DISH SERVINGS

Savoy

SPECIALTIES

Civet, a rich stew, often of hare
Gratin of crayfish made with the local cheese
Farçon, a sweetened potato pudding
Rissoles, fried or baked pastry turnovers filled with ground veal
Cardoons, a vegetable, often served with cheese
Matefin, a thick pancake eaten either sweetened or salted
Tartiflette, cheese dish baked with potatoes and bacon
Fondues, melted cheese into which bits of food are dipped
Raclette, melted cheese served with boiled potatoes, cornichons, and ham

CHEESES

Reblochon, mild and creamy
Tamié, similar to Reblochon

DESSERTS

Honey-flavored candies
Almond nougat
Gâteau Savoy, a light sponge cake

WINES

Whites include Crepy and Seyssel
Reds include Gamay and Mondeuse

MOUNTAIN PURITY

Even the shortest visit to this region of the French Alps remains vivid in the mind. We drove to Lake Annecy and the medieval town of Talloires, where no road is level until you work your way down to the lake itself. And what a lake it is, dazzling in its beauty and purity now, despite a painful history of abuse and irony. The lake was so polluted in the early part of this century and so unappealing that by the 1950s the citizens knew they had to do something to cure a touristic nightmare. At great expense, they purified it, rigorously regulated the way it might be used in the future, and in the process they made it so clean that not even the tiny plants called plankton were left to feed its fish. That meant that the lake, having been done in by pollution and presumably now resurrected, was still unable to sustain life. It was virtually sterile. It took determination and know-how to induce the water to gain sufficient natural nutrients that it could support plankton again, without allowing pollution to return. Today, even though it is reputedly the cleanest lake in all of Europe, the traditional fish are back—trout, pike, perch, and, in particular, the *omble chevalier,* a close relative of trout, remarkable for its moist delicacy and still rare and expensive, a culinary prize that carries with it a certain stature when it shows up on menus of three-star restaurants at some distance from Lake Annecy.

But there is more in this area than a magnificent lake surrounded by snowcapped mountains. Just outside Annecy, we met one of the most colorful chefs we would encounter, Marc Veyrat, at his restaurant Auberge de l'Eridan. His claim to fame— and it is absolutely stunning to me—is that four years earlier he had been working as a shepherd and now this self-taught cook runs a restaurant that has already earned two stars in the Michelin guide. The sudden recognition set him on a wild ride of

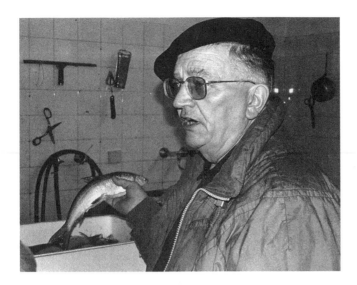

Fernand Bise, a hotel and restaurant proprietor in Talloires, shows off the fish of Lake Annecy.

expansion as he remodeled an impressive lakeside villa built in the 1930s and made it his new restaurant. He still wears a crinkled black shepherd's hat to remind himself and anyone else of his origins.

When you walk into his establishment a sign declares that the chef is a *cuisinier aux plantes,* reflecting his true and deep spiritual attachment to the land and its flora. He still heads up into the mountains in a mud-splattered Jeep to collect herbs and plants like thyme, rosemary, fennel, and celery. The *Gault Millau* guide rhapsodizes about his use of wild celery in a sauté of smoked trout and potatoes and warmed *foie gras* with *aili* berries, a rare mountain fruit. When we visited, he prepared a vegetable ravioli with mountain herbs that was as distinctly his as his own name. The chef does cook with nonvegetarian ingredients, like fish fresh from the lake, but he is so devoted to vegetation that he employs no veal or chicken stock in his sauces, only an intense vegetable stock. As innovative as his approach may be, it is one that fits in well with the current desire in the United States to use more herbs and more vegetables and cut down on meats and fats. His success is the sort that is likely to prove how flavorful and satisfying food can be, even without the large amount of protein we have become used to, and to embolden others to become ever more lavish in their use of a wide variety of herbs.

Marc's creativity, of course, diverges from what is strictly traditional in this region, but for those who crave the old-time warmth of the fondue and the raclette there is certainly no shortage—thanks to an abundance of cheese—of those dishes and oth-

The Reblochon cheese of Savoy, which inspires reverence from its admirers in the region, is made from the milk of cows especially suited to climbing in the rough Alpine landscape.

ers. Most notable of the local cheese is the mild, creamy, smooth Reblochon. It is a cow's milk cheese that was once the peasants' offering to the monks who came to bless their fields. Now, the residents—and I am reminded here, especially, of Fernand Bise, the area's best-known hotel proprietor and our guide much of the time—speak of it only with the greatest reverence: they melt it for certain dishes but even melting it seems a bit sacrilegious to them.

The fact that it is made from cow's milk rather than that of goats is stranger than it might seem: the mountains are steep here, and cows aren't normally built to climb mountains, but those here are bred to do just that (talk about survival of the fittest). They must move to the higher Alpine elevations to graze in the summer and back down to the lower areas when winter sets in. On the cooler, damp days of spring and fall, fog rules, slipping through the valleys and around the mountains, making driving more adventurous than one might want. But on warm days, the sun is so clear and pure that it reminds you of the lake down below.

It was summer when we visited the *alpages,* the high-mountain grazing area, of Christine and André Perillat Merceroz in Le Clusaz. Once there we found we had stumbled into Heidi-land (the region is, after all, bordered by Switzerland)—the farmhouse is a small chalet with windowboxes full of geraniums, and the entire scene is framed by deep green mountain slopes. The cows are moved to the higher pasture in the warm months not only because the grazing is richer there (and will produce better cheese) but also because hay can then be harvested on the lower pastures for the wintertime. André tends the cows, milking them twice a day, and Christine makes the cheese in the evening (she is somewhat unusual in that respect since many modern women now head for the towns and cities to work in other occupations and leave their traditional cheesemaking work to the men alone). The cheese is mild and soft because it is sold very young, after just three or four weeks of aging, during which time it is regularly turned and wiped with a cloth to remove some of the moisture that escapes as it solidifies.

❦ *One of the dishes that is perfect for the cold and rugged Savoy region is the* tartiflette, *a body-fueling combination of Reblochon cheese, potatoes, and bacon. It is one of the few dishes in which the local people allow this nearly sacred cheese to be cooked rather than eaten in its natural, raw state. Here is the recipe that Christine Perillat Merceroz offered us.*

Tartiflette
(POTATOES WITH BACON AND REBLOCHON CHEESE)

2 pounds red potatoes
Salt and freshly ground pepper
   to taste
3 slices bacon, cut in ¼-inch
   strips across

1 teaspoon finely chopped garlic
2 tablespoons butter
1 round Reblochon cheese,
   about ½ pound, skinned and
   shredded

1.   Wash the potatoes, place them in a saucepan with salted water to cover, and simmer for 15 minutes or until tender. Drain and allow to cool. Remove the skins and slice the potatoes into ¼-inch rounds.

2.   In a nonstick skillet sauté the bacon until lightly brown. Add the potatoes, garlic, and salt and pepper to taste. Sauté briefly. Grease a *gratin* dish with the butter. Place the potato mixture in the dish.

3.   Sprinkle the potato mixture with the cheese. Place under a broiler until the cheese is thoroughly melted but not browned. Serve hot.

YIELD: 4 SERVINGS

❦ *When Marc Veyrat prepares his vegetable ravioli he employs vegetable slices instead of pasta and fills the ravioli with as many as eighteen different herbs, laying them out in neat little piles as he prepares to use them. But re-creating it just as he does it would be impossible at home, so this is a simplified version. The recipe is for a total of 12 vegetable ravioli, 6 carrot and 6 turnip.*

Ravioli de Legumes aux Herbes
(VEGETABLE RAVIOLI WITH HERBS)

4 very thick carrots, about 6 inches in
   length, peeled and trimmed

2 large, round white turnips, peeled
   and trimmed

¼ cup of a combination of herbs, finely chopped (use any readily available fresh herbs such as chives, thyme, oregano, or lemongrass)

¼ cup melted butter

Salt and freshly ground pepper to taste

2 teaspoons sugar

18 thin slices of black truffles

Vinaigrette (recipe follows)

1.   Cut the carrots into 3-inch lengths and trim the outer edges of each piece to make approximate rectangles. Slice very thinly (less than ⅛ inch) on a vegetable slicer or mandoline, making sure the slices are of an even thickness.

2.   Remove and discard the narrow ends of the turnips and slice the rest to the same thickness as the carrots. There should be 12 large slices.

3.   Arrange the vegetable slices on the rack of a steamer in a single layer and cook about 1 minute. Cook in batches, if necessary.

4.   Brush a clean, level work surface lightly with melted butter. Lay the carrot slices on the buttered surface, overlapping them slightly to create 12 3-inch squares. These squares will serve as the tops and bottoms of the carrot ravioli. Brush the squares lightly with butter, and sprinkle with salt and pepper.

5.   Place 1 teaspoon of the mixed herbs in the center of 6 of the carrot squares. Make sure they remain in the center; any excess should be scraped away from the edges with a small paring knife.

6.   Pick up the remaining carrot squares carefully with a steel spatula and place them over the herbs to form ravioli. Make sure the slices forming the covers do not come apart as they are moved; they should continue to overlap slightly.

7.   Brush the covers lightly with butter, and sprinkle them with salt and pepper and a very little sugar.

8.   Butter the work space and make the turnip ravioli, using only the 6 widest slices for the bottoms. Only a single slice will be required for each top and bottom. Place 3 truffle slices precisely over the center of each of the turnip ravioli bottoms. Brush with butter, season, and cover them with herbs as above. Place 6 turnip slices on top, again brushing with butter and sprinkling with salt and pepper, and this time using slightly more sugar to compensate for the bitterness of the turnip.

9.   Place a 2-inch-round cookie cutter carefully over the center of each ravioli and press down firmly so that the edges are removed evenly.

10.   Just before serving, heat the oven broiler to high.

11.   Using a metal spatula, place carrot and turnip ravioli alternately on individ-

ual ovenproof serving plates. Set each plate under the broiler, about 3 inches from the heat source, for about 1 minute or until lightly browned.

12.   Brush each ravioli with vinaigrette (recipe follows) and serve 3 carrot and 3 turnip ravioli on each plate.

YIELD: 2 SERVINGS

Vinaigrette aux Framboises
(RASPBERRY VINAIGRETTE FOR VEGETABLE RAVIOLI)

1½ tablespoons raspberry vinegar
1 tablespoon water
Salt and freshly ground pepper
    to taste

2 tablespoons vegetable oil
2 tablespoons olive oil

1.   Combine ingredients in blender for 30 seconds.

YIELD: 2–4 SERVINGS

❧   *The wild herbs in the Savoy region include sage, chervil, and rosemary, so I offer three dishes that make good use of them. If chervil is not available, parsley is always a possible substitute.*

Foie de Volaille à la Sauge
(CHICKEN LIVERS WITH SAGE)

4 tablespoons butter
1 cup onions, finely chopped
Salt and freshly ground pepper to
    taste
2 tablespoons peanut or vegetable oil

1 pound chicken livers, split in half
    and with any tough veins removed
1 tablespoon fresh chopped sage, or
    2 teaspoons crumbled dried
2 tablespoons grated Parmesan cheese

1.   Melt 2 tablespoons of the butter in a nonstick saucepan over medium heat and add the onions with salt and pepper to taste. Mix thoroughly, then cover and cook for 10 minutes; the onions should become quite soft.

2.   Heat the oil in a large nonstick skillet. When quite hot add the livers, sprinkle with salt and pepper, and cook over high heat for 2 to 3 minutes, shaking the skillet and tossing the livers so that they brown lightly on all sides. Drain in a colander.

3.   Heat the remaining 2 tablespoons of butter in the skillet and when very hot add the livers and onions. Sprinkle with sage and cook, stirring, for 3 or 4 minutes. Sprinkle with Parmesan cheese. Serve with rice.

YIELD: 4 SERVINGS

Purée de Pommes de Terre au Cerfeuil

(MASHED POTATOES WITH CHERVIL)

2 pounds Idaho, Maine, or Yellow
    Gold potatoes
Salt to taste
3 tablespoons butter at room
    temperature

¼ teaspoon freshly grated nutmeg,
    or to taste
¼ cup chopped chervil (or substitute
    parsley)
1 cup warm milk

1.   Peel the potatoes and cut them into 2-inch cubes.

2.   Place them in a saucepan with salted water to cover. Bring to a boil and simmer for 20 minutes or until the potatoes are tender. Do not overcook.

3.   Drain the potatoes and put them through a food mill or potato ricer. Return them to the saucepan.

4.   Using a wooden spoon, beat the butter into the potatoes. Add the nutmeg and the chervil. Beat in the warm milk.

YIELD: 6 SERVINGS

Tomates Grillées au Romarin
(GRILLED ROSEMARY TOMATOES)

8 ripe plum tomatoes
Salt and freshly ground pepper
   to taste
1 tablespoon garlic, minced

3 tablespoons fresh rosemary,
   chopped, or 2 tablespoons dried
2 tablespoons olive oil

1.   Preheat broiler to high.

2.   Core the tomatoes and slice them in half lengthwise.

3.   Place the tomatoes cut side up in a baking dish large enough to hold all the tomato halves in one layer. Sprinkle with salt and pepper.

4.   Sprinkle each half with the garlic and the rosemary. Sprinkle the olive oil over each half and place under the broiler about 3 to 4 inches from the source of heat for 5 minutes, or until done. Do not overcook.

YIELD: 8 SERVINGS

❧   *In this journey from one stupendous meal to another, the one we were served at the home of Philippe Revillon, of Le Bourgeat Cookware (not too far a drive from Annecy), took second place to none. When we arrived at the house, Revillon's cook of twenty or so years, a man named Giovanni, was basting a twenty-pound suckling pig, stuffed with rice, ground meats, and vegetables. It would be cooked slowly for several hours on an outdoor spit. The trick, Giovanni said, was to start it far from the flames, so the skin would not burn. The servings came large and often. And we ate it all; I have no regrets. The preparation of a suckling pig requires professional equipment that some home cooks buy for their backyards.*

Cochon de Lait à la Broche Farci
(BARBECUED SUCKLING PIG WITH RICE STUFFING)

¾ cup olive or vegetable oil
3 cups onions, thinly sliced

4 tablespoons garlic, minced
2 pounds lean ground beef

2 pounds lean ground pork

4 sprigs fresh thyme, or 2 teaspoons
    dried

4 bay leaves

2 sweet red peppers, cored, seeded,
    and cubed

2 green peppers, cored, seeded, and
    cubed

12 cups cooked rice

1 whole, dressed suckling pig, with
    head and feet removed, about
    30 pounds

Salt and freshly ground pepper
    to taste

2 whole tomatoes, cored

1. Prepare and heat barbecue with a rotating spit.

2. In a large saucepan or kettle, heat ½ cup of the oil. Add the onions and garlic and cook, stirring, until wilted. Add the beef, pork, thyme, bay leaves, and peppers and continue stirring for about 10 minutes more. Add the cooked rice and blend well. Remove thyme sprigs and bay leaves.

3. Sprinkle the inside of the pig with salt and pepper to taste. Stuff half of the rice mixture into the pig's belly. Add the 2 whole tomatoes and then the remaining stuffing. Sew the belly closed with fishing line or fine wire.

4. To prevent the seam from breaking open during cooking, and to maintain the shape of the pig during cooking, wrap the mid-section between its shoulders and legs with a piece of chicken-wire fencing. Secure the fencing tightly with fishing line or fine wire.

5. Secure the suckling pig to the spit with more wire and brush it with the remaining oil. Season the outside of the pig with salt and pepper to taste. Add about ½ cup of water to the drippings pan.

6. Place the pig far enough from the source of heat that its surface will not burn, and roast it for 5 to 6 hours. Baste often with the drippings that collect beneath the roast.

7. To test for doneness, insert a meat thermometer into the thickest part of the leg. It should reach 155°.

8. Carve the pig and serve it with the stuffing on warmed plates. Serve a tomato salad on the side.

YIELD: 20–30 SERVINGS

Alsace

SPECIALTIES

Choucroute garnie, sauerkraut cooked with a variety of smoked meats, such as bacon, smoked pork, and sausage

Cabbage, braised, cured for sauerkraut, sautéed, and in other preparations

Sausages and *charcuterie* include liver sausages; *boudin noir,* or blood sausages; *foie gras,* usually made into *pâté*

Freshwater fish, especially carp, trout, and salmon

Tarte flambée, also known as *flammekueche,* a simple thin-crusted Alsatian pizza topped with onions, cream, and bacon

Riesling-braised poultry, served with egg noodles or spaetzle (dumplings)

Baeckeoffe, a casserole of potatoes baked with marinated pork, beef, and lamb

CHEESE

Munster cheese, aromatic and moist, from Munster

DESSERTS

Kugelhopf, a yeast-risen coffee cake with almonds and raisins

Tarte au fromage blanc, a slightly sweet, very rich cheesecake

Plums, such as the *quetsches* and the tiny yellow *mirabelles,* baked in cakes and their juice distilled into fruit brandy

WINES

Sensational whites, including steel-crisp Rieslings, spicy Gewürztraminers, and the musky Tokay (or Pinot Gris)

ROUTE DE LA CHOUCROUTE

I n many areas of France, one finds wine routes, maps, and brochures to direct you from one major vineyard to another, but leave it to Alsace to have a Route de la Choucroute. It is after all the *choucroute garnie*—sauerkraut cooked with a variety of smoked meats, such as bacon, smoked pork, and sausage—that has become the best-known dish of the region. The reputation is well warranted. I believe a good *choucroute* is a wonderful, soul-warming dish, and that is especially true here, where the chefs all have their own individual approaches and present their creations with great pride. (Potatoes can be added at the end, or liver dumplings; some cooks will boldly offer a seafood *choucroute,* the furthest thing from tradition.)

Even the cabbage is a matter of choice and discussion. The cabbages that might go into one *choucroute* or another number eight different kinds of white and red. But more important than the type of cabbage, I think, is the quality of the other ingredients a chef chooses and the customary use of goose fat to cook it all. (Many Alsatian chefs say that they smoke all their own meats, and I do think that kind of care will show up in the caliber of the final production.) It's a lot of fun—if more than a little filling—to try one chef's version against another.

One of the promotional brochures for the region declares that Alsace and cabbage are synonymous: "*L'Alsace C'est Chou!*" Since *choucroute* is such a big business here, you'll see little plots of cabbage wedged in just about anywhere, right among the houses, as you drive through the towns and cities. *Choucroute* has been famous in the region since Napoleon's soldiers, marching through on their way to the Russian front, found that it cures scurvy.

The word *choucroute* itself is a reflection of a people who, to this day, carry the scars of living in disputed territory, the control of which was fought over right up until World War II. They live on the German border, and their architecture reminds

A stroll around Strasbourg, where Tudor-style houses line the canals, reveals a profusion of dining possibilities—both indoors and out.

you of Germany; they are fiercely French and yet, even so, they speak a version of French that is really their own, Alsatian. The word *choucroute* derives from *sürkrüt,* an Alsatian word meaning sour grass.

But in a way all this carrying on about *choucroute,* justified though it may be, masks other virtues of Alsace, which is certainly one of France's richest regions in the food it has to offer, as well as the great beauty of its landscape and cities. It is a place of marked contrasts: the sensibilities of high refinement and lusty rustic life mix and blend in a way that, if you are patient and spend enough time here to take it in, leaves you tingling with astonishment. Take Strasbourg, for instance, a truly handsome city, soaring and cosmopolitan, yet down to earth, too. A meal at Restaurant Le Crocodile can star an awfully good and lusty *choucroute* by the chef, Emile Jung, but on one of the days we were there, our table was graced with a wonderfully moist and delicate stuffed quail, tidbits of smoked eel over a bed of leeks, and strips of cèpes sautéed perfectly in butter.

The graciousness and the poise at Crocodile remind me so much of the old ways—except that in a strikingly modern manner women play a larger role than they would have decades ago in a restaurant of such high esteem. Over to the side, I saw Emile's wife, Monique, genteel and confident, serving a table of diners from a cart we call the *chariot* in French. The *chariot* is literally no more than a mobile serving table, but beyond that it is a stage for the skills of the dining room staff, encouraging a certain bravura. It's perfect for carving a large roast or chicken, or to *flambé* a dish like duck in a liqueur-based sauce. (It also allows for the last-minute preparation that enhances the quality of food that otherwise might be forced to languish beneath warming lights somewhere in the kitchen.)

Turning to the other side of the room, I let my glance linger on a stunning waitress (women servers are still unusual in high-cuisine establishments) as she moved through the restaurant with feline grace, tall and with the posture of a runway model—but dressed in severe black as the waiters were. There was a tranquillity in her movements that enhanced the experience of the meal.

Later, Emile Jung invited us along to see the city through his eyes. He described the Tudor-style houses, constructed in such a way that they could be disassembled and delivered, along with furnishings, as part of an inheritance or a dowry. Pointing this way and that as we moved across the Ill River, over the canals and through the streets, Émile took us to see the great cathedral of the city, marveling out loud—as he must have done with many another guest, too—at the light piercing through the sculpted spire. From there we walked a brief way to visit some immaculate *pâtisseries* and colorful, working-class eating-and-drinking establishments called *winstubs*. At a place called Hailich Graab we found sufficient appetite (even though lunch was still a vivid memory) to dig into an onion tart. We dropped in on another *winstub* called Strissel, built in 1564; Emile had taken us there to get a sense of the sort of place his father, who was also a cook, would bring him to when Emile was a boy: simple food, like the big ham baked in a crust waiting to be carved—and the ambience warmed by uninhibited, joking, laughing people.

In the town of Enzheim, we got to sample more of the earthy fare of Alsace at a charming hotel and restaurant called the Hôtel Père Benoit. The restaurant, downstairs and across a courtyard from our rooms, is called the Steinkeller. In its kitchen, standing before a brutally hot wood-burning stove, is Denis Masse, the young chef (and son of the owner), as he rapidly cooks a *tarte flambée,* a sort of simple Alsatian pizza—topped with onions, cream, and bacon—thrusting it into the oven for only a few seconds until the dough cooks. Each one is made just as it is ordered, and in the dining room, the customers are ordering a great many, the pressure causing Denis's face to redden in the heat and beads of sweat to form on his brow. The Steinkeller also offers another of the great dishes of rural Alsace, the *baeckeoffe,* a casserole of potatoes baked with marinated pork, beef, and lamb.

The whole region is an enormous market basket of rich food—we knew we had to arrive here with an appetite or not bother at all. Among Alsace's other offerings is a deeply flavored cheese that will come as a surprise to anyone who has encountered the processed variety in the United States. That sumptuous cheese is Munster, and the town of Munster is its home (the name derives from the word "monastery," and the twelfth-century monks who inhabited the valley). While we were there, we were diverted by a huge outdoor aviary for stork breeding—another interest of these remarkable Alsatians, who seem determined to single-handedly, if necessary, keep the magnificent stork around for the sake of the future.

Denis Masse prepares the Alsatian pizza called a tarte flambée.

And through all this, I have so far neglected to men-

tion the wines of Alsace, most of them whites, and perhaps the most underappreciated of the regional trea-
sures, at least among Americans. Although many of us
are well-acquainted with the beautiful, delicate Rieslings of the region and perhaps the spicy Gewürz-

*Alsatian wine, from
Gewürztraminer to Riesling,
is produced by standards
that are demanding even
for France.*

traminer, there is still so much more to what the Alsatians can do: the fresh Sylvaner,
which goes so well with seafood; the fruity (but dry) Muscat, a wonderful *apéritif*—
and one we just don't see very often in the United States; the Tokay or Pinot Gris, a
full-bodied wine that is worth searching out. I have always been an admirer of the
Trimbach wines of Alsace in particular, partly because they are readily available in
the United States (the Trimbach family has been making wine here since 1626, across
twelve generations), but there are many other fine vintners in Alsace as well.

A notable difference between the way wine is judged and labeled in Alsace and in
the rest of France—a reflection of the fact that beneath their good humor and hos-
pitality, these are precise, demanding people—is that every year before any wine can
be awarded the highest designation, a Grand Cru apellation, it is examined by an
official committee. In other words, unlike the convention in other regions of France,
where a Grand Cru vineyard simply remains one, here the winemakers must prove
themselves over and over again.

❧ *Among the most pleasant and most capable chefs we met in France were René Flo-*
ranc and his son Patrick at the Auberge du Père Floranc, just outside the stunningly per-
fect Alsatian city of Colmar, a place that is literally chock-a-block with museums,
churches, and mansions. The Florancs are serious about their work, curing their own
meats and choosing especially young and tender cabbage for their traditional choucroute. *The ingredients will provide a big one, just the thing for a cold-weather party.*

Choucroute Garnie

(SAUERKRAUT WITH PORK)

8 pounds sauerkraut
½ cup goose fat or lard
3 cups onions, thinly sliced
1 bottle Riesling, or comparable
    white wine
2 pounds pork shoulder (bone in),
    cured and smoked
2 pounds pork loin, cured and salted,
    about 4 ribs
1 pound lean slab bacon
1 pound lean salt pork
4 salted pig's knuckles, about
    1½ pounds
Salt to taste

2 tablespoons garlic, finely chopped
Bouquet garni, tied together with
string and consisting of:
    2 tablespoons coriander seeds
    2 tablespoons juniper berries
    1 tablespoon cumin seeds
    ¼ teaspoon whole cloves
    4 bay leaves
    10 peppercorns
12 red-skinned potatoes, well washed
10 to 12 all-beef frankfurters
6 large knockwurst or veal-and-pork
    sausages, cut in half

1.   Preheat the oven to 375°.

2.   Place the sauerkraut in a large bowl, cover with water, and let soak for 5 minutes. Drain well.

3.   In a large cast-iron pot or soup kettle, melt the goose fat over medium heat
and add the onions. Cook, stirring, until wilted but not browned. Add the wine and
half of the sauerkraut and blend well with a wooden spatula. Add the shoulder, loin,
bacon, salt pork, knuckles, salt, and garlic. Pour enough water to cover (about 4
cups) over this mixture and add the *bouquet garni.* Stir in the remaining sauerkraut.

4.   Cover the pot tightly and bring to a boil over medium-high heat, then transfer it to the oven and cook for 1½ hours, or until the meat is done. Do not overcook.

5.   Meanwhile, place the potatoes in a large saucepan with water to cover.

Bring to a boil and simmer for 15 minutes. Remove from the heat and keep warm.

6.   Place the frankfurters and sausages in a saucepan with water to cover. Bring to a boil and simmer for 2 minutes. Remove from the heat and keep warm.

7.   To serve, slice the stewed meats into serving-sized portions. Drain the sauerkraut and put it in the center of a large platter with the meat, frankfurters, sausages, and potatoes arranged neatly on top and around the sides. Serve with mustard.

YIELD: 12 SERVINGS

✢   *One of the more adventurous uses of sauerkraut combines it with fish instead of the traditional meats. Emile Jung of Crocodile likes the way the mildness of the fish contrasts with the acidity of the sauerkraut, and this is his recipe. He used the freshwater fish* sandre, *but lemon sole will do as well.*

Note: The garni *recipe that follows the main recipe for the roulade must be prepared first.*

Roulade de Choucroute et Sandre d'Emile Jung
(FRESHWATER FISH ROLLS STUFFED WITH SAUERKRAUT)

4 small red waxy potatoes, peeled
1 large carrot, peeled, trimmed, and
    cut into ⅛-inch slices
2 cabbage leaves
¾ pound *sandre* (or lemon sole)
    fillets, skinless and boneless
Salt and freshly ground pepper
    to taste
1½ cups sauerkraut garnish (see
    recipe page 289)
2 tablespoons white wine vinegar

6 tablespoons Riesling, or other
    dry white wine
3 tablespoons finely chopped
    shallots
¼ teaspoon cracked black
    peppercorns
2 tablespoons water
¼ teaspoon juniper berries
2 tablespoons gin
2 tablespoons heavy cream
4 tablespoons butter

1.   Place the potatoes in a saucepan with salted water to cover. Bring to a boil and cook for 15 minutes, or until done. Drain and keep warm. Repeat this process with the carrot slices and the cabbage leaves, reducing the cooking times as necessary.

2.   Season the fish with salt and pepper to taste.

3.   Cut an 8-by-6-inch piece of paper to serve as a guide to the size of the fish fillets when aligned in a layer. Unroll a length of plastic wrap at least 3 times as long over the paper. Place half of the fish fillets on the plastic wrap, using the paper underneath as the pattern. Reserve the remaining fish for a second roll.

4.   Place ¾ cup of the sauerkraut garnish in a neat strip lengthwise down the middle of the fish rectangle, reserving the remaining garnish for the second roll. Roll the fish around it, creating a compact cylinder wrapped in plastic as you go. Roll the cylinder in several layers of plastic wrap. Repeat with the remaining ingredients to form the second roll.

5.   Place the rolls in a steamer, cover tightly, and cook for 20 minutes. Remove and keep warm in the plastic.

6.   Meanwhile, combine the vinegar, wine, shallots, peppercorns, and 2 tablespoons water in a saucepan over medium-low heat. (Adding the water will allow you to cook the sauce longer, extracting more flavor from the shallots before too much liquid has evaporated.)

7.   Reduce the sauce, simmering until almost all the liquid has evaporated and the shallots are thoroughly cooked. Add the juniper berries, gin, and cream. Return to a boil and reduce heat. Swirl in the butter and salt to taste. Strain the sauce through a fine sieve.

8.   Unwrap the fish rolls and cut each into ½-inch slices. Cut the cabbage leaves into strips ½ inch wide. Arrange slices of fish roll on 2 warmed serving plates and place the potatoes, carrots, and cabbage strips decoratively around the fish. Spoon sauce around.

YIELD: 2 SERVINGS

Choucroute pour Garniture

(SAUERKRAUT GARNISH)

1½ pounds sauerkraut

2 tablespoons goose fat, duck fat, or lard

1 cup onions, finely sliced

½ teaspoon garlic, minced

½ cup Alsatian white wine, such as Gewürztraminer or Pinot Gris

½ cup fresh chicken broth (see recipe page 108), or good quality canned

Bouquet garni, tied together with string and consisting of:

    3 sprigs parsley

    2 sprigs fresh thyme, or ½ teaspoon dried

    1 bay leaf

    2 whole cloves

    6 juniper berries

Salt and freshly ground pepper to taste

1.   Put the sauerkraut in a bowl and cover generously with water. Let stand for 10 minutes.

2.   Turn the sauerkraut out into a colander and drain well. Press with your hands to extract the excess liquid.

3.   Heat the goose fat in a heavy casserole or saucepan. Add the onions and garlic and cook, stirring, until wilted. Then add the sauerkraut, wine, chicken broth, *bouquet garni,* and salt and pepper to taste. Cover tightly and bring to a boil, then simmer for 20 minutes. Do not overcook.

4.   Pour the sauerkraut through a strainer, pressing firmly to extract all the liquid. Allow to cool. Remove *bouquet garni.*

YIELD: 4 SERVINGS

❧ *When in Alsace, I can't easily stop thinking about cabbage. Here is another dish that I know you will enjoy trying. It's terrific with the pork dish that follows, but serve it with anything you like.*

Chou à l'Alsacienne

(ALSATIAN CABBAGE)

1 medium-sized cabbage, cored and
    with the green leaves trimmed
1 tablespoon butter
1 tablespoon olive oil
½ cup onions, thinly sliced
1 teaspoon garlic, chopped
Salt and pepper to taste

2 whole cloves
¼ cup Gewürztraminer, or
    comparable white wine
1 bay leaf
2 sprigs fresh thyme, or ½
    teaspoon dried

1.   Remove the core from each cabbage leaf and slice the leaf thinly. You need about 6 cups.

2.   Heat the butter and olive oil in a large skillet and add the onions and garlic. Cook, stirring, until wilted, then add the cabbage, salt, pepper, and cloves and continue cooking for another minute.

3.   Add the wine, bay leaf, and thyme. Bring to a boil, cover, and simmer for 15 minutes or until tender. If there is too much liquid, remove the cover and allow the liquid to reduce. Remove bay leaf and thyme sprigs.

4.   Serve with pork cutlets (recipe follows), if desired.

YIELD: 4 SERVINGS

❧ *The spiciness of Gewürztraminer was meant for pork, so in this dish I arranged for the marriage.*

Côtelettes de Porc au Gewürztraminer

(SAUTÉED PORK CUTLETS WITH WHITE WINE SAUCE)

4 pork cutlets, about 6 ounces each,
    trimmed of excess fat

Salt and freshly ground pepper
    to taste

2 tablespoons vegetable oil
2 teaspoons ground cumin
2 sprigs fresh thyme, or 1 teaspoon
   dried
¼ cup shallots, finely chopped
½ cup Gewürztraminer, or
   comparable white wine

¼ cup fresh chicken broth (see
   recipe page 108), or good quality
   canned
2 tablespoons butter
¼ cup fresh coriander leaves

1. Flatten each cutlet slightly with a meat pounder or mallet and sprinkle with salt and pepper.

2. Heat the oil in a nonstick skillet large enough to hold the cutlets in one layer. When the oil is hot, add the meat, cumin, and thyme and cook over medium-high heat for about 5 minutes, or until brown. Turn the cutlets and cook for 5 minutes more. Then reduce the heat and continue cooking for 2 minutes longer, turning the cutlets occasionally.

3. Transfer the meat to a platter and keep warm. Pour off the fat from the skillet, add the shallots, and cook, stirring, until wilted and lightly browned. Add the wine and broth and stir to dissolve the browned particles that cling to the bottom of the pan. Cook until this sauce is reduced by more than half. Add the butter and blend well. Remove thyme sprigs.

4. Serve the cutlets with the sauce poured over them, garnished with the fresh coriander and accompanied by braised cabbage (recipe follows).

YIELD: 4 SERVINGS

Chou Rouge
(BRAISED RED CABBAGE)

1 2½-to-3-pound head of red cabbage
4 tablespoons butter
2 tablespoons brown sugar
½ cup water

¼ cup red wine vinegar
1 teaspoon caraway seeds
1 apple, peeled, cored, and grated
¼ cup red or black currant jelly

1. Preheat the oven to 350°.

2. Cut the cabbage into quarters, then remove and discard the core from each quarter.

3. Grate the cabbage leaves into fine shreds.

4. Heat the butter in a large, heavy casserole and add the sugar, water, vinegar, and caraway seeds. Stir to blend, then add the cabbage, stirring to coat it in the butter-and-sugar mixture. When well blended, cover closely and cook for 10 minutes, stirring occasionally.

5. Place the casserole in the oven and bake for 1 hour. Stir occasionally, taking care that it does not burn.

6. Add the grated apple and the jelly and stir to blend. Bake for 10 minutes longer. Serve immediately.

YIELD: 8–10 SERVINGS

❊   *I always say that I like to cook with good wine, rather than inferior "cooking wine" that so many people seem to think will be just fine. The fact is that the character of the wine does impart its virtues to the food. So here is a chicken and vegetable recipe meant to show off a fine Alsatian Riesling. It goes well with buttered noodles, the recipe that follows.*

Suprême de Volaille au Riesling et Légumes
(CHICKEN BREASTS WITH ALSATIAN RIESLING AND VEGETABLES)

24 pearl onions, peeled
2 large carrots, peeled, cut into
    1½-inch strips and quartered,
    or 12 baby carrots, peeled and
    uncut
4 skinless boneless chicken breasts,
    about 5 ounces each
Salt and freshly ground pepper
    to taste
4 tablespoons butter

1 cup cèpes (or any other wild
    mushrooms such as chanterelles
    or morels), sliced
1 tablespoon shallots, finely chopped
1 cup snow peas, trimmed
½ teaspoon garlic, minced
1 cup Riesling
¾ cup heavy cream
¼ teaspoon dried thyme
1 tablespoon chives, finely chopped

1. Blanch the pearl onions and carrots in boiling salted water for 3 to 4 minutes. Do not overcook. Drain and reserve.

2.   Sprinkle chicken with salt and pepper to taste.

3.   In a nonstick skillet large enough to hold the chicken breasts in one layer, melt 3 tablespoons of the butter over medium-high heat. Add the chicken breasts and cook until lightly browned, about 2 to 3 minutes on the first side and 3 to 4 minutes on the second. Remove from skillet and keep warm.

4.   To the same skillet add the remaining butter, the mushrooms, shallots, pearl onions, carrots, snow peas, garlic, and wine. Stir the vegetables over medium heat until the wine is reduced by more than half. Add the cream and continue to cook for 3 to 4 minutes until slightly thickened. Sprinkle in the thyme. Add the chicken breasts and any juices that may have accumulated around them and bring to a boil. Check for seasoning.

5.   Arrange the chicken breasts on warmed plates, spoon the sauce and vegetables over them, and sprinkle with chives. Serve with noodles (recipe follows).

YIELD: 4 SERVINGS

Nouilles au Beurre

(BUTTERED NOODLES)

½ pound flat noodles
Salt and freshly ground pepper
   to taste
1 tablespoon butter

1 tablespoon shallots, finely chopped
1 tablespoon fresh parsley, finely
   chopped

1.   Fill a large saucepan with enough salted water to cook the noodles and bring it to a boil. Cook 7 to 8 minutes, or according to package instructions, then drain the noodles and reserve ¼ cup of the cooking liquid.

2.   In the same saucepan, heat the butter, add the shallots, and cook, stirring, until wilted. Add the reserved liquid and the noodles. Bring to a simmer. Sprinkle with parsley and toss well. Cook until heated through and season with salt and pepper.

YIELD: 4 SERVINGS

During the visit to Alsace I became so enamored of the wines that while cooking at La Cheneaudiere I even turned to a Riesling for a dish that might normally be more evocative of the Mediterranean. And I do think the crisp, high-quality wine made a significant contribution. Here's a simplified version of the dish.

Pavé de Saumon en Bouillon de Huile d'Olive Douce

(SALMON STEAKS IN AN OLIVE OIL–FLAVORED BROTH)

⅓ cup carrots, peeled, trimmed, and cut into 1-inch matchstick shapes

⅓ cup zucchini, trimmed, and cut into 1-inch matchstick shapes

⅓ cup leeks, white part only, washed and trimmed into 1-inch matchstick shapes

Salt and freshly ground pepper to taste

¾ pound salmon, skinless and boneless, cut into 2 steaks about 1 inch thick

4 tablespoons olive oil

⅓ cup shallots, finely chopped

1 teaspoon garlic, finely chopped

¼ cup Riesling

½ cup fish stock

2 tablespoons butter

10 pitted Niçoise olives

Sprigs of fresh chervil for garnish

1. Place the carrots, zucchini, and leeks in a saucepan with salt to taste and water to cover. Bring to a boil and simmer for 3 minutes. Drain and keep warm.

2. Season the salmon with salt and pepper to taste.

3. In a nonstick skillet, heat 2 tablespoons of the olive oil over low heat and add the salmon. Cook the fish for about 7 minutes on one side only. The top should remain moist and pink. Remove from the heat and keep warm.

4. Bring the shallots, garlic, and white wine to a boil in a small saucepan over medium heat and simmer them for about 3 minutes, or until little liquid remains. Add the fish stock and reduce again by a bit more than half. Briskly whisk in the remaining olive oil, swirl in the butter, and check for seasoning.

6. Place each portion of fish in a warmed soup plate and top with olives. Spoon sauce around the salmon and sprinkle with the vegetables. Decorate with sprigs of chervil and serve.

YIELD: 2 SERVINGS

❧ *A typical Alsatian side dish, a kind of dumpling that can be served in place of rice, noodles, or potatoes, is called spaetzle. Here is my recipe.*

Spaetzle

(ALSATIAN EGG DUMPLINGS)

2 cups sifted all-purpose flour
2 whole eggs
⅔ cup milk
Salt and freshly ground pepper
    to taste

½ teaspoon freshly grated nutmeg
2 tablespoons butter
2 tablespoons parsley, finely chopped

1. Pour the flour into a mixing bowl. Beat the eggs separately and then add them to the flour, stirring with a wire whisk or electric beater. Gradually add the milk, salt, and nutmeg and beat until smooth.

2. Bring a large quantity of salted water to a boil. Pour the batter into a colander and hold the colander over the boiling water. Press the batter through the holes of the colander with a rubber spatula or a large spoon. Stir the spaetzle gently. They are done when they float to the top of the water; this should take about 1 minute. Drain and transfer them for a brief time onto a clean towel to dry them.

3. Heat the butter in a nonstick skillet and, when it is bubbling, add the spaetzle. Sprinkle with salt and pepper, and toss for a few minutes. Add the chopped parsley. Serve immediately.

YIELD: 4 SERVINGS

❧ *Here's a version of the* tarte flambée *we enjoyed so much at the Hôtel Père Benoit;
I know you don't have the wood-burning stove they use there, but this should prove to be
a fair approximation of the* tarte. *Speed is very important; even though this is a recipe
for six portions, it will be necessary to serve them one, perhaps two, at a time as you keep
cooking.*

Tarte Flambée Denis Masse

(DENIS'S THIN-CRUSTED PIZZA WITH BACON AND ONIONS)

Classic bread dough (recipe follows),
    divided into 6 4-ounce pieces
6 tablespoons heavy cream
6 tablespoons sour cream
6 tablespoons softened cream
    cheese

Salt and freshly ground pepper
    to taste
½ cup slab bacon, in strips ½ inch
    long and ¼ inch wide, blanched
    and drained
½ cup onions, very thinly sliced

1.   Preheat the oven to 500°.

2.   For each *tarte*, roll the dough into a thin 10-inch circle (a dinner plate will be
useful in gauging the size) and transfer to a cookie sheet.

3.   In a mixing bowl, combine the heavy cream, sour cream, and cream cheese.
Season with salt and pepper to taste. This quantity is intended to suffice for all six
tartes.

4.   Spread some of the mixture evenly over the dough and sprinkle with bacon
and onions.

5.   Bake on the lowest rack in the oven for 2 to 3 minutes, or until the dough is
crisp, rotating the *tarte* from time to time to assure even cooking. Serve immediately,
repeating the procedure until all six have been cooked.

YIELD: 6 SERVINGS

Classic Bread Dough

1 envelope active dry yeast
1¼ cups warm (90°) water

3 cups unbleached all-purpose flour
1 tablespoon salt

1.   Place the chopping blade in the food processor bowl. Add the yeast and ¼ cup warm water. Mix by turning the chopping blade by hand. (Turn the stem without touching the sharp blade. Just to be extra cautious, unplug the machine.) Add all the flour. Turn on the machine and blend for 5 seconds. Add the salt and blend for 5 seconds more. While the blade rotates, add the remaining cup of water. Blend until the batter begins to form a large ball, 20 to 25 seconds.

2.   Flour a board and knead the dough on it, forming it into a ball. Flour a large mixing bowl and place the ball of dough in it. Sprinkle the top with flour. Cover with a dish towel. Let the dough rise in a warm place until it doubles in size. The time required varies with environmental conditions, but at a room temperature of about 75° it will take at least an hour.

3.   Remove the dough from the bowl and punch it down. It is now ready for use in the preparation of *tarte flambée.*

Note: To use the same dough to prepare a loaf of bread, it is necessary to form it into a loaf, let rise again until double in size (about 1 hour), and bake it for 30 minutes at 400°, then 10 minutes at 375°.

Champagne

SPECIALTIES

Mussels steamed in wine
Dandelion salad with bacon
Flamiche au Poireaux, leek tart
Potée Champenoise, a stew made with pork, cabbage, and vegetables
Andouillettes (chitterling sausages) fried with potatoes
Matelotes (fish stews) incorporating Champagne
Pig's trotters à la Sainte-Menehould, braised with garlic and wine,
then breaded and fried
Mutton and lamb, roasted, braised, also in sausages
Roast thrush with cabbage and beans

CHEESES

Brie and Brie de Meaux, Chaourse (a rich white cheese), and Maroilles
(a sharp, hard cheese)

DESSERTS

Beignets au fromage blanc, fritters with white cheese
Almond confections, including meringues; tarts; and *rocaillons,*
chocolate candies shaped like pebbles

WINES

Champagne

PRECIOUS BUBBLES

The traffic was bad on our way to Reims in Champagne, and we were an hour late for a filming segment. The Champagne makers who had gathered to meet us for a tasting had evidently begun already, which was all to the good. They were enjoying themselves and soon, in the swing of things, so were we. We met at a bistro called Le Vigneron, where homage is paid to Champagne everywhere your eye falls, all over the walls and in every empty space—huge posters advertising the famous Champagne houses, a wine press in the middle of the floor, antique Champagne buckets. The extensive tasting was good for getting into the spirit of things in more ways than one; it allowed us to appreciate the array of Champagnes, from the opulent and creamy to the delicate and fruity and to see the energy and delight the people here put into their careers.

The use of Champagne in cooking, which has been something I've turned to often in my life, almost always imparts a lighter, fruitier taste to a sauce: in other words the Champagne taste and quality are not lost in the process (as long as you remember to cook briefly; lengthy contact with heat will certainly flatten it and then you've wasted the money). It is therefore the perfect accompaniment for fish, and the white meats, especially chicken. That light fruitiness combined with sweet cream is an especially fine marriage of smooth flavors.

Among the tours we were offered in Champagne was a stunning one of Ruinart, one of the noble houses here, to see how Champagne is made. We got the chance to observe the bottling process as each bottle paraded by, military fashion, on a conveyor belt, but we were told to keep our distance; you never know when one of these pressurized bottles will explode. Down steep steps (lighted only with dim yellow sulfur lights chosen, we were told, because they would not damage the wine) and through tunnels, we reached a place where we could observe the process known as

Le Vigneron, a bistro in Reims, is also something of a museum dedicated to Champagne.

riddling, which, because of the sediment produced in the Champagne-making process, proves to be necessary only with this wine and no other. In riddling, each bottle is rotated exactly one-quarter turn every day, so that the sediment will drift, ever so gently, down the inverted bottle toward the neck (heavy particles will descend with relative ease; it's the pesky lighter ones that require this delicate process). Once all the sediment is in the neck it will be frozen, trapped in a block of ice that is then expelled by the gas in the bottle.

A riddler will turn, on average, 40,000 bottles in a day and will, as a result, have wrists that are thick and strong beyond imagining—before a riddler can take on this job he must strengthen his wrists through specialized exercises. But the job is not just one of endurance and strength. It also requires Zen-like patience—he must learn to be so precise that his concentration is never lost: one-quarter turn, that's all, over and over again.

The riddler, a worker who precisely turns each Champagne bottle to dislodge sediment, must possess tireless wrists and unflagging concentration.

In Champagne, the predominant grape is the Chardonnay, the same one that produces Chablis, but here the climate and soil are much different than those of Burgundy, and, of course, the Champagne makers believe that their Chardonnay grapes are distinctive, unmatched anywhere. They believe that the secret behind the delicacy of Champagne is some quality inherent in the deep seam of chalk that underlies the clay soil of the vineyards. (The Romans mined the chalk, and now it is in these naturally climate-controlled mines that Ruinart stores and processes its wine.)

If you ever wondered where the fizz comes from, it is produced during a second fermentation of the wine, during which the sugar in it is transformed into alcohol and carbolic gas. It is the carbolic gas that breaks into a billion bubbles.

Many of the Champagne houses are open for visits, but often only by appointment, so if you intend to see some of this for yourself be sure to stop at the local tourist office to get the phone numbers for all of them.

❧ *One place I couldn't miss—because I have friends among its owners, the Budin family, and because I admire their Champagne in any case—is the house of Perrier-Jouët. It was at the company's guest house, La Maison Belle Epoque, that I prepared this chicken in Champagne sauce. One bit of advice I need to underline: do not brown the chicken too thoroughly or it will fight the sauce in both taste and color.*

Fricassée de Poulet au Champagne

(SAUTÉED CHICKEN IN CHAMPAGNE CREAM SAUCE)

1 whole chicken, about 3 pounds
Salt and freshly ground white pepper
   to taste
2 tablespoons butter
1 cup pearl onions
2 cups white mushrooms
1 tablespoon shallots, finely chopped
1 tablespoon flour

Bouquet garni, tied together with
string and consisting of:
   4 sprigs parsley
   2 sprigs thyme
   1 bay leaf
1 cup Champagne
½ cup heavy cream

1.   Cut the chicken into 10 pieces. The best way to do this is to separate the wings (allowing some of the breast meat to adhere to each), the drumsticks, and the thighs into individual pieces; fillet the breast meat away from the bone so you have two fillets, and then cut each fillet in half.

2.   Season the chicken pieces on all sides with salt and pepper to taste.

3.   In a nonstick skillet large enough to hold the chicken pieces in one layer, melt the butter over medium heat. Add the chicken pieces—thighs and drumsticks first—skin side down and cook until lightly browned. Turn and cook until lightly browned on other side.

4.   To the same skillet, add the onions, mushrooms, and shallots. Cook, stirring,

for about 3 minutes. Add flour, blend well, and continue to cook for about 2 minutes. Add the *bouquet garni* and Champagne and simmer for about 10 minutes. Turn the pieces from time to time to assure even cooking. When the meat comes away from the thigh bone easily and no blood runs, the chicken is cooked.

5.   Add the cream, bring to a boil, and blend well. Cover, remove from heat, and let rest 5 minutes. Remove the *bouquet garni,* check for seasoning, and transfer to a warmed serving platter. Serve with rice with red pepper (recipe follows).

YIELD: 4–6 SERVINGS

Riz aux Piments Doux

(RICE WITH RED PEPPER)

2 tablespoons butter
¼ cup onions, finely chopped
1 garlic clove, peeled
1 cup parboiled (converted) rice
1½ cups fresh chicken broth (see recipe page 108), or good quality canned

2 sprigs fresh parsley
1 cup sweet red peppers, cored, seeded, and cut into ¼-inch cubes
Salt and freshly ground pepper to taste

1.   Melt 1 tablespoon of the butter in a medium-sized saucepan over medium heat. Add the onions and garlic and cook, stirring, until just wilted. Do not burn.

2.   Add the rice and stir well until each grain is coated with butter. Add the chicken broth, parsley, red peppers, and salt and pepper. Cover and simmer for 17 minutes. Do not allow the rice to return to a boil. When there is no moisture remaining, the rice is done.

3.   Fold in the remaining butter gently, being careful not to crush the peppers. Check for seasoning.

YIELD: 4–6 SERVINGS

We stayed at the Royal Champagne hotel between Epernay and Reims, a stately place fronting the road but whose rear looks out across the verdant countryside. The name is that of the famous regiment that used the building as a stopover when this was a major military area standing between Paris and France's enemies to the east. In those days, the officers would not bother to pull the corks from the Champagne bottles; in traditional military fashion, they would cleanly decapitate the bottles at the neck with their sabers. Today there are still antique pistols and sabers all around the place. One of the dishes we prepared there was a dessert, using demi-sec Champagne, the sweetest of these wines. Although specific fruits are called for in the ingredients list, seasonal fruits can be substituted.

Salade de Fruits au Sabayon de Champagne

(FRUIT SALAD WITH CHAMPAGNE SABAYON SAUCE)

1 cup kiwi, peeled and cut into
   ¼-inch cubes
1 cup figs, peeled and cut into
   ¼-inch cubes
1 cup grapes, sliced in half

1 cup fresh strawberries, sliced in half
1 cup fresh raspberries
2 egg yolks
⅓ cup granulated sugar
1 cup demi-sec Champagne

1.   Heat broiler to its highest setting.

2.   Divide the cut fruits into 4 soup plates, arranging them decoratively in each.

3.   Make the sabayon sauce by combining the egg yolks and sugar in a large mixing bowl. Whisk together briskly until the yolks begin to turn a light lemony color. Add the Champagne a little bit at a time, whisking constantly until well blended.

4.   Place the mixing bowl in a pot or pan and pour about 1 inch of water around it. Bring the water to a simmer and continue to whisk vigorously until the mixture becomes light and foamy. Once the mixture starts to thicken, remove the bowl from the heat. Do not overcook. Continue to whisk for 10 seconds.

5.   Pour equal amounts of the *sabayon* sauce over each portion of fruit salad. Place the plates under the broiler about 3 inches from the source of heat and allow them to cook just until they are lightly browned on the surface. Rotate them from time to time to assure even browning.

6.   Serve immediately, with a glass of Champagne to accompany the dessert if desired.

YIELD: 4 SERVINGS

✤ *The chef at the Royal Champagne, Alain Guichaoua, smokes his own salmon, but of course you don't have to in order to prepare this robust salad.*

Gratin de Saumon Fumé avec Pommes de Terre

(WARM SMOKED SALMON AND POTATO SALAD)

1 pound smoked salmon, thinly sliced
4 tablespoons coriander seeds, crushed
4 tablespoons fresh dill, finely
   chopped
Salt and freshly ground white
   pepper to taste
1 pound waxy red potatoes

½ cup heavy cream
Juice of ½ lime
2 tablespoons chives, finely
   chopped

1.   Heat broiler to its highest setting.

2.   Season the salmon slices individually with the coriander, dill, and pepper, pressing seasonings lightly into the fish.

3.   In a large saucepan, add the potatoes and salted water to cover. Bring to a boil and cook for about 15 minutes, or until tender. Drain the potatoes and cool enough to be able to handle them. Peel the potatoes, cut them into ¼-inch slices, and divide them evenly onto 4 serving plates, arranging them in a circle in the center of each plate. Season with pepper to taste.

4.   Arrange the salmon slices in an overlapping fashion to cover the potatoes on each of the 4 plates.

5.   In a small mixing bowl, combine the cream, lime juice, chives, and salt and pepper to taste. Blend well with a wire whisk.

6.   Pour the sauce evenly over the salmon and potatoes. Place each plate under the broiler just until the sauce is warmed through and begins to bubble.

YIELD: 4 SERVINGS

APPENDIX

In the course of creating this book and the television series it accompanies, I visited many fine restaurants, hotels, shops, and other points of interest in France. Here are the addresses and telephone numbers for many of those mentioned in this volume. For certain of the establishments, especially the wineries and distilleries, it is always a good idea to call ahead to learn when they are open to the public and whether formal reservations are required.

Paris

RESTAURANT LES AMBASSADEURS
(at the Hôtel de Crillon)
10, place de la Concorde,
75008 Paris (8th arrondissement)
tel. 44.71.15.00, fax 44.71.15.02

LA COUPOLE
102, boulevard du Montparnasse,
75014 Paris (14th arr.)
tel. 43.20.14.20, fax 43.35.46.14

E. DEHILLERIN (KITCHEN SUPPLY STORE)
18 & 20, rue Coquillère,
75001 Paris (1st arr.)
tel. 42.36.53.13, fax 45.08.86.83

CAFÉ-RESTAURANT CHEZ DENISE À LA TOUR
DE MONTELHÉRY
5, rue des Prouvaires, 75001 Paris (1st arr.)
tel. 43.36.21.82

LAPÉROUSE
51, quai des Grands-Augustins,
75006 Paris (6th arr.)
tel. 43.26.68.04, fax 43.26.99.39

BISTRO CHEZ PAULINE
5, rue Villédo, 75001 Paris (1st arr.)
tel. 42.96.20.70, fax 49.27.99.89

RESTAURANT LA RÉGALADE
49, avenue Jean Moulin,
75014 Paris (14th arr.)
tel. 45.45.68.58

HÔTEL RITZ (HOTEL-RESTAURANT)
15, Place Vendôme, 75001 Paris (1st arr.)
tel. 42.60.38.30, fax 42.60.23.71

LA TOUR D'ARGENT
15, quai de la Tournelle,
75005 Paris (5th arr.)
tel. 43.54.23.31, fax 44.07.12.04

Normandy

Boulangerie Ancienne Osmont
18, rue Jacques Lelieur, 76000 Rouentel.
35.07.18.18, fax 35.73.12.99

Calvados Coeur de Lion
(Calvados distillery)
RN 177, Pont l'Evêque-Deauville,
14130 Coudray-Rabut
tel. 31.64.30.05

Restaurant Gill
8 & 9, quai de la Bourse, 76000 Rouen
tel. 35.71.16.14, fax 35.71.96.91

Ferme des Poiriers Roses
(bed and breakfast)
St.-Pilibert-des-Champs,
14130 Pont l'Evêque
tel. 31.64.72.14, fax 31.64.19.55

Ferme Saint-Siméon (hotel-restaurant)
rue Adolphe-Marais, 14600 Honfleur
tel. 31.89.23.61, fax 31.89.48.48

Brittany

Restaurant Beau Rivage
40, promenade de Georges Clemenceau,
85100 Sables d'Olonne
tel. 51.32.03.01, fax 51.32.46.48

Auberge Bretonne
2, Place Duguesclin,
56130 La Roche-Bernard
tel. 99.90.60.28, fax 99.90.85.00

Crêperie Madame Christianne Gatin
place de Bouffay, La Roche-Bernard
tel. 99.90.63.60

Hostellerie le Domaine d'Orvault
(hotel-restaurant)
chemin des Marais du Cens,
44700 Orvault (Nantes)
tel. 46.76.84.02, fax 40.76.04.21

Charente

Restaurant La Belle Etoile
115, quai Maurice Métayer, 79000 Niort
tel. 49.73.31.29, fax 49.09.05.59

Cognac Marnier Château de Bourg-Charente (Cognac distillery)
16200 Bourg-Charente
tel. 45.81.30.22

La Chapelle Saint-Martin
(hotel-restaurant)
87510 Nieul près Limoges
tel. 55.75.80.17, fax 55.75.89.50

Hôtel de la Monnaie
3, rue Monnaie, 17000 La Rochelle
tel. 46.50.65.65, fax 46.50.63.19

Le Moulin de Marcouze
(hotel-restaurant)
17240 Mosnac par St.-Genis-de-Saintonge
tel. 46.70.46.16, fax 46.70.48.14

Restaurant Richard Coutanceau
plage de la Concurrence,
17000 La Rochelle
tel. 46.41.48.19, fax 46.41.99.45

Loire Valley

Hostellerie du Château de Pray
(hotel-restaurant)
Chargé 37400 Amboise
tel. 47.57.23.67, fax 47.57.32.50

LES HAUTES ROCHES
(HOTEL-RESTAURANT)
    86, quai de la Loire, 37210 Rochecorbon
    tel. 47.52.88.88, fax 47.52.81.30

S.C.E.A. DE LA FERRIÈRE
(CHEVIGNOL GOAT-CHEESE FARM)
    Crésancy en Sancerre
    tel. 48.79.04.89

CHÂTEAU DE LA VERRERIE
    Oizon, 18700 Aubigny-sur-Nère
    tel. 48.58.06.91, fax 48.58.21.25
    Private château that accepts guests

Bordeaux

CHÂTEAU CORDEILLAN BAGES
(HOTEL-RESTAURANT-VINEYARD)
    33250 Pauillac
    tel. 56.59.24.24, fax 56.59.01.89

CHÂTEAU HAUT-BRION (WINERY)
    33602 Pessac
    tel. 56.98.75.14, fax 56.98.75.14

CHÂTEAU LANGOA ET LEOVILLE BARTON
(WINERY)
    St.-Julien-Beychevelle, 33250 Pauillac
    tel. 56.59.06.05, fax 56.59.14.29

CHÂTEAU LYNCH-BAGES (WINERY)
    33250 Pauillac
    tel. 56.73.24.19, fax 56.59.26.42

RESTAURANT LE SAINT-JAMES
(AT HAUTERIVE HÔTEL)
    3, Place Camille Hostein,
    33270 Bordeaux-Bouliac
    tel. 56.20.52.19, fax 56.20.92.58

Périgord/Dordogne Valley

LA BELLE ETOILE (HOTEL-RESTAURANT)
    24250 La Roque-Gageac
    tel. 53.29.51.44, fax 53.29.45.63

CHÂTEAU DE CAZENAC
    24220 Le Coux et Bigaroque
    tel. 53.31.69.31, fax 53.28.91.43
    Private château that accepts guests; meals
    on prior notice

LE MOULIN DE LA TOUR (WALNUT-OIL MILL)
    Ste.-Nathalène, 24200 Sarlat
    tel. 53.59.22.08

LE VIEUX LOGIS (HOTEL-RESTAURANT)
    24510 Tremolat (Dordogne)
    tel. 53.22.80.06, fax 53.22.84.89

Toulouse and Languedoc

HÔTEL ALTEA (HOTEL-RESTAURANT)
    41, rue Porta, 81000 Albi
    tel. 63.47.66.66, fax 63.46.18.40

RESTAURANT LA BARBACANE
(AT HÔTEL DE LA CITÉ)
    place de l'Eglise, 11000 Carcassonne
    tel. 68.25.46.47, fax 68.71.50.15

RESTAURANT CHÂTEAU ST. MARTIN
TRENCAVEL
    290, avenue du Gal-Leclerc,
    11090 Carcassonne
    tel. 68.71.09.53

LE DOMAINE D'AURIAC
(HOTEL-RESTAURANT)
    BP 554, route de St.-Hilaire,
    11000 Carcassonne
    tel. 68.25.72.22, fax 68.47.35.54

RESTAURANT LE LANGUEDOC
32, Allée d'Iéna, 11000 Carcassonne
tel. 68.25.22.17, fax 68.47.13.22

HÔTEL LONGCOL
(HOTEL-RESTAURANT)
La Fouillade, 12270 Najac, Aveyron
tel. 65.29.63.36, fax 65.29.64.28

L'OUSTAL DEL BARRY
(HOTEL-RESTAURANT)
12270 Najac
tel. 65.29.74.32, fax 65.29.75.32

RESTAURANT LE PORTANEL
La Placette "Passage du Portanel"
11100 Bages
tel. 68.42.81.66

LA RÉSERVE (HOTEL-RESTAURANT)
Fonvialane, route des Cordes, 81000 Albi
tel. 63.47.60.22, fax 63.47.63.60

CHÂTEAU DE VILLEFALSE
(HOTEL-RESTAURANT)
Le Lac, 11130 Sigean
tel. 68.48.54.29, fax 68.48.34.37

Gascony and the Basque Country

HÔTEL DE FRANCE (HOTEL-RESTAURANT)
place de la Libération, 32003 Auch
tel. 62.61.71.84, fax 62.61.71.81

RESTAURANT LES PLATANES
32, avenue Beausoliel, 64200 Biarritz
tel. 59.23.13.68

HÔTEL LES PYRÉNÉES
(HOTEL-RESTAURANT)
19, place du Général de Gaulle,
64220 St.-Jean-Pied-de-Port
tel. 59.37.01.01, fax 59.37.18.97

RESTAURANT AUBERGE DU CHÊNE
64250 Ixtassou
tel. 59.29.75.01

Provence

RESTAURANT BRUNO
Campagne Mariette, 83510 Lorgues
tel. 94.73.92.19, fax 94.73.78.11

DOMAINE CASTEL ROUBINE (WINERY)
BP 117 83510 Lorgues (Var)
tel. 94.73.71.55, fax 94.73.29.34

RESTAURANT LA FONTAINE D'AMPUS
place de la Mairie, 83111 Ampus
tel. 94.70.97.74

BOULANGERIE JOEL BERTAINA
place de la Mairie, 83111 Ampus

FERME AUBERGE CHEZ MARCELINE
04240 Argenton
tel. 92.83.22.29

LE MOULIN DU MAÎTRE CORNILLE
(OLIVE-OIL MILL)
rue Charloun-Rieu,
13520 Maussane les Alpilles
tel. 90.97.32.37

LE BISTROT DU PARADOU
13125 Le Paradou
tel. 90.54.32.70

V&S DOMAINE RABIEGA (WINERY)
Clos Dière Méridional,
F-83300 Draguignan
tel. 94.68.44.22

LE VIEUX CASTILLON (HOTEL-RESTAURANT)
Castillon-du-Gard Remoulins
tel. 66.37.00.77, fax 66.37.28.17

Côte d'Azur

AUBERGE DU COLOMBIER
(HOTEL-RESTAURANT)
    06330 Roquefort-les-Pins
    tel. 93.77.10.27, fax 93.77.07.03

AUBERGE DU JARRIER
    30, passage de la Bourgade, 06410 Biot
    tel. 93.65.11.68, fax 93.65.50.03

RESTAURANT LE LOUIS XV
(AT THE HÔTEL DE PARIS)
    place du Casino, Monte Carlo,
    98000 Monaco
    tel. 92.16.30.00, fax 93.15.90.03

BISTROT DE MOUGINS
    06250 Mougins
    tel. 93.75.78.34, fax 93.90.18.55

LE PETIT NICE
(HOTEL-RESTAURANT)
    Anse de Maldormé, Corniche J. F.
    Kennedy, 13007 Marseille
    tel. 91.59.25.92, fax 91.59.28.08

Lyon

BERNACHON (PÂTISSERIE)
    42, Cours Franklin-Roosevelt, 69006 Lyon
    tel. 78.24.37.98

RESTAURANT LE GARET (BOUCHON)
    7, rue du Garet, 69001 Lyon
    tel. 78.28.16.94, fax 78.00.06.84

RESTAURANT LÉON DE LYON
    1, rue Pléney, 69901 Lyon
    tel. 78.28.11.33, fax 78.39.89.05

LE BISTROT DE LYON
    64, rue Mercière, 69002 Lyon
    tel. 78.37.00.62, fax 78.38.32.51

RENÉE & RENÉE RICHARD (FROMAGERIE)
    Halle de Lyon, 102, Cours Lafayette,
    69003 Lyon
    tel. 78.62.30.78, fax 78.71.75.09

SIBILIA SALAISONS (CHARCUTERIE)
    Halle de Lyon, 102, Cours Lafayette,
    69003 Lyon
    tel. 78.62.36.28

Rhône Valley

HOSTELLERIE DU BOIS PRIEUR
    Domaine de Granjean-Galafray,
    42360 Cottance
    tel. 77.28.06.69, fax 77.20.06.55
    Meals available on prior request only.

RESTAURANT PIERRE GAGNAIRE
    7, rue Richelandière, 42000 St. Etienne
    tel. 77.42.30.90, fax 77.42.30,91

RESTAURANT MICHEL CHABRAN
    26600 Pont-de-l'Isère
    tel. 75.84.60.09, fax 75.84.59.65

Burgundy

L'ABBAYE SAINT-MICHEL
(HOTEL-RESTAURANT)
    Montée de Saint-Michel, 89700 Tonnerre
    tel. 86.55.05.99, fax 86.55.00.10

HOSTELLERIE DES CLOS
(HOTEL-RESTAURANT)
    rue Jules-Rathier, 89800 Chablis
    tel. 86.42.10.63, fax 86.42.17.11

CONTINENTAL DE CROISIERES (BARGES)
    9, rue Jean Renaud, 21000 Dijon
    tel. 80.30.49.20, fax 80.30.27.01

LA CÔTE D'OR
(HOTEL-RESTAURANT)
    2, rue d'Argentine, 21210 Saulieu
    tel. 80.64.07.66, fax 80.64.08.92

ETS FALLOT SARL
(DIJON MUSTARD MANUFACTURER)
    31, Faubourg Bretonnière, 21200 Beaune
    tel. 80.22.10.02, fax 80.22.00.84

HOSTELLERIE DE LEVERNOIS
    route de Verdun-sur-le-Doubs,
    21200 Beaune
    tel. 80.24.73.58, fax 80.22.78.00

J. MOREAU ET FILS GRANDS VINS DE
CHABLIS (WINERY)
    route d'Auxerre, 89800 Chablis
    tel. 86.42.40.70, fax 86.42.44.59

Charolles and Auvergne

CHÂTEAU LA CHAIZE (WINERY)
    69460 Odenas
    tel. 74.03.41.05, fax 74.03.52.73

CHÂTEAU DE CODIGNAT
(HOTEL-RESTAURANT)
    Bort-l'Etang, 63190 Lezoux
    tel. 73.68.43.03, fax 73.68.93.54

CHÂTEAU DE PIZAY
(HOTEL-RESTAURANT)
    route Villie Morgon,
    69220 St.-Jean-d'Ardières
    tel. 74.66.51.41, fax 74.69.65.63

HÔTEL RESTAURANT TROISGROS
    Place Jean Troisgros, 42300 Roanne
    tel. 77.71.66.97, fax 77.70.39.77

Franche-Comté (Jura)

HÔTEL DE FRANCE
    51–53, rue Pierre Vernier, 25290 Ornans
    tel. 81.62.24.44, fax 81.62.12.03

FRUITIÈRE DE FRASNE (CHEESEMAKERS)
    25560 Frasne
    tel. 81.49.82.26

JEAN-MICHEL TANNIÈRES
(HOTEL-RESTAURANT)
    25160 Malbuisson
    tel. 81.69.30.89, fax 81.69.39.16

Savoy

LE COTTAGE FERNAND BISE
(HOTEL-RESTAURANT)
    route du Port, au bord du Lac d'Annecy,
    74290 Talloires
    tel. 50.60.71.10, fax 50.60.77.51

L'AUBERGE DE L'ERIDAN
    13, Vieille Route des Pensières,
    74290 Veyrier-du-Lac
    tel. 50.60.24.00, fax 50.60.23.63

Alsace

HOSTELLERIE LA CHENEAUDIÈRE
(HOTEL-RESTAURANT)
    67420 Colroy-la-Roche
    tel. 88.97.61.64, fax 88.47.21.73

SALON DE THÉ CHRISTIAN (PÂTISSERIE)
    12, rue de l'Outre, 67000 Strasbourg
    tel. 88.32.04.41

RESTAURANT LE CROCODILE
    10, rue de l'Outre, 67000 Strasbourg
    tel. 88.32.13.02, fax 88.75.72.01

HAILICH GRAAB (WINSTUB)
    15, rue des Orfèvres, 67000 Strasbourg
    tel. 88.32.39.97

JEAN (PÂTISSERIE)
    6, place de l'Ecole, 68000 Colmar
    tel. 89.41.24.63

KIREN TRAITEUR (DELUXE MARKET)
    19, rue du 22 Novembre, 67000 Strasbourg
    tel. 88.32.16.10, fax 88.32.08.65

NAEGEL (PÂTISSERIE)
    9, rue des Orfèvres, 67000 Strasbourg
    tel. 88.32.82.86

HÔTEL PÈRE BENOIT (HOTEL-RESTAURANT)
    34, route Strasbourg, 67960 Enzheim
    tel. 88.68.98.00 (restaurant),
    tel. 88.68.91.65, fax 88.68.64.56

AUBERGE DU PÈRE FLORANC
(HOTEL-RESTAURANT)
    9, rue Herzog, 68000 Colmar
    tel. 89.80.79.14, fax 89.79.77.00

RESTAURANT STRISSEL (WINSTUB)
    5, place de la Grande Boucherie,
    67000 Strasbourg
    tel. 88.32.14.73, fax 88.32.70.24

F. E. TRIMBACH
(VINEYARDS)
    15, route de Bergheim, 68150 Ribeauvillé
    tel. 89.73.60.30

CHEZ YVONNE (WINSTUB)
    10, rue du Sanglier, 67000 Strasbourg
    tel. 88.32.84.15

Champagne

LA MAISON BELLE EPOQUE
(GUEST HOUSE AT PERRIER-JOUËT)
    11 & 26, avenue de Champagne,
    51200 Epernay
    tel. 26.55.20.53, fax 26.54.54.55
    Open to the public only for tours

HOTEL ROYAL CHAMPAGNE
(HOTEL-RESTAURANT)
    51160 Champillon-Bellevue
    tel. 26.52.87.11, fax 26.52.89.69

RUINART
(CHAMPAGNE MAKERS)
    4, rue des Crayères, 51100 Reims
    tel. 26.85.40.29

LE VIGNERON
    Place Paul Jamot, 51100 Reims
    tel. 26.47.00.71, fax 26.47.87.66

INDEX

All recipes are indexed
by English subtitles. Numerals
in *italics* indicate illustrations.

PHOTOGRAPHIC CREDITS

A NOTE ON THE TYPE

The text of this book was set on the Macintosh in a
digitized version of Garamond, a rendering of the type
first cut by Claude Garamond (c. 1480–1561). Garamond
was a pupil of Geoffrey Tory and is believed to have
based his letters on the Venetian models, although he
introduced a number of important differences, and it is
to him we owe the letter which we know as "old style."
He gave to his letters a certain elegance and a feeling of
movement that won for their creator an immediate
reputation and the patronage of Francis I of France.

Composed by North Market Street Graphics,
Lancaster, Pennsylvania
Printed and bound by Arcata Graphics/Martinsburg,
Martinsburg, West Virginia
Color insert printed by Arcata Graphics/Kingsport Press,
Kingsport, Tennessee
Maps and spot drawings by Claudia Carlson
Design by Anthea Lingeman